GINNY GOOD

ALSO CREATED BY
GERARD JONES

Everyone Who's Anyone in Adult Trade Publishing
the online directory of literary agents, editors and publishers.
http://www.everyonewhosanyone.com

GINNY GOOD
A MOSTLY TRUE STORY

GERARD JONES

MONKFISH BOOK PUBLISHING COMPANY
RHINEBECK, NEW YORK

Monkfish Memoirs, Volume 3

Library of Congress Cataloging-in-Publication Data

Jones, Gerard, 1942-
Ginny Good : a memoir (a mostly true story) / by Gerard Jones.
    p. cm.
ISBN 0-9726357-5-0
1. Jones, Gerard, 1942- 2. Good, Ginny, b. 1941. 3. Hippies--
United States--Biography. 4. Ashland (Or.)--Biography. 5. Califor-
nia--Biography. I. Title.
CT275.J746A3 2004
979.4'053'0922--dc22   2003028197

Book and cover design and cover art by Georgia Dent

Bulk purchase discounts,for educational or promotional purposes, are available. Contact
the publisher for more information.

First edition

First impression

10 9 8 7 6 5 4 3 2 1

Monkfish Book Publishing Company
27 Lamoree Road
Rhinebeck, New York 12572
www.monkfishpublishing.com

ACKNOWLEDGMENTS

Other than the love of my life and my long-suffering mother and my no longer suffering dad and my best buddy, Michelle Salts, who can turn a sow's ear into a silk purse like nobody's business, and my baberific literary agent, Laura Strachan, and the boss of Monkfish Book Publishing Company, His Holiness Paul Cohen, and their all too modest book designer and graphic artist, Georgia Dent, and their ever so erudite editor, David Stanford, the rest of you know who you are. Thanks! Oh, except for Michelle's daughter, Katie. She might not quite know who she is yet, due to still being kind of a kid. She will though, I have every confidence in her. Thanks, Katie!

"I think you should make the title: 'Once There Was a Girl Called…GINNY GOOD.' It sounds sort of wistful and poignant, the way Ginny used to talk with her eyes all amazing and blue."
—Laurie L. Jones (my mother)

"Stay me with flagons,
Comfort me with apples:
For I am sick of love."
—Song of Songs, 2:6

"By writing a book, a man frees his mind from an overwhelming impression."
—Eugen Rosenstock-Huessy

LIST OF CHAPTERS

CHAPTER ONE

Ashland

I'm using everyone's real name. They can all sue me. I hope they do. I could use the excitement. It gets kind of boring living up here with my eighty-year-old mother in Ashland, Oregon. She likes having me around, though. She was sick of being by herself. My dad died…wow, a while ago…going on something like nine years now. Sometimes it feels like yesterday; other times it feels like he's still alive. We keep finding scribbled notes in his ninth-grade handwriting here and there—like when I change a fuse in the fuse box or my mother digs through the glove compartment looking for a map. Plenty of other people seem to think he's still alive too. They keep sending him mail—brochures from hearing aid companies and long letters on good bond paper explaining to him how he might want to consolidate his debt. Hey, his debt's as consolidated as it gets. It's paid, paid in full—going on nine years now.

I do the things my father used to do: mow the lawn, get the car fixed, put in new light bulbs, change the furnace filters, take the lids off jars that are on too tight for my mother's arthritis. Other than that, I pretty much just play golf. I play golf every day, rain or shine. The rainier, the better—wind, sleet, hail, snow, I don't care. Sometimes I get to feeling a little like King Lear out there, talking to thunder, flipping off gusts of wind. Ha! The other day I held my putter up like a lightening rod, daring the elements to do their worst, but usually I just play golf.

I play golf with anyone who shows up. Ford. Wallace. Bergeron. Johnny Pelosi. Felix. Knapp. Tyrone. Tyrone's a black guy from the Shakespeare Festival. He was the King of France last year. We all play golf at a cheap, hilly little municipal golf course called Oak Knoll. It's out of town a ways, south on Highway 66, toward Emigrant Lake. Standing on the ninth tee, you can see everything for miles around. Pilot Rock's directly in front of you, off in the distance toward California. Mt. Ashland's a little to the right; Grizzly Peak and Pompadour Bluff are to the left.

The golf course is home to five families of Canadian Geese. Nobody fucks with them. They poo on the greens with impunity. Even the feisty mallards and wood ducks and the seagulls that fly over from Klamath Lake stay out of their way. The five families of Canadian Geese correspond roughly with the five families of the New York Mafia. Well, according to Johnny Pelosi, anyway. He knows all about that sort of thing. Johnny Pelosi isn't his real name. I don't know for a fact that he got it as part of a witness protection program; all I know is you don't want to beat him out of more than a couple of bucks a round unless you want to wake up with your parakeet's head in your bed.

It's an eclectic group. Wallace drives a Winnebago. He's also a direct descendent of William Wallace, that *Braveheart* guy, so you want to watch how much money you beat *him* out of too. Ford has trouble keeping his trousers on. Bergeron has a twinkle in his eye. Knapp carries beer in a blue cooler in the summer and drinks whisky in the winter. Felix hangs drywall and thinks he's Lee Trevino. We all make up Mexican sounding things to say to him. Felix was one of my dad's buddies at the Elks. My dad used to make up Mexican sounding things to say to him, too.

Besides the five families of Canadian Geese and a few pesticide-resistant burrowing animals, there are flowering bushes and white birches and yellow birches and oak trees with mistletoe in their branches and willow trees. The groundskeepers prune them down to bare nubs in the fall but they always grow back into huge weeping willows by the time summer rolls around again. Then, on top of all that, there's the sky—all different kinds of sky, changing from one minute to the next; dark clouds, white clouds, mist, rainbows, double rainbows, you name it—anything you'd ever want to see in the way of weather.

If none of the guys I usually play golf with shows up, I play golf all by myself. Nor do I play golf well. I play golf badly. I've been playing golf badly every day for the last two and a half years. I shot a 76 once, but that was a gigantic fluke. The wind kept changing direction. It was with me on every hole. Calm zephyrs gently guided my 90 compression Titleist straight toward the pin every time I hit the thing. If I'd been any good it would have been a 66. But I'm not any good. That's part of the reason I quit playing golf and decided to write this book instead —well, that and just to get it the hell over and done with once and for all.

I'm not worried about getting it published. What publisher wants to get sued? No publisher, that's what publisher.

I suppose I could get my sister to stick it on the Internet for me. She has a web-design company. One of her clients is the World Elephant Polo Association, which, according to *People Magazine*, was one of the hot sites of the week awhile back, so you never know. Someone I knew thirty years ago might just be idly browsing the web, stumble across his or her name, and decide to sue me for something. Hey, it could happen— Sandy Good, Donna McKechnie, Gordon Lish—any one of them might just up and sue my ass. I hope one of them does. I hope they all do.

"Hey," I'll say, "get in line."

I might even throw in some people I *didn't* know, just to increase my chances of getting sued—Mia Farrow, maybe, Jill Clayburg, Elizabeth Clare Prophet, Courtney Love. I sort of *did* know Courtney Love, actually. She would only have been around two years old at the time, but I'll put her in anyway. Her father brought her over to where Ginny and I were living on Shrader Street in something like 1966. He needed a babysitter. We were on acid. Her angelic little towhead two-year-old glow lit up the whole room. So, yo, Courtney, sue me, man. Bring it on.

The prospect of some hard working process server showing up at my mother's front door with a summons on behalf of some long forgotten friend or acquaintance just somehow warms the cockles of my heart. Duchess, my mother's little black ragamuffin dog, will bark her fool head off when the process server knocks on the door, but I'll be so glad I'll practically kiss the guy. The summons will tell me that I should get a lawyer, but I won't. Ha! I don't need no stinking lawyer. I'll be my own lawyer. That will be the exciting part.

4

The last job I had was as a paralegal. I got fired, but I was a paralegal all the same. I'll totally know how to defend myself if it ever comes to that. I've got plenty of pleading paper and exquisite answers to all the complaints anyone might want to make. That's how I got the money to play golf every day for the last two and a half years, as a matter of fact—by suing the law firm that fired my ass. Shafer, Kirloff, Isaacson & Barish. Those twerps. They were what you might call a mid-sized San Francisco labor and employment law firm. It all started out innocently enough. I had run out of money. My whole life I've been running out of money. I knew one of the associates. She recommended me. The partners took her word for it that I wasn't some kind of whacko—and I wasn't. Well, not right away.

When I first started working there, I wasn't sure what a paralegal was supposed to *do*, exactly, but my predecessor left a pile of stuff on his desk, which gave me clues. Call people on the phone. Make lists. Look up things on *Westlaw.* Write memos. Come up with chronologies.

I worked there around a year and a half. I *liked* working there. I got good at it. Everyone loved me; well, *almost* every-one. By my standards, I made plenty of money. I rode through Chinatown on the crowded California Street bus, jay-walked across Montgomery Street, went into the lofty marble lobby through a chrome-plated revolving door and got free coffee in the company coffee room. I liked getting free cof-fee. Another thing I've always been is cheap. How do you think I've managed to play golf every day for the last two and a half years on the paltry settlement money I finally managed to squeeze out of those Bozos? By being cheap, that's how.

The partners billed me out at eighty-five bucks an hour. I had my own office. We took up the whole 22nd floor. My window looked out across the red roofs of Chinatown. I ate lunch in the park next to the Transamerica Pyramid—usually with one or another of the secretaries. They were all pretty cute, too. Terri. Stephanie. Tess. Barbara! I flirted with them. They flirted back. I was happy.

In my spare time I wrote thinly disguised fictional stories about the place. That's another thing I've always done—my whole life I've been writing thinly disguised fictional stories about stuff. In the stories I called the place "Sadler, Cristlieb, Altschule & Beckwith" or "SCAB." That's one of the slick things about fiction; you can thinly disguise stuff to suit your own clever, ironic purposes.

The reason Shafer, Kirloff, Isaacson & Barish fired my ass was that I tried to organize a union among the support staff. Organizing a union totally pissed them off. The partners prided themselves on being big time union busters. That was their job. That was what they were paid to do. It would have been hard to charge the kind of money they charged to keep unions out of other businesses if they couldn't keep a union out of their own damn business—hey, don't think I hadn't thought of that.

Organizing a union was *intended* to piss them off. They had pissed us off. Mainly by making us work longer hours without increasing our pay. Personally, I was happy to be getting the money I was getting, but the secretaries were all up in arms. *They* were the ones who wanted the stupid union in there. I couldn't have cared less. But I'd written some seminar material about how to *avoid* union organizing and therefore knew a little something about the mechanics.

The first thing you have to do when you're organizing a union is shut up about it. We had surreptitious planning sessions after work. Stephanie and Terri and I all took pictures of each other sitting in Kirloff's office with our feet on his desk, leaning back in his chair, and wearing a baseball hat that said, "Union, Yes!"

I called the local Teamsters Organizing Committee. They said they'd back us up—and the next day, on behalf of all the cute secretaries, I wrote a memo to the partners informing them that it was our intention to form a duly recognized labor union affiliated with the International Brotherhood of Teamsters.

That got their attention. The partners had a healthy respect for the Teamsters. Gary Barish used to work over there. He'd recently been made managing partner, although it was Rick Shafer who started the company and still really ran the place. Shafer looked like Lenin—Vladamir Ilyich, without the goatee. Barish looked like the guy from the Men's Warehouse. He turned the task of dealing with me and our union organizing efforts over to Walter Reynolds. Wally, he was called. Wally looked like the gray-haired guy on *The Nightly Business Report*.

With their fear of the Teamsters backing me up, I told the partners all they had to do was increase our pay to compensate for the increased hours. It seemed simple enough to me, not to mention fair and just and reasonable. Barish and Reynolds objected to the "tone" of my memo. That was it. We didn't get our raise.

It took them another couple months, but the partners finally got the secretaries to give up on the idea of joining a union. Then they sent me a "warning" memo which included a bunch of cockamamie reasons they were going to use to fire me for so-called "good cause." One of the things the memo mentioned was that I had said, "Gary Barish eats shit," to someone in the elevator. I drafted an answer which pointed out that it wasn't in the elevator, it was in the coffee room, and that, furthermore, it was a fact, Gary Barish *did* eat shit— not only due to the USDA finding that there's a certain amount of fecal matter in most commercially prepared foods, but in the more traditional meaning of the phrase, as well. My letter started out: "If you're reading this, I've been fired."

I carried it around with me wherever I went so I could whip it out on them when they finally got around to actually giving me the ax. In the meantime, just for practice, I whipped it out on Barbara Kalinowski. She was Wally Reynolds's secretary. Her cubicle was just outside his office. She had overheard some of our more heated conversations and liked the way I stood my ground.

I liked the way Barbara Kalinowski looked, period: green eyes, red hair, big juicy mouth all lipsticked up. She wasn't quite twenty-five but had been on her own since she was fifteen. Her husband produced pornographic movies. She was allowed to have sex with women, but not other men. Her husband was allowed to have sex with other women and didn't want to have sex with men. It didn't seem fair.

We went out for drinks after work one night. She had four or five gin and tonics. I sipped a Glenfiddich on the rocks. She read my memo out loud to me and kept getting all breathless with laughter and cracking up in the middles of sentences.

After we'd taken a cab to my apartment, I went across the street to get her a six-pack of Michelob. When I got back, she was on my bed with no clothes on. She had a single body piercing—a small, tasteful, 24 carat gold clit ring. She had multiple orgasms. I forget how many. Sixteen? Seventeen? Some astronomical number. She must have had some sort of gynecological condition. It wasn't anything I was *doing*, exactly, she just kept having orgasms, one after another—you barely had to breathe in her direction and, whoops, there she was, having another orgasm. She said it wasn't quite a record, but record or no record, it was all the orgasms I ever wanted any chick I ever had anything to do with to have.

The next day, I was summoned to Gary Barish's office and was told I was being "let go." Fired. Terminated. Given the old heave ho. Shafer was on vacation. Barish and Reynolds did the actual axing of my ass. I whipped out the letter I'd already whipped out on Barbara Kalinowski on them. It had a few gin and tonic stains on the first page. Barish and Reynolds weren't particularly impressed with my Pleistocene understanding of labor law. Oh, well. I signed up for unemployment and wrote a letter to Rick Shafer. He said I should get on with my life. Guys like Shafer always say that. What it means is that they would like you to go away and leave them alone so they can get on with their own damn lives.

A few months later, after I turned all our correspondence over to the National Labor Relations Board and filled out a formal complaint, Shafer and Kirloff met me at the Cadillac Bar and Grill and I agreed to take around ten thousand dollars, in exchange for dropping the thing. It was kind of anticlimactic. I could have gotten a lot more, but I'd mainly just wanted to prove my point. Then I moved up to my mother's house in Ashland and played golf every day for the last two and a half years.

Barbara Kalinowski came up for a visit last summer. She was in the middle of getting a divorce. We played golf. I introduced her to some of the guys I usually play golf with. She had on a yellow tank top. When we got to Felix, he said, "Ay, Chihuahua." He didn't mean to say it. He couldn't help himself. She's a pretty good golfer, too. I can't think of anything Barbara Kalinowski's not good at.

Later on she and I took a blanket and a flashlight and a bottle of Scotch up to the cemetery where my father's buried. It's called Scenic Hills. It was still around eighty-five, even at night. During the day it had been up to a hundred and six— not quite a record, but close. We passed the Scotch back and forth and shined the flashlight on my dad's tombstone:

"Many Dreams Came True"

That's what the tombstone says. My mother picked it out. It was the truest thing she found among the samples she'd been shown. Under the words, there's a picture of a guy fly fishing beside a lake with snow-capped mountains in the background and fluffy clouds chiseled into the smooth gray granite.

Barbara Kalinowski turned off the flashlight and stretched out on the blanket. There was a sliver of moon and about a billion bright shining stars shimmering in the huge black cemetery sky. She watched the stars for a while. Then she rolled me over and I watched the stars for a while.. There were times when neither of us watched the stars. Then we watched the stars together for a while. It wasn't all that comfortable, even with the blanket. Plus, I kept getting the eerie feeling that my father was going to rise up from the grave to find out what the hell was causing all the commotion. He never did like a lot of commotion. But he didn't rise up from the grave. Not ever.

Barbara Kalinowski has a new boyfriend now. The last I heard, they were getting married. As for me, my meager settlement money's just about gone. I probably ought to be thinking about getting another job, but I've decided to conserve what little money I have left and take a stab at writing this book I've been threatening to write for longer than I can remember. I'm not exactly starting from scratch. I've started what amounts to the same book on and off for the last thirty years or so and have, in the process, accumulated a little stack of stuff I thought might come in handy someday—the oldest surviving scrap goes back to the spring of 1960. I also have a bunch of old letters and things—part of a diary, a few pictures, a Valentine's card. But, basically, the book's about four people—Elliot Felton, Virginia Good, Melanie and me—and what we all tried to do with each other back in the summer of 1972.

I suppose I need to start with Ginny. She was the first hippie, in case anyone's ever wondered. That tidbit of information probably never made its way into any history books, but it's true. I have proof. Documentary evidence. She was also the older sister of Sandra Good, the same Sandra Good who used to be one of the chicks in the so-called Manson Family. Sandy's *still* one of the chicks in the so-called Manson Family. I saw her on TV a while ago, talking about how she and Squeaky had set up a website to show what a bum rap poor Charlie got. When I get my sister to stick this on the Internet for me, I'll have her link it to the Charlie Manson site.

11

I'm pretty sure I still have a letter Ginny sent me about her sister and the so-called Manson Family back before anyone had ever heard of them. I've got all kinds of letters and things, stuff I haven't looked at in years. I think I'll go ahead and start with a biography of sorts—just write down whatever I vaguely recollect Ginny telling me about what happened to her before I met her. I always used to tell her I was going to write a book about her someday. That may have been why she even liked me in the first place. Oh, well. Better late than never.

CHAPTER TWO

Del Mar

Virginia Dixon Good was born on March 5, 1941. She spent her childhood in one or another of those sleepy little seaside communities down along the Southern California coast, just north of San Diego. Her mother was too busy for kids. She had three daughters. Ginny was her second daughter. Sandy was the third. I forget the first daughter's name. I can't remember Ginny's mother's name, either. I might have blanked it out. Her father's name was George. George F. Good. I never knew what the "F." stood for. There were so many things I never knew.

Ginny's mother couldn't have said for sure why she'd even *had* kids except that having kids was what one *did*. Kids were annoying. She couldn't understand what the hell they were talking about, for one thing. She didn't know what the Salvadoran maid was jabbering about half the time either, but at least the maid understood what *she* was saying:

"Rosalie! God damn it! If I find one more grain of sand in this kitchen, I'm going to *kill* you! Do you understand?"

As long as it had just been she and her husband, Ginny's mother had always been the center of attention, but when she started churning out daughters one after another, the kids seemed to think that *they* were the center of attention. That got to be god damned *annoying* after awhile—and that it wasn't their *fault* just made it all the more annoying. Here she was, a bright, attractive, capable woman, stuck in a marriage she had known wasn't going to last since before her *first* daughter was born, but who could she blame for that? Herself? That would have been absurd. Her husband? He was happy. Her parents? God? So Ginny's mother took her wretchedness out on her children and disguised it as altruism. She *wanted* to be a lousy role model. She *wanted* her kids to rebel. The way she seemed to have it figured was that the best thing she could do for her daughters in the long run was to see to it that they *hated* the idea of ever getting married and having kids—and if by some silly extension of childish logic that made *them* feel somehow unwanted or unloved, well, so be it, it was a small price to pay.

Ginny's mother simply had more important things to do than care for her daughters—her commitment to the local theater group, for example. Who else in Del Mar could act worth a damn? And who was better suited to preside over the Junior League? Ginny's mother had responsibilities to the state, to the country, to the world. Staunch Republican causes kept cropping up all the time—the struggle for freedom in Hungary, circulating petitions to impeach Earl Warren—so that, all in all, Ginny's mother stayed too *busy* to be bothered with kids, and Ginny and her sisters were mostly raised by their father (while he was still around), by Rosalie Rosales and by Jolly, the good-natured black Lab who followed them down to the tide pools and barked at fiddler crabs and whipped his tail like a stalk of seaweed and panted and drooled and shook salty water off his shiny wet coat into their flushed, sunburned faces and carried sand between his toes into every corner of the house, which needless to say pissed off Rosalie Rosales beyond her ability to express in English.

* 𝒢 𝒢 *

When she was old enough, Ginny went to a private pre-school. They could afford it. Her father was rich. That was why her mother had married him. He also worshipped the ground she walked on, of course, was educated at Princeton, had his own airplane, was quiet, thoughtful, soft-spoken and kept to himself for the most part—all of which had seemed like good enough reasons to have married him at the time, but none of which would have been worth a damn if he hadn't been rich.

The marriage lasted until Ginny was five. What finally ended it was that her father was simply too *nice*. He loved his family. He loved his wife and his house and his dog. He loved reading to his daughters at night and listening to what they had to say during the day and was patient with the tangles in their hair. It was all too much for Ginny's mother to bear. She divorced him for mental cruelty.

Ginny's father didn't contest it. Which exactly proved her mother's point—the guy had no balls! How could she bear to live with a guy with no balls? What she wanted, he wanted. He suffocated her. So what if he went to Princeton—he was a fool. He was short and stocky and wore coke bottle glasses with wire rims like Harry S. Truman, the haberdasher—and, on top of everything else, he was a stamp collector!

Ginny's mother had long since chosen to forget that she had felt truly comforted and loved and relieved when she had allowed Ginny's father to think that, in his quaint, quiet, soft spoken way, he had talked her into marrying him, for better or worse, and chose instead to remember only that she'd had her whole life ahead of her when along came this soft-spoken guy with a two-bit Beechcraft Bonanza who had charmed her mother and had played golf with her father and had utterly fucked up her life but good with his unremitting niceness! This twerp!

Her mother chose to forget all kinds of things and remembered only what she needed to remember in order to divorce her husband without regret. Her father sadly loaded his books and his golf clubs and his stamp collection into the trunk of the second car and drove away two days before Ginny's fifth Christmas...and left the sound of the car driving away reverberating in her brain and rumbling through the pit of her stomach for the rest of her life.

* $\mathcal{G}$ $\mathcal{G}$ *

I used to have a picture of Ginny when she was a kid. I had it for a long time. I don't know what's become of it. I've looked for it. It was just an ordinary, black and white snapshot taken in front of the house she and her family were living in when she was four. It's probably good I lost it. I kept it in my wallet so long you could hardly make out what she even looked like anymore, but the way I remember it is as fresh and crisp as the day she gave it to me.

She was sitting on the bottom step of a front porch in a pair of bunny rabbit bedroom slippers and a pair of overalls.

16

It was hard to tell they were still even bunny rabbits anymore; their ears had fallen off and their eyes were missing and they had no noses. Ginny's face was tan. Her hair was streaked blond and curly. She was squinting into the sun, smiling a shy, cockeyed smile and holding up some imaginary something for whoever was taking the picture to see—her father, I presumed.

Ginny's father took off two days before her fifth Christmas and never came back. He was gone. Period. There was no changing that fact. But that didn't stop her mind from *trying* to change it. Minds are a determined bunch of neurons and ganglia and unknowable stuff. They're like skin or bones, they get cut or broken, and right away they set about the mindless task of making themselves whole again. Skin and bones grow new cells, scab up, scar over; minds blank things out, compensate, make things up, and pretty soon they're good as new—and that was what Ginny's mind did. There was no stopping it. Somewhere along the line, she hit on the idea that if she *stayed* four years old, her father wouldn't be gone! It was simple and logical and elegant and unassailable. So she did that. Somewhere in her mind, Ginny Good stayed four years old for the rest of her life, and somewhere in her mind, her father read her books at night and listened to what she had to say and was patient with the tangles in her hair, and when she grew up and got cute as hell there were plenty of guys who were willing to perpetuate the idea that she was *still* a four year-old kid. I was one of them, sure, but I wasn't the only one.

* 𝓰 𝓰 *

I'm not explaining this well. There's a reason for that. I never really knew Ginny's mother, see. I heard a lot about her but never met her. I lived with Ginny on and off from the end of 1964 to the beginning of 1969 and kept in pretty close touch with her for a long time after that, but I never laid eyes on her mother except in pictures. Elliot knew her. He and Ginny's mother were buddies. They hung out with each other when he and Ginny were living together down in L.A. Ginny's mother and Elliot hit it off. They liked each other. They laughed at each other's jokes. La dee dah. He thought she was funny and smart and entertaining and thoughtful and artistic, so, like, if you really want to know more about what Ginny's mother was like, Elliot's the guy you should be talking to—go dig his dead ass up and ask him. If I knew where he was buried, I'd go dig his dead ass up and ask him myself.

But, wait a minute. I've got a letter Ginny wrote me—I've got a small pile of them, actually. I used to have hundreds. I don't know what the hell happens to everything. There's this one letter I'm thinking of in particular, though. Ha! Got it! Okay, here's what *Ginny* had to say about her mother:

I can't write long 'cause I've got to write a paper. I had a neat fantasy with Dr. Crockett's dollhouse. In the living room (this part's real) the little girl doll was upside down in the playpen. The Mummy and Daddy doll were headed toward the door that leads to the bedroom. There were two mirrors on the walls and a picture of a rose. There was a door and two windows. I looked and said, 'Why's that girl upside down in the crib?' Laughed—'Oh my God—she's me. I can't get out. But I should be the woman. I'm not. I'm still stuck in the crib.'

Then I really started in…The Mummy and Daddy bashed her head in, she's five, and threw her in the crib. The dad is going to leave forever.

He does. What can the girl do? She must escape. She can't go through the door nor through the windows. The only way out is through the mirrors or the rose. If she goes through one mirror she will be in cavernous labyrinths underground. If she goes through the other, she will be in a wondrous garden. If she goes through the rose she will go through the stem to the caverns, which she may explore and eventually she will emerge, into the garden. She picks the rose.

Here I proceeded to minutely describe the sensuous qualities of the rose. She then went down through the stem. It was moist gooey and smoothly fibrous. She slipped down in the direction of the fibers. She found herself bedded in the moist black fertile soil. She stayed there for a while and then began to grow. She grew right up into the garden—her face the center of the rose—the stem, her body. When her feet were on the ground the petals fell away and she could walk. How beautiful it was! She followed a melodic path until an acorn dropped upon her shoulder. Dink! She opened it up, half from half, and there sat a little man. 'Hello.' 'Hello.' They exchanged. 'I'm so glad you found me,' he said. 'An old ogre imprisoned me long ago and I have been subsisting on the inner substances of this acorn.' 'Oh!' said she, 'May I have a taste?' Here I stopped and went back to say what I felt.

Obviously, the first thing was I was bashed when Daddy left. I had to escape but couldn't face reality way outs—the door, the windows. It had to be fantasies. What the caverns and garden is is too much to explain. It's probably obvious anyway. Most of the thing speaks for itself, except the stem is really interesting. I associated it with anal tubes and a penis both at once. 'Why?' I asked. Of course! I came from a penis—the sperm that grew. My dad is both my father and mother. Why an anal tube? I reject the idea that I came from a mother. The anal tube was a woman's. Mother's. She is doo doo—and I, if born from her, am doo doo too. Of course the soil is obvious and the garden and me. Pretty optimistic, Huh! I can hardly wait for the next session, it's like tune in tomorrow…

As something of an aside, here's part of that letter I mentioned earlier, the one that talks about some of Sandy's "adventures" with the so-called Manson Family:

Sandy is a total hippie who was living with the Beach Boys in Malibu and now is with prospectors in the desert teaching Dean Martin's daughter how to lose her ego. They cluck their tongues about what bad shape Mia Farrow and Nanci Sinatra's heads are in, altho Miss Farrow gave away her clothes and is living ascetically, 'she just can't give up her image.' I would certainly like to see my sister after reading her letters. She hikes barefoot in the desert forever, and she used to deride my mystical propensities. She is an Aquarian—Pisces cusp—which goes right along with what she is now doing. An absolutely rebellious, unconventional mystic. I sort of envy her.

All I personally remember about Sandy is that she used to work as a sales clerk at the Emporium on Market Street. She sold scarves and plastic headbands and was a lot less charismatic than Ginny—less compelling, more drab. That was before she shaved herself bald, carved a swastika into her forehead and hung out with the rest of the Manson chicks chanting spooky stuff outside the Hall of Justice in L.A., and way before she and Squeaky set up their own website.

* 𝒢 𝒢 *

After the divorce, Ginny's mother was rich all by herself, and Ginny went to a private grammar school. Then her mother married some other rich guy, some military-industrial rich guy, and they were even richer still. Ginny went to a private high school, stole a bulldozer, lost her virginity, was raped by the cop investigating the incident of the stolen bulldozer and got dumped by the guy to whom she'd lost her aforementioned virginity as a consequence of telling him she got raped by the cop.

Then she went to Sarah Lawrence College…briefly. She was, after all, bright and talented and charming—a poet, an actress, a dancer, an incisive, witty, sparkling conversationalist—and her parents, all three of them, had more money than God. While she was at school she hung out with Jill Clayburgh and fell in love with a guy who was in grad school at Brown. His name was Roger Singmaster. She went too crazy one Christmas and he dumped her. That broke her heart.

She quit school, cut her wrists, went into a private psycho ward for a little over a month, lived with her father in Piedmont for awhile, then moved to San Francisco, got an apartment on 45th Avenue, enrolled at San Francisco State, had dates with two different guys on New Year's Eve of 1962, and ended up at the Jazz Workshop. Jimmy Witherspoon was there. So was I. So was Elliot.

Wait. Now that I think about it, I probably ought to have started with Elliot. Damn. It was actually *Elliot* I knew first. But, you know what? In order to get to how I got to know *him* and all that, I guess I have to start with me—which means that I have to start in Michigan. Crap. Okay, I'm starting in Michigan, but go ahead and remember all the stuff about Ginny. It'll come in handy later.

CHAPTER THREE

Royal Oak

I grew up in Michigan. Royal Oak, Michigan. Ten miles north of Detroit. That was how the main roads got their names—by how far north of Detroit they were: Ten Mile Road. Eleven Mile. Twelve Mile. Like that. Starting down by the Detroit River, Woodward Avenue cut across each of the Mile Roads clear out to the lakes we went to in the summer; Orchard Lake, Cass Lake, Walled Lake. That was what you did in Michigan. You swam in lakes in the summer and ice-skated on lakes in the winter. The farther away from Detroit you got, the better the neighborhoods became. I lived a block from Ten Mile myself, not far from the Detroit Zoo.

Royal Oak was famous in the thirties and early forties as the home base of a radio program put on by a guy named Father Coughlin. Father Coughlin was a Catholic Priest whose virulent anti-Communist, anti-Semitic tirades went out over the airwaves to every city in conservative America from the pulpit of the Shrine of the Little Flower. The Shrine of the Little Flower was on the corner of Twelve Mile and Woodward. According to my grandmother, anyone who listened to Father Coughlin ought to have been stood up against a wall and shot.

Not long after I was born, the Catholic Church pulled the plug on his radio program. Practically speaking, I don't think my birth had much to do with it, but you couldn't convince my grandmother of that. She thought me getting born was the cat's pajamas. She spoiled me rotten and doted on me to distraction. Not much happened in Royal Oak after that. It was known for a while in the eighties as a hotbed of deranged postal workers. Now the only thing famous about Royal Oak is it's where Jack Kevorkian lives.

I had an idyllic childhood. There were kids of every ethnicity under the sun on my block; Welsh kids, Polish kids, English, Irish, French, German, you name it. Well, there weren't any colored kids, of course, or Japs or Chinks or Mexicans—and the Jews all lived over in Huntington Woods. That was just the way things were.

We built forts in trees, dug forts in the ground, played kick-the-can, knocked the street lights out with slingshots, had block parties on Halloween and hung out American Flags on the Fourth of July. Everybody knew everybody else. My whole family, including my grandfather and my grandmother, all lived in a big mournful-looking old house with a coal furnace and a fireplace and a backyard full of trees and a side yard full of trees—elm trees, oak trees, and a big black ash with a blue jay's nest in its uppermost branches. Morning glories climbed the chimney, clinging for dear life to the smooth red bricks with their tough little green sucker feet.

My father put up storm windows in the fall and took them down in the spring. He had a system. Nobody else knew what it was. My mother tended her peony beds, pruned her rose bushes and kept the spirea trimmed. She picked lilacs and lilies-of-the-valley and made them into bouquets and put them into carnival glass vases on the mantle and at either side of the window seat in the dining room.

There was a cherry tree in the backyard. Cherry blossoms blossomed in the spring. Bumblebees hovered among them. White butterflies landed in them. My grandmother baked cherry pies. I picked the cherries myself. I climbed up onto a rickety old paint ladder with a stainless steel pan. The cherries plinked and echoed inside the pan for a while, then got quieter and quieter as the pan filled up and up, higher and higher.

Beyond the cherry tree were my mother's whitewashed clothes poles and my father's horseshoe pits and my grandfather's vegetable garden. My grandfather grew tomatoes and rhubarb and radishes and green beans and a row of sunflowers. I ate tomatoes off the vine, while they were still warm from the sun. When I bit into one, it popped. Hot tomato juice dripped down my throat, soaked the neck of my T-shirt, turned cold, dried, left tomato seeds sticking to my chin.

My grandfather chewed Red Man Tobacco and listened to the Cleveland Indians on the radio because he was originally from Canton, Ohio. He brought me home Clark Bars and Butterfingers in his lunch box. He let me chin myself on his biceps, rubbed dandelions on my cheek to find out whether I liked butter or not, and got killed by a car on Main Street across from Sid and Wally's. Sid and Wally's was a beer garden. My mother and my father and my grandmother all told me my grandfather was color-blind. That didn't make any sense. He'd been color-blind all his life. He had to know a red light from a green light. Red was on top. Green was on the bottom. I didn't get to go to his funeral.

There were ups and downs, but my idyllic childhood went on and on, summer after summer—fall, leaves, winter, snow—spring after spring. There were hand-painted pictures of Bambi and Thumper on my curtains and gold lariats on the blue blanket on my bed. I believed in Santa Claus until I was eleven. I *still* believe in the Tooth Fairy, but that's only because I saw her with my own eyes, flitting around my pillow one night. She looks kind of like Tinkerbell, but she's way more serious. And shy. Every year, when it finally got to be the middle of June and my birthday rolled around again, I got so excited I made myself sick.

* 𝒢𝒢 *

But the only really pertinent thing about growing in Michigan is that I flunked government and didn't graduate from high school. Mrs. Miller flunked me. She called herself "Mrs." Miller, but had never been married. Everyone knew she'd never been married.

The first day of class she pushed herself away from her desk, stood up, licked the tip end of a little nub of chalk, wrote "Mrs. Miller" in chubby white letters across the center panel of a clean slate blackboard, dropped the chalk back into the chalk tray, dusted her chubby white hands together and said, "This is U.S. Government. If you flunk Government you don't graduate high school." Here she paused to let the idea of not graduating from high school sink in awhile—or maybe to give some of her chins a chance to stop quivering—then said, "I'm Mrs. Miller."

Chalk dust hovered in shafts of morning sunlight.

Mrs. Miller pushed her glasses deeper into the indentations at either side of her chubby nose, gave herself a hug and asked, "Are there any questions?"

Nope. Not me, Mrs. Miller, we all said silently. There wasn't so much as a smirk. We didn't even *think* things that might have made us smirk. She was on the lookout for smirks. She was on the lookout for thoughts that might lead to smirks. Row by row she zoomed in on us, one by one, bristling at the possibility that some mental retard might, however fleetingly, look like he or she was in any degree of doubt about the marital status Mrs. Miller had chosen to bestow upon herself, and row by row, we watched the second hand click its way around the face of the clock and listened to the last of the chalk dust settle onto the floor.

Finally, she almost smiled and said, "Good."

What Mrs. Miller got out of her thirty year career as a teacher was those first few minutes at the beginning of each new semester when she had twenty-five fresh little half-formed souls to bully into corroborating the lie of a lifetime, and what we got out of being in her class was a visceral appreciation of the better part of valor and self-control enough to last us at least through the rest of puberty. We would have gone along with anything. She could have called herself Marilyn Monroe and we all would have sworn up and down that we saw Joe DiMaggio dropping her fat ass off in front of school that morning.

But the truth was that Mrs. Miller *wasn't* married and hadn't ever *been* married and wasn't bloody likely to ever *get* married, and the reason for that was that nobody *liked* the old bat; whereas I, on the other hand, well, everyone had always adored me since the day I was conceived—which was no doubt the *real* reason she flunked my ass. Out of spite. She didn't say so, of course. She *said* she flunked my ass because I slept in class and didn't do the work.

That was what she told my mother, at any rate. But what would you expect her to say? That she was jealous? Pfssh. She wouldn't have admitted she was jealous any more than she would have admitted she'd never been married—besides which, it was all my mother's fault, anyway. *She* was the one who used to read out loud to me before I was born—long rambling passages from *Anna Karenina* and *Kristin Lavrensdatter* and *The Good Earth*. It wasn't *my* fault that the way I learned how to learn was by listening. What that meant vis-à-vis Mrs. Miller, however, was that I didn't take notes in class or anything, but just leaned back in my chair and *listened* and presumed what was worth knowing would stick in my mind and what wasn't wouldn't take up limited space.

Sometimes I listened with my eyes closed.

Mrs. Miller accused me of sleeping while she was explaining some rigmarole about the separation of powers. "Wasn't that why people even *came* to this country?" I frowned convincingly. "To *have* religious freedom."

"Nice try," she said, but flunked my ass anyway.

I had to take another semester of high school when my family moved to California. Then, even though I wrote a paper that correctly predicted Kennedy would win the 1960 presidential election…and by how many electoral votes from which states (including astutely allowing for voting irregularities in Cook County), the crew cut Nazi government teacher in California almost fucking flunked my ass *again*, and I almost didn't graduate from high school that time either.

I still have nightmares about it. I find myself stuck in long, complicated dreams of living the rest of my life in one great big endless government class with Mrs. Miller standing over me like Winston Churchill in drag, wagging a churlish, spiteful, self-satisfied finger in my face, telling me that I never will know the separation of powers from the separation of church and state. I wake up in cold sweats…but the only thing that really matters about any of this is that that was how I got to know Elliot Felton. If Mrs. Miller hadn't flunked my ass, none of this would have ever happened.

* 𝓖 𝓖 *

Elliot was my friend. We were in a drama class together at Hillsdale High School in San Mateo, California. His parents were Mormons. He'd grown up in Salt Lake but had moved to San Mateo when his father was transferred to the San Francisco office of the FBI the previous year.

By the time I got there, Elliot already had something of a reputation. He'd almost killed one of the school's star football players, for one thing. It was an accident, I found out later, but almost killing an all-conference defensive end gets you something of a reputation whether it was an accident or not. Then he got the part of Clarence Darrow in *Inherit the Wind*, won first prize in an art contest put on by the *San Mateo Times* and started going steady with Dru Davidson, the cutest girl in the senior class, all while he was still just a junior. Obviously there had to be something sort of cool about the guy, but nobody seemed to be able to figure out quite what.

Yeah, he could draw pictures and act, but the only thing he ever really *did* was shuffle up and down the hallways in a pair of dusty Wellingtons, never saying a word to another living soul and smoking close to three packs of Camels a day. Rumors flew. People thought he could read minds or that he knew voodoo or that he could hypnotize people. How else could he have gotten Dru Davidson to go steady with him? He must have put some kind of whammy on her. Dru dumped him the summer before I got there, but Elliot had a reputation when I met him nonetheless.

The second week of school we had to do a scene together in drama class. Why I signed up for a drama class I'll never know. Elliot and I were complete strangers to one another—and total opposites in every way. The drama teacher, Donald Ralston, just sort of arbitrarily stuck Elliot and me up on the stage together. Well, it seemed arbitrary, but I think Ralston thought Elliot and I might "do each other good." He seemed to think Elliot was some kind of budding genius, but the only thing he could have known about me was that, thanks to Mrs. Miller, I was a year older than everyone and seemed to have something of a chip on my shoulder.

He was right about the chip. I mean, not to change the subject or anything, but not only was I a year older than everyone, I didn't belong there, period, not in high school or California, either one. I'd already been on my own the whole summer, working on a yacht down in Newport Beach, and had no intention of ever going to any kind of school again, let alone back to *high school*.

I barely remember how it all happened. I was having a hard life, I remember that much. I'd been having a hard life ever since my girlfriend in Michigan dumped me and went to New York to get rich and famous. She did, too—get rich and famous, that is. Well, somewhat rich and famous, I guess. I don't know quite how one measures these things. She ended up thinking quite a lot of herself, if that's the criteria.

Her name was Donna McKechnie. You don't hear much about her anymore, but for a while there, she was like the hottest ticket on Broadway. She won a Tony Award for her role as Cassie in *A Chorus Line* and did all kinds of movies and TV shows and things. She was The Rose in *The Little Prince* and Sam Malone's girlfriend on *Cheers*. I think she may even have been elected Miss Turnstile of the New York City subway system at some point—but that all came way after I ever knew her. She dumped me right around the time that Ritchie Valens song about some chick named Donna dumping him was playing on every radio and jukebox in the country. There was nowhere you could go to get away from it.

Crap. I really don't want to get into any of this, but it's true, and probably even sort of pertinent; ever since old Donna dumped my ass, I really never *have* been quite the same—so I guess maybe I ought to start with *that*.

CHAPTER FOUR

Fifteen Mile

Donna didn't used to think quite so much of herself. Not when I first got to know her. She was a new kid, from a different school. She didn't live in the same district as the rest of us. No one knew why that was, but we suspected it was something sinister, something adult, a situation of some sort. She didn't fit in. I found out later that it was simply more convenient for her to go to our school because of its proximity to her dance studio. But there was still something sort of fishy about her—like she had webbed feet or something. Damn! That was our first conversation.

I broke my collarbone is how it all started. I was playing football on Tommy Malden's front lawn. Paul Grey and Jimmy Mattern were tackling me. I was trying to gain an extra yard or two, as if so much depended on it. I heard the bone break. It was a muffled crack, like sitting on a couch with a pencil in your back pocket. Dr. Steinberg put a figure eight cast under my arms and referred to my broken collarbone as a fractured clavicle. When the cast was ready to come off, Donna McKechnie and her mother happened to be at the doctor's office, too.

Donna and I were both sixteen. I was six months older than she was. I'd seen her around school. We were in the same homeroom. And if you think she was hot as Cassie in *A Chorus Line*, you should have seen Donna McKechnie when she was barely sixteen, wearing a modest red plaid skirt and a lacy white blouse buttoned up to the indentation at the base of her throat and dangling a dusty black penny-loafer off the ends of her toes in the waiting room of the only orthopedist in town. Her calves rippled under a pair of white tights. Muscular thighs. Sparkly brown eyes. Dimples. Waist like a wasp. Her breasts were small but not so small that they didn't cause the tiny translucent buttons to strain against the buttonholes up the front of her blouse.

"What are you here for?" she asked.

"Fractured clavicle," I said smartly, hoping to sound as though I was someone with whom she could discuss her own medical condition if she so chose. "I broke my collarbone," I said then, in case she thought "fractured clavicle" was too technical. "The thing's been itching like crazy. It's driving me nuts. What about you?"

"I have webbed feet." Her eyes filled with inexplicable mirth.

The comment was meant as a sort of inside ballet joke, I found out later. Dancers walk like ducks. It has something to do with all the gyrations they do—the positions, the repetition. Their pelvises become deformed. Their feet turn out. They walk like ducks. Ducks have webbed feet. Ha, ha. Joke. Funny, funny. But I thought she really *did* have webbed feet and for some reason the idea of primordial little folds of skin between her toes was mildly repulsive.

My father furthered our friendship. He saw a picture of her in *The Royal Oak Tribune*, all dressed up in a medieval costume of some sort, like she might have been Cinderella. One of her legs was bent up behind her at an awkward angle. Her arms were over her head, hands relaxed, fingers touching. He thought she was pretty cute and dared me to call her up. I didn't, not for a long time, but I *did* start paying more attention to her in homeroom. She seemed sad, like she didn't have any friends, but also aloof, like she didn't *want* any friends. The thing that cinched it was I saw her riding to school with Larry Burlison one morning.

Larry Burlison was one of the local hoods. He kept a pack of Lucky Strikes rolled up in the sleeve of his white T-shirt and drove a cool car—a gunmetal gray '52 Hudson Hornet, lowered, and fitted with some sort of custom exhaust system which made it purr like a kitten—but car or no car, if Donna McKechnie would be seen in public with Larry Burlison, she'd be seen with anyone. So I called her up. We went out on dates.

By February of 1959, we were making out in the back seat of Ron Metcalf's dad's Olds '88, listening to Chet Baker sing *My Funny Valentine*. After that, we were on our own. Once we knew all we really wanted to do was make out, we stuck to ourselves, listening mostly to make out music—Johnny Mathis and Nat King Cole and *Who Wrote the Book of Love?* Hm. I wonder.

Donna used to come over to my house. I used to go over to her house. We sat in the car. We didn't care where we were. I remember she had a big mirror in her basement. The mirror had a bar in front of it—or *barre*, I guess you'd say. There was a couch across from the mirror. We used to sit on the couch and watch ourselves hug and kiss and neck and pet.

We cut school and took the streetcar to downtown Detroit—sat on benches by the Ambassador Bridge and snuck into Briggs Stadium and wandered the marble hallways of the golden-domed Fisher Building, talking and talking and necking and talking—we talked and necked ourselves silly. And even when we *did* go to school, all we ever did was write each other love letters. She had a favorite pen. It was a fountain pen with lavender ink. Later on, whenever anyone talked about purple prose, I always thought of Donna and the ink in that pen.

I used to go to her dance studio with her. I even played the part of the director in one of her recitals. Everyone was auditioning for me. It was like *A Chorus Line.* I read somewhere that Donna had had a hand in the writing of *A Chorus Line.* The mirror she danced in front of in *A Chorus Line* was very likely the same mirror she used to dance in front of down in her basement, and the premise probably came from that dance recital where I played the part of the director—hey, I was Michael Bennett before Michael Bennett was Michael Bennett. Ha!

Back then, though, Donna McKechnie was just another sixteen-year-old kid taking dance classes at The Rose Marie Floyd School of Ballet. She worked up a sweat. It soaked her tights and leotard and dripped down her throat. She flicked salty drops of sweat into my face from the bottom of her chin with the backs of her fingernails and laughed with her eyes and sucked in her cheeks and made her lips move in and out like a goldfish. We were kids. She was Mitzi Gaynor. I was

James Dean. Nobody understood us. They called it puppy love.

When she changed back into her street clothes, she always put on extra perfume. The perfume was *L'Aimant*, by Coty. I don't think they even make it anymore, but if they do, go down to the cosmetics counter at Macy's sometime and take a whiff of *L'Aimant*, by Coty—it smells like Donna McKechnie when she wasn't quite seventeen.

At some point I finally saw her with her shoes and socks off. There weren't any primordial folds of skin between her toes, thank God, but her feet were all gnarled up with corns and bunions. They bled. She couldn't dance in toe shoes. She thought she'd never be able to dance. That was all she ever really wanted to do.

Our teenage romance went on and on, getting more and more tempestuous. By Easter we were going steady...and breaking up...and going steady again. The first time we broke up was because I put my hand down the front of her blouse. She took the chain with my class ring on it, sullenly, solemnly, from around her neck and put it into the palm of my wayward hand. I threw it over my shoulder into the back seat of my father's lime-green '57 Plymouth Belvedere. We had a tearful chat. We were always having tearful chats. She crawled over the seat, found my ring, put it back around her neck...and from then on it was okay to put my hand down her blouse.

The next time it was her panties. They weren't even panties, actually, but the bottom half of a white terrycloth bikini bathing suit she had ordered from an ad in the back pages of a *McCall's Magazine* which turned out to have been far too "risqué" to wear in public, so Donna wore them for panties. This too had its price. Off came the ring. Out the window it flew.

And we had to spend the next half hour in a tangle of black-berry bushes looking for the thing again.

Toward the end of June, Donna thought she was pregnant. I was watching Rod Steiger slur his way through *Al Capone*. I had just turned seventeen. She found me in the theater. I never saw how the movie ended. We had another of our tear-ful chats, during which it was somehow concluded that we were going to get married. Then she wasn't pregnant. We were going to get married anyway. Then we weren't. We were too young. She and her mother had too much invested, and personally, I didn't think much of the idea of working at some crappy job the rest of my life in order to buy baby formula or whatever. So we weren't. Then we were again. I'd go from one crappy job to the next, twenty-four hours a day, buying baby formula by the boxcar. We were in love. We couldn't live without one another. We would die if we couldn't be with each other forever. It was fraught.

GG

All that fraughtness came to a head one night toward the end of August. We were going to go see *Imitation of Life* at the drive-in. I parked my dad's car in Donna's dirt driveway. The McKechnie's lived on Fifteen Mile Road. Out in the sticks. I went in the back door, up the stairs and into the kitchen.

Her mother was doing dishes. It was around seven. The sun was still up. The kitchen was dim. There was a small, open window above the sink. Because of the angle of the sun-light, her mother's face was wrinkled in ways I'd never seen before. Usually she looked pretty cute. She'd only been around sixteen when Donna was born. Her husband hadn't

36

been much older than seventeen himself. Her mother's hands were shiny and red from the dishwater. The hem of her skirt was unraveling. Her blouse wasn't tucked in all the way around. She looked like Donna would look after we'd been married for twenty years. The family dog was asleep at her feet—some sort of nondescript flop-eared Maltese Pomeranian.

Donna came into the kitchen. She was wearing a skirt the color of celery and a white sweater with fake pearls around the collar. We didn't say anything to her mother and she didn't say anything to us and we didn't say anything to each other but just walked silently down the back stairs. She led the way; it was like a dirge, like a death march.

I didn't open the car door for her. She slammed it when she got in and stayed as far away from me as she could get— slumped down, with her arms hugging the front of her white sweater. That was anathema, by the way. Back in the summer of 1959, the girl didn't sit by the door. She sat by the boy, as close as she could physically get. Those were the rules. That was all there was to it. I made a quick U-turn and squealed the car back up the driveway. I wasn't going to work myself to death the rest of my life for some...dame...who was going to sit next to the god damn door on our way to the drive-in movies.

Hot August dust from the driveway invaded the inside of the car when she jumped out. Good riddance, I sat there thinking. The celery-colored skirt went down maybe six inches or so below her knees, which made it awkward to run at full speed, but she ran as fast as she could, in through the back door and up the stairs. I sat there with my ears ringing the way they do when you're pissed off and brokenhearted at the same time. It was over. Done. All she wrote.

Then I heard the dog squeal, like maybe it had gotten in her way, and right after that, I heard Donna screaming—nothing intelligible, just screaming. Her mother was looking out the kitchen window at me with a sort of plaintive, helpless expression. My inclination was just to throw the car in reverse and get the hell out of there, but it would not have been chivalrous to have done that, so I went up to the door again. Donna came back down. She had composed herself. She got into the car again and we ended up at the drive-in movies after all.

Imitation of Life was the saddest movie ever made. It was about some black chick trying to pass for white—trying to be someone she wasn't, trying to leave her humble past behind and make a name for herself. It was a total tearjerker. We cried and cried and kissed each other's sopping, sobbing faces with the fatal certainty that our true love, which we knew for sure would last for all eternity, was doomed forever. Dead. Impossible. Hopeless. And the more doomed it was, the deader, the more impossible, the more passionate our sadness grew, and the sadder our passion became.

We ended up in the back seat with most of her clothes tangled up in a tear-soaked wad around her eighteen-inch waist. I don't know whether we ever found the bottom half of that terrycloth bikini bathing suit she wore for panties or not. They may still be stuck up behind one of the heater hoses, for all I know, sitting in an abandoned junkyard somewhere, rotting into dust—the faint odor of doomed true love and *L'Aimant*, by Coty, still lingering after all these years.

Somewhere along the line, the movie must have ended. My car was the only one left in the lot—and the cop shining his flashlight through the steamed-up window wasn't in any hurry to turn the thing off. What a dick! Well, I guess you could hardly blame the guy. I mean, who, if they ran across Donna McKechnie when she was still sixteen and all but stark-ass naked in the back seat of a '57 Plymouth, *wouldn't* keep the flashlight on longer than absolutely necessary?

"What do you kids think you're doing?"

"We're engaged," I said. "We're going to get married."

"Well. Better see to it you do, then."

We put on as many of our clothes as we could find, got back up into the front seat again, and drove out of the bumpy drive-in movie parking lot.

Then I had to stop at a red light. That was the thing I remember most of all. There weren't any cars anywhere. I thought about not stopping, but I stopped anyway. Donna jumped out of the car and ran. I parked on someone's front lawn and chased her. She could really run, too, even in that skirt. I caught up to her, yeah, but we were pretty far away from everything by then. We were out of breath, panting, sweating, still trembling from the brouhaha back at the drive-in.

"Let's just go back to the car. I'll take you home."

"I'll take myself home." She turned to run away again. I grabbed her wrist. "Don't *touch* me!" She looked frantic. A porch light went on.

"People are going to call the cops or something, okay?"

"I don't *care!*"

"Would you just listen a second."

"No."

"I love you."

"Shit!"

39

That was pretty definitive back in 1959. When the boy said, "I love you," to the girl and she said, "Shit," well, there really just wasn't all that much left to say. She took off again. I didn't try to stop her. She hadn't even bothered to throw my class ring anywhere, this time. I think that was the last time I ever saw the thing. She might still have the son of a bitch, for all I know. Maybe it's hanging around her Tony Award. I doubt it, but, hey. I mean, who knows? Not me.

When I got back to the car, some old guy in a frayed bathrobe was standing there with a ten-gauge shotgun. The engine was still running. The driver's side door was still open. The headlights were shining at cockeyed angles up into the limbs of an elm tree. The guy hoped I had a good explanation for the tire tracks on his lawn. I didn't. I had no explanation whatsoever. I got in the car and drove away. If he was going to shoot me, he could go ahead and shoot me.

I went home and waited for Donna to call. I had it all pictured. She'd be all tearful and cry and beg my forgiveness and make it up to me in ways neither of us had ever thought of before. She didn't call, however. I kept waiting. School started. I thought we'd be in the same homeroom again. We weren't. She was no longer enrolled in school. I asked at the office. I saw her early one morning. She was riding with her mother in their old bronze Chrysler New Yorker. They were headed in the opposite direction from the school, going south on Woodward Avenue toward downtown Detroit. Her mother looked sleepy. Donna didn't see me.

I *still* kept waiting for her to call. Whenever the phone rang, I got palpitations. It was never her. Finally, around Christmas, Donna came back to spend the holidays with her mother and gave me a call. That was a surprise. We went to the Shrine of the Little Flower for midnight mass on Christmas Eve. Neither of us was Catholic. I found out that during the four months I'd been waiting for her to call, she'd gone with a friend who was auditioning for the traveling company of *Guys and Dolls* and ended up getting the part herself. Then she dropped out of school, went to New York and—blah, blah, blah—the rest is Broadway history.

After mass was over, we parked in her driveway and talked some more, then started making out a little, like for old time's sake. Pretty soon, she started to cry and, naturally, I thought, hey, hey, here we go—but then she stopped right in the middle of kissing me and started sobbing uncontrollably.

"What's the matter?"

"I miss Michael," she said.

That was it. There's only so much a person can forgive. Who the fuck was Michael? I didn't even ask. My poor heart was utterly crushed and broken forever.

* *♫ ♫* *

I did manage to see her a few times in the intervening years, but she kept getting more and more uppity every time. It was like *Imitation of Life* all over again, like I was part of some humble past she wanted to put behind her. One of the times I saw her, she was in San Francisco with the traveling company of *A Chorus Line*. She and Marvin Hamlish were sitting in the orchestra seats at the Curran Theater. He wanted to know what she was like in the back seat of a '57 Chevy. I told him it was a Plymouth. Then all he wanted to talk about was ice cream. Another time I saw her, she was prattling on about how she was going to marry Michael Bennett. I presumed

Michael Bennett had been the Michael she'd been crying about in her driveway lo those many years ago, and it pissed me off a little that I'd been aced out by some fag, but I didn't mention that either.

The last time I saw her was around twenty years ago. We were eating ice cream cones in Sausalito. I told her that when it came to women, I sure knew how to pick them. She took that as a compliment. I'd meant it as a compliment. Since the last time I saw her, Donna had married Michael Bennett in Paris and had divorced Michael Bennett in New York. That was kind of a sore subject. I asked if she got anything good out of the divorce. The question pissed her off. She told me I was like a crass *tabloid* reporter. She got extra uppity about it, like maybe she thought I was going to go on *Geraldo* and tell the whole world how she used to ride around in Larry Burlison's '52 Hudson Hornet. I don't know what the hell she thought. And, frankly, I didn't much care. I had troubles of my own by then—which I'll get to soon enough if I can somehow manage to get back to how I got to know Elliot Felton.

CHAPTER FIVE

Pacifica

Okay. So. After I was convinced that I was definitively dumped forever, I drowned my sorrows by writing the senior play. I've always drowned my sorrows by writing stuff. If I had no sorrows I wouldn't ever write diddly. Writing the senior play was my big claim to fame. The school didn't have the money to buy the rights to a real play, so I said I'd write one. I stuck in a scene about a guy who had recently had his heart utterly crushed and broken forever. Then I played the part of the brokenhearted guy and gave myself lots of good advice. Ha! I was the student director, too. I did it all.

The play was a big success. I had to take a bunch of bows. People kept clapping. And all of a sudden all kinds of new chicks started coming up to me in the hallways, batting their eyelashes, bumping their breasts into my bare arms—cheerleaders, actresses, smart chicks with glasses.

Then, right in the middle of all that, Mrs. Miller flunked my ass and I didn't graduate. What chick's going to mess with some guy who flunked out of high school? No chick, that's what chick. No wonder I had a chip on my shoulder. I've still got a chip on my shoulder. I'll always have a chip on my

shoulder. Talk about completely fucking up a person's life forever. Oh, well. My life probably would have gotten fucked up
forever somehow or other anyway.

* 𝒢 𝒢 *

The day after I didn't graduate from high school, we all,
me and my two younger sisters and my mother, flew out to
California to join my father. He'd been transferred there in
April, and the insurance company he was working for gave
everyone a free plane ticket. How could I pass it up? The picture I had in mind of California was row upon row of sun-
bleached blond girls in bikini bathing suits lying around on
sandy white beaches waiting for random guys to come rub
Coppertone on them—and my father had written a letter telling us that the house he'd rented was three blocks from the
ocean! Where there was an ocean there had to be a beach,
right? Hot sand? Damp towels? Salty sweat and a melting
cherry Sno Cone dripping down some cute little California
surfer chick's suntanned throat?

Wrong.

What my father's letter didn't mention was that the house
he'd rented was in a place called Pacifica, which, next to maybe
Baffin Island and Tierra del Fuego, is easily the third most
inhospitable place on the planet. According to the people
who live there, Pacifica stays "socked in" all summer, and what
"socked-in" means is that it's so fucking freezing-ass cold and
foggy and windy that you can't see across the street let alone
down to the ocean, and even if you could see down to the
ocean, which you can't, you still couldn't see any beach
because, number one, there isn't any beach and, number two,

what passes for a beach is nothing but jagged rocks with huge cliffs towering above them, so that even if you could see what passes for a beach, there wouldn't be any girls on it unless some poor blind paraplegic chick accidentally rolled her wheelchair over the edge of one of the cliffs, and even then she wouldn't have on a bikini bathing suit unless she was also so hopelessly crazy you wouldn't want to have anything to do with her anyway.

I didn't blame my father. None of us did. Well, not for that. We took his word for it that the weather had been nice the day he'd rented the place, and besides, there were plenty of other things to blame him for—like those three blocks from the ocean he'd bragged about. What the letter didn't say was that each block was half a mile long and went straight up the side of a mountain, so that if you were ever stupid enough to risk life and limb by venturing out into the blinding wind and fog long enough to try to make it down to the tawdry little shopping area at the bottom of the street, you'd have to be Edmund Hillary to get back home again.

My father was having kind of a hard life himself. His job wasn't what it was cracked up to be. What had sounded like a lot of money in Michigan wasn't much in California. I don't know which of us was the most disappointed. I think it was a five-way tie. We all had different ideas of what things were going to be like in California, and none of them was anything like what we found in Pacifica.

My sister Nicki, who'd just turned fifteen, did nothing but sit on the bare floor in her room, wearing every stitch of clothing she owned and listening to Buddy Holly sing *Everyday* over and over so often she wore out the grooves on the record. My father tried to cheer her up as best he could, first by trying to play *Peggy Sue* on the mouth organ, then by getting her her own phone—both of which turned out to be about as disastrous as everything else he'd tried to do so far that year. If anyone could have played *Peggy Sue* on the mouth organ it would have been my dad, but the fact is it can't be done, and as for getting Nicki her own phone, yeah, she always *had* wanted a phone of her own, but the son of a bitch never *rang*, and she didn't know anyone she could *call* except back in Michigan, which nobody could afford to pay for, and it only would have made her more homesick than she already was even if anyone *could* have paid for it.

My poor mother. All she ever did was try not to cry in front of my five-year-old sister, Tuney…and poor Tuney! She thought for all the world that we were going to be living next door to Disneyland. Ha! The only thing remotely resembling Disneyland that we could reasonably get to on the best of days was a drafty, overpriced, one-screen movie theater down in the tawdry shopping area at the foot of that bloody mountain. I didn't help matters much.

Tuney had heard that *The Snow Queen* was playing at the movie theater at the bottom of the mountain. I told her that I'd take her to see it but that I didn't have any money to buy myself a ticket. She got all excited and jumped up and down and begged and pleaded and, in short, convinced me that she wanted to see *The Snow Queen* so excruciatingly badly that she gladly agreed to pay my way with the silver dollar she got from her grandmother that Christmas.

The story has become something of a family legend. The way Tuney tells it is that I tricked her into giving me her silver dollar then took her to see *The Apartment*, instead. And, on the face of it, that's true. I did. Well, not the "tricked her" part. I didn't trick her. *The Snow Queen* had been replaced by *The Apartment* just that day, is all, and I truly did not think that she would really want to turn around and walk all the way back up the side of that god damn mountain again without seeing *some* movie, *any* movie, so I took her to see *The Apartment*. I thought I was being considerate, but, no, no, no, she ended up thinking that I was the asshole of the universe. We still go around and around about it. Every few years or so we have some version of the same general conversation:

"Gave it to you, my ass!" Tuney says. "I did not *give* it to you. You flat-out stole the silver dollar I'd been saving since my *grand*mother gave it to me for Christmas…on her *death*bed."

And I say, "Hey, I took you to the movies, right?"

"Yeah, to *The* fucking *Apartment* ! Why would I want to see some shitty movie that gave me nightmares the rest of my life?"

"It wasn't her deathbed."

"It was the last time I saw her *alive*, the last Christmas I was in Michigan, the last Christmas it *snowed*."

"So why'd you spend it?"

"I *didn't* spend it, you fucking asshole. You fucking stole it off of me! To see *The* fucking *Apartment*."

"I didn't *steal* it."

"Oh, no? Oh, no? I had a silver dollar. It was mine. I owned it. I loved it. I kept it under my pillow at night. And I never would have spent it on anything except to see *The Snow Queen*. And I never *saw The Snow Queen*."

"Why don't you just go rent *The* god damn *Snow Queen*?"

"I did. It was stupid."

"So I saved you from seeing a stupid movie."

"It wouldn't have been stupid when I was five!"

"Yeah, well the way I see it is if I hadn't taught you the value of a dollar at such a tender age you never would have gone to law school."

"Oh, so I *owe* you? For what? Deadbeat clients' deciding it's easier to sue my ass for malpractice than it is to pay their bills? Bloated old judges *admonishing* my ass? Prissy little *paralegals differing* with the way I punctuate my sentences?"

"Hey, I was a prissy little paralegal."

"Yeah, until you got fired for being an asshole."

"I got fired for conducting legitimate union organizing activities."

"That's what I said. You got fired for being an asshole."

"A lot you know."

"That's right. I do. Remember that the next time you try tricking a five-year-old into seeing some shitty movie that gives her nightmares the rest of her life."

* 𝒢 𝒢 *

Oh, well. The day after our disastrous trip to see *The Snow Queen,* I got the hell out of there and hitchhiked down along the coast highway until I came to the California I'd had in mind back in Michigan. It started just past Malibu. I didn't have any money. I ate food out of garbage cans, slept on beaches and feasted my eyes on sun-bleached blond girls in bikini bathing suits from dawn to dusk—until having no money and a third-degree sunburn had me heading back up toward Pacifica again.

That was when I got the job on that yacht I was talking about. This colored guy picked me up. He was driving a white Cadillac and had a white girlfriend. His name was Lucius. His girlfriend was a nurse, "A noyse," he called her. Lucius told me to show up at the Lido Shipyard in Newport Beach the next morning and he'd see to it that I got a job. I did. I slept behind a billboard, hitchhiked back down to Newport Beach and started work that same day. I was a good worker. I did everything no one else would do, like paint the inside of the chain locker. I had Rustoleum in my eyebrows for weeks.

Toward the end of the summer, when we were just about through renovating the whole huge boat from stem to stern, the captain told me I could stay on as part of the crew when they took it on a trip around the world. I had it all pictured. Hawaii. Fiji. Bali. Bangkok! Then I don't know what the hell happened.

Well, I got fired, is what happened—for going for a ride on the Ferris Wheel on Balboa Island with the owner's son's girlfriend. Her name was Paris. She had blond hair, freckly thighs and zinc oxide across the bridge of her nose. I didn't know she was anyone's girlfriend. She didn't *say* she was anyone's girlfriend—and she sure didn't *act* like she was anyone's girlfriend. But she was. And the owner's son told the owner to tell the captain to tell the foreman that I was fired and that was that—no trip around the world, no job, no money, no place to live, no nothing. I hitchhiked back up to my parents' house.

GG

It was September. My family had moved from Pacifica to San Mateo by then and were living in a modest little three bedroom house in a place called San Mateo Village—which was how I ended up at Hillsdale High School doing this scene in a drama class with some stuck-up Mormon kid from Salt Lake City.

I was the cop. Elliot was the crook. I had to give him the third degree. That was the scene. I forget what play it was from. The script had been run off on a mimeograph machine. The ink was purple; the ink *smelled* purple. He had on a black and maroon striped shirt and was sitting in a metal folding chair pulled up next to a green cardboard card table. There was an open pack of Camels in his shirt pocket.

I stood over him with my sleeves rolled up and the stub of a pencil behind my ear. A hundred and fifty watt light bulb glared into his face. Sweat beaded up on his scalp. His hair was dark brown, almost black, and straight, and stringy. He had the beginnings of a widow's peak, but his hair was so long in back it curled up at the ends like fish hooks. A muscle twitched in his cheek. Blood wiggled through an artery in his temple. The corners of his mouth jerked into inappropriate smiles. His lips trembled. I could see each individual follicle of the sparse whiskers on his chin and the pores on the sides of his nose and the veins in his nostrils and the hair inside his ears. A drop of sweat trickled down his temple. His hands were shaking. His *ears* were shaking. His eyelids were puffy.

And his eyes. I still can't say what his eyes looked like. Well, they were brown, but I can't describe the expression in them. It was pure fear—abject panic. He was scared to death. His eyes darted back and forth, into and out of every murky corner of the fidgeting auditorium, getting more and more terrified. Then he looked up and directly at me for the first time. That was the last straw. There were tears in his eyes. He looked like he was about to wet his pants. I wanted to stop everything right there and tell him, hey, man, come on, it's a *drama* class. Yeah, sure, I knew he was supposed to be *acting* like he was scared, but he wasn't acting, he was really scared, he was *terrified*—and even if he *was* acting, there comes a point when it doesn't matter; like if you wet your pants in front of whole god damn drama class, how could it possibly matter whether you were just acting or not?

I burst out laughing. I couldn't help it. I couldn't read the lines. I tried, but when he looked up at me, I had to laugh. They had to close the curtain on us. We had to start all over. That happened three times—him looking up at me, me laughing, them closing the curtain. The fourth time, Elliot lurched out of his seat, kicked his chair across the stage, tossed the script out into the audience and stormed over to the emergency exit door, leaving sheets of mimeograph paper rocking slowly back and forth down through the sudden utter silence of the cavernous auditorium.

I felt sort of bad that I was screwing up the scene for him, sure, but on the other hand, what the hell did he think, it was Carnegie Hall? It wasn't. It was a two-bit drama class in a high school I never should have been at in the first place. My girlfriend was in New York, dancing on Broadway, getting rich and famous. And, as for me, I should have been in Bali by then. I should have been halfway to Bangkok.

Over in the wings, Elliot took a few deep breaths, whipped out a comb, slicked back his hair, and came back out onto the stage. One of the kids in the front row offered him a new script. Elliot waved it off. He brought his chair back, sat down again, and we tried doing the scene one last time. The curtain opened. The light bulb glared. Sweat beaded up. His cheek twitched. His mouth trembled. He looked at me. There were tears in his eyes. He was about to wet his pants. I laughed. The curtain closed. We were alone back there.

"Sorry," I said.

Elliot didn't say anything. He hadn't said anything the whole time. He *wanted* to say something. It was plain to see that he was trying to think of something suitable to say, but by the time I got around to telling him I was sorry, he couldn't have said anything even if he'd thought of something to say, and finally he just *hissed* at me. He bared his teeth and hissed at me like a cat—but not even a cat, something more primitive than a cat—a lizard, or a snake, or a sea urchin.

A current of electricity shot through me. It felt for a second like I was going to hiss back at him, but then it dawned on me that I didn't have to put up with some California dipshit hissing at me like a fucking sea urchin no matter what I did, and I *winked* at him, instead—just a quick little wink with my right eye.

That was the best thing I could have done. It caught him so completely off guard he had to smile. Then he caught himself trying not to smile and that made him almost have to laugh. It was like the sun coming out. All of a sudden his eyes were so full of such affection for me it felt like he was about to jump out of his chair and dance me around the stage like a rag doll—as if his whole life he'd been waiting for someone to wink at him and nobody ever had. Elliot couldn't just let it go at that, however, and acted like he felt sort of sorry for me.

"How about I play the cop?" he asked.

"You should just get someone else, man. I can't act worth a shit. I don't know why I even signed up for this stupid class in the first place."

"There's nothing to it. Just be a cop. Be thinking about what your wife's going to be cooking for dinner while you ask me questions."

"I can't. I'd be picturing her cooking snakes or something. They'd be jumping out of the pot. She'd have to keep hitting them on the head with a spoon."

"Hey, that's *King Lear* ! 'Down, wantons, down.' That's my favorite line. 'Cry to it, nuncle, as the cockney did to the eels when she put 'em i' the paste alive; she knapped 'em o' the coxcombs with a stick, and cried, "Down, wantons, down!" 'Twas her brother that, in pure kindness to his horse, buttered his hay.'"

"Yeah, well, I don't know about any of that. All I know is trying to do something I can't do makes me laugh."

"So, quit trying." He shrugged.

I made him feel superior. He liked that. He made me laugh. I liked that. We got to be friends. That was all there was to it. We stayed friends forever—or for however long forever might have been back then. I don't know the meanings of words anymore. Forever seems about right.

CHAPTER SIX

San Mateo

$\mathcal{E}$lliot's parents lived in a custom-built turquoise and white ranch style house at the end of a cul-de-sac up in the hills above the southern part of San Mateo. I liked going up there. The living room had plush, pearl gray carpet that smelled like it had just been installed and soft cream-colored love seats and a soft cream-colored couch, all with matching end tables and table lamps with three-way bulbs.

The furniture in the living room was centered around a combination television and high-fidelity record player. Sliding glass doors opened onto a redwood deck with a panoramic view—north up past the airport to San Bruno Mountain, south down almost to San Jose and east across the bay to Oakland and Hayward and over the hills to Mt. Diablo. Beyond the deck there was a path of flagstones leading over to some jasmine bushes and a Cost-Plus waterfall. In the kitchen there was a huge new two-door refrigerator full of all sorts of things I'd never seen outside a grocery store.

My own parents, by way of contrast, had bought a house in San Mateo Village, like I said, down in the flatlands by the bay, with the same floor plan as all the other houses in the flatlands; the same hard grass yards, with short, newly planted trees. Instead of carpet, we had rugs. Nothing matched. Nothing was new. And the only good thing in the refrigerator was maybe a bowl of browned potatoes left over from one of my mother's pot roasts. There was nothing in the world my father liked better for breakfast than leftover potatoes from one of my mother's pot roasts, sliced razor thin and fried in sizzling bacon grease along with his eggs—two, sunny-side up. I adore my dad. He's dead. As I've said.

The other thing I liked about going up to Elliot's house was his mother. She used to get a kick out of wearing skimpy clothes around the house. There was this one sheer white silk robe I remember in particular, with a sash she always had trouble keeping tied when she answered the door.

They had a mat on the front porch with the word WEL-COME spelled out in pieces of pink rubber held together with short lengths of wire, and there was a brass doorknocker on the door with the name "FELTON" etched into it. The door-knocker was actually a doorbell *disguised* as a doorknocker. When you picked it up and pushed it back down again, it was supposed to go "Ding...dong!" But there was something wrong with the dong. It sounded like it had a piece of broken Popsicle stick stuck down inside it. The ding was okay, but the dong just went "thunk."

𝒢 𝒢

I remember going up there this one day. I rang the bell, "Ding...thunk," wiped my feet on the welcome mat, and waited breathlessly for his mother to come to the door. Elliot never answered the door himself. His mother always did. I think it might have been some sort of a deal they had. I heard her fumbling with the dead bolt. Moths fluttered around my heart like it was a three-way light bulb. The door opened a crack and I saw one beguiling green eye peeking out at me. She unhooked the chain and pulled the door wide open with a big whoosh, and the vacuum created by the door opening sheathed her thighs and the nipples of her breasts in sheer white silk for a second. When I looked up, she was looking at me with her head cocked, like she knew exactly the effect she was having on me.

I melted.

I couldn't help but melt.

She was pretty from the top of her head to the tips of her painted toenails—short, fine, coppery-red hair, pouty lips, creamy red lipstick. Her mouth turned down at the corners; she looked perpetually sad. She licked her lips before she spoke. I could see the wetness of her mouth.

"Elliot's in listening to his weirdo music," she said and pointed toward the living room. Then she sauntered slowly down the hallway toward the open door of her bedroom with shafts of bright sunlight shining through her sheer white silk robe.

* *G G* *

When I got to know him better, I found out how Elliot had almost killed the football player. The football player had been drunk. He and some other football players had been drinking beer in the parking lot next to McDonald's. One of them tossed an empty beer bottle over by where Elliot was waiting for a bus. Elliot kicked the empty beer bottle into the gutter. That wasn't the right thing to have done. There wasn't any right thing to have done.

One thing led to another. The football player took a swing at him. All Elliot did was duck. The football player lost his balance and cracked his face against the edge of the curb. Three teeth broke off at the root. Blood puddled up. His eyes stayed open. He was trying to swallow. He looked like a fish. Elliot threw up.

He went over and over it and over it in his mind for months. He got obsessed with ways he could have prevented it and ended up making a vow to himself that he wouldn't ever fight anyone again, no matter what, not even to defend himself—next time he wouldn't even duck. He was as close to being an absolute pacifist as a person could reasonably be. The idea of hurting living things made him sick to his stomach.

Being such a pacifist made Elliot do things differently from other people—like take out his aggressions, for example. A normal person would just hit a wall or kick a hole in a door or something, but Elliot had to resist such simple solutions for fear of wiping out whole civilizations of microscopic wall dwellers. That wasn't the case when it came to Dru Davidson, however; when it came to Dru, all bets were off.

Elliot presumed he and Dru would be getting back together any day. The way he saw it was that pretty soon he'd be making a name for himself as an actor or an artist or a guitar player and she'd come crawling back, make it all up to him in ways they'd never thought of before. They'd get married and live happily ever after in a house he was going to build for her on one of those huge outcroppings of rock that juts out into the ocean down around Big Sur.

Then Elliot's imagination started falling apart. First Dick Joseph saw Dru playing tennis with some Japanese guy at the tennis courts behind Burlingame High. Not long after that, someone else saw her with the same guy at a party in Eichler Highlands and mentioned they thought the guy might be in dental school.

Elliot didn't believe anything anyone told him. He knew Dru wouldn't be caught dead with no sorry-ass Jap, period, and especially not with no sorry-ass Jap who was going to spend the rest of his life mucking around in people's *mouths* for a living. What kind of person would pick at putrefaction and decay and muck around in root canals all day? Would his darling Dru want to share a life like that? No. What would they talk about? Plaque? Gingivitis?

It certainly wouldn't be the sort of life she and *Elliot* would have together. Would some Jap dentist take her to Spain to see the sublime shadows and lights of El Greco? Would they go to the Prado to marvel at *The Garden of Earthly Delights*? Would they worship at the altar of Antonio Gaudi? Or listen to Segovia? Or Charlie Bird? Or Charlie Parker? Or Miles? Or Mozart? Would he read to her from *The Book of Ecclesiastes* or sing to her from *The Song of Songs*? Would she be his Cordelia? Would they live and pray and sing and tell old tales and laugh at gilded butterflies?

Then, with his own eyes, he saw her arm in arm with the selfsame Japanese guy he'd been hearing about, and Elliot *knew* the guy. It was Jerry Takahashi. He wasn't in dental school. He was taking classes at the College of San Mateo—in Dental Technology. He wanted to make false teeth for a living. That was just the beginning. Not much more than a week after he'd seen Dru with Jerry Takahashi, Elliot saw her again, this time all snuzzled up to Steve Goldner by the front window of Sherman & Clay, looking at pianos. There wasn't anything extraordinary about Steve Goldner. He was a Jew. He worked in his father's jewelry store—he was a Jew jewelry clerk in his Jew father's Jew jewelry store!

I have no reason whatsoever to believe that up until then Elliot had an ax to grind with the Japanese or Jews, either one. (well, his father spent a year or so in a Japanese prison camp, but I doubt that had much to do with it). All I know is that from then on, all Elliot thought about was hunting down Japs and Jews indiscriminately and hacking them to pieces with the machete his father had brought back as a souvenir from the war in the Pacific. This was at odds with Elliot's strict pacifism, however, and he ended up painting strange, disturbing pictures instead.

At first the pictures were nothing but bloody piles of body parts, but they got more sophisticated as time went on, subtler, more refined. I think I was the only person besides him who ever actually *saw* any of the pictures. Elliot wasn't *proud* of them. They were necessary. They were therapeutic. I kind of liked them myself. I mean, however objectionable the subject matter, the pictures themselves were just plain pretty to look at. They were like Russian Orthodox icons; they were so gorgeous they almost glowed. One was all in dull reds and yellows and somber browns, depicting bodies being loaded into a row of fiery furnaces. That one he simply called, "Hitler's Ovens." Another, with the fragile outlines of a Japanese family vaporized like spider webs against one of the interior walls of a house in Hiroshima, he called, "Roll On, Enola."

In addition to acting and painting pictures, Elliot played flamenco guitar and sculpted. He sat out in his backyard, sweating under a prickly red Indian blanket in the ninety-degree sun for hours, staring at a blank rock until some combination of dehydration and incipient sunstroke caused him to hallucinate something he could chisel into permanence. His backyard crawled with the gruesome little things. He called them his lobotomies.

* *GG* *

After his mother let me in the front door that day, I finished watching her walk down the sunlit hallway and made my way into the living room—and there he was, Elliot Felton, rocking back and forth on a Persian prayer rug, listening to music with his eyes closed and his legs folded under him in a sort of half lotus position. He was wearing a shiny green quilted brocade smoking jacket with black satin lapels. There was a yellow silk cravat tucked down the front of the jacket. He was smoking a meerschaum pipe. His mother had made the smoking jacket for him for his seventeenth birthday. The pipe had the head of a bearded gnome carved into it. His father had brought it home from the property room at the FBI. He told Elliot that the pipe had belonged to some famous crook.

Elliot had no idea I was there. I just watched him for a while until I felt myself start to chuckle so deep inside my chest it brought tears to my eyes. I didn't say anything—I just walked over and sat down across from him and listened to whatever he was listening to. It could have been most anything—*Sketches of Spain*, Segovia, *The Magic Flute*, Charlie Parker, Beethoven, Bach.

That day it was Yma Sumac. People might not know much about Yma Sumac anymore. Not many people knew much about her then, but Elliot worshipped Yma Sumac. She was supposed to have been an Incan Princess whose voice had a range of around nine octaves, lower than thunder on the low end and so high only bats could hear it on the high end. Well, either that or she was some Puerto Rican chick from the Bronx named Amy Camus who spelled her name backwards and *masqueraded* as an Incan Princess.

Whoever or whatever she was, however, her voice did more things than any human voice I ever heard before or since, and Elliot flat-out adored her. He listened to her records so often he knew the words to her songs by heart. Whatever Yma Sumac did with her voice, Elliot tried to do too. They sang duets together. While everyone else was singing along with Mitch Miller, Elliot was singing along with Yma Sumac. She'd growl like a jaguar and hoot like a howler monkey, and he'd try to match her syllable for syllable.

He and Yma Sumac *stalked* each other. The living room was a Peruvian jungle. He peeked out from behind a philodendron, then pounced like a jaguar out from between the couch and the coffee table, tipping over lamps and crashing into a set of brass fireplace tools. It was funny. *He* was funny. *They* were funny; Elliot and Yma, an odder couple you never did see.

* $\mathcal{GG}$ *

His mother worried about Elliot. She was proud of him, but she thought he was odd. Quirky. She didn't think he fit in. We talked about him in their kitchen one afternoon. We were looking out the window at Elliot sitting outside under his Indian blanket. She was wearing a pair of tight white tennis shorts. Her legs were tan. Sunlight sparkled through pretty red highlights in her hair.

"Elliot's always been...exceptional," she said.

"Everybody's exceptional," I told her.

"Yeah, but he's always been so—I don't know...difficult, I guess—even when he was little. He thought he could do things nobody can do. He thought he brought a bird back to life. It was just a sparrow, a little fluff of a thing."

She stopped and seemed to be picturing him as a curly-headed little three-year-old with his baseball cap on sideways, then went on in a faraway voice:

"It flew into the screen door of our house in Salt Lake— probably the first time the poor thing had ever been out of its nest. I'm sure it was only stunned, but Elliot thought it was dead. He picked it up and cupped his hands around it and blew into his hands and pretty soon the sparrow started chirping. He was so proud. He beamed up at me. His eyes were happier than anything I've ever seen. I said something silly, like, 'Now it thinks you're its mother.' And do you know what he said then?" she asked.

The color of copper glinted in her hair. She wet her lips and there was a sad, baffled, smolderingly sexual look in her eyes, like if I could come up with the right answer, she'd be grateful beyond words.

"No," I said. "What did he say?"

"He asked me...he said, 'Are you my mother?'"

"Most kids wonder about stupid stuff like that," I said.

"Sometimes I don't feel like I've been a good mother."

"He never says anything *bad* about you."

"I was so young."

"You must have been," I said.

* 𝒢 𝒢 *

During his last week of school, Elliot went back home to get the gym stuff he had to take back in order to graduate and walked in on his mother and a Lebanese real estate agent having deliberate, consensual sexual intercourse on the drain board next to the kitchen sink. He told me about it later. He trusted me. I trusted him. The real estate guy's pants were around his knees. He hadn't even taken off his tie. That bothered Elliot more than anything else. His mother spoke to him only with her eyes. She pretended it wasn't happening. Elliot got his gym stuff and went back to school.

Elliot spent the better part of the next year in bed. He still hadn't gotten over Dru. His mother and the Lebanese guy had been the last straw. Every time I went up there, he hadn't moved since the last time I'd been there. He was always in bed. His room had sliding glass windows with drapes that didn't close all the way. There was a half finished painting on an easel over in one corner, a bare bones rendering of the kitchen sink. The dishes were all washed and stacked neatly in the dish drainer and there was a fancy silk tie draped around the silverware.

I sat on the edge of his bed. The ceiling sparkled where sunlight came through the crack in the drapes. His bed was a mattress and box springs on the floor. He flicked the ashes from a cigarette into a teacup. The cup had morning glories on it. The ashes sputtered. He coughed. Veins stood out at his temples and in his forehead. His skin was so thin I got the feeling he could see me with his eyes closed.

With his eyes open, it hurt to look at him. He didn't know what to do. He was thinking about maybe cutting his vocal cords and playing flamenco guitar in the gutters of Madrid. He was thinking about maybe taking a kayak to the source of the Amazon River. I brought him a *National Geographic* map of Brazil. According to it, the Amazon River had several sources.

"Hey, so, go up them all," I suggested.

"Which one should I start with?"

"Throw a dart."

But he couldn't make up his mind, period, not about anything. He was close to catatonic. He just stayed in bed, smoking cigarettes. His skin turned yellow and his muscles atrophied and his fingernails grew long and his fingers turned the color of the empty packs of Camels strewn around his room. He didn't want anything from anyone.

His mother thought it was her fault. She implored me with her eyes, what should she do, what should she do?

What could I tell her?

Then, one fine morning, without saying a word to anyone, Elliot got out of bed and joined the Special Forces before anyone had ever heard of the Special Forces and was going to Vietnam before anyone had ever heard of Vietnam. This time it was his father's turn to be proud. He'd known the kid had had it in him all along. He bragged about his son, the Green Beret, to his buddies at the FBI.

Elliot's decision to go into the military crushed his mother. She thought he was trying to hurt her in the worst way he knew how. She thought it was a conspiracy, that Elliot and his father were in on it together, that they were punishing her, that they wanted her to die of pain and shame and guilt and sorrow and regret.

Personally, I didn't get it at all. I thought he was nuts—why an absolute pacifist would join the army, I did not know.

"What are you going to do in the army? Grow up? Liberate people? Stop communism? Get laid? What?"

"Special Forces," Elliot said.

"Yeah? What makes them so special? They don't kill people?"

"How will anyone know whether I kill people or not?"

"What are you going to do, *pretend?*"

"Maybe," he said. Then he smiled the way he had when I'd winked at him back in drama class. It had been almost two years since then.

Yeah, well, during those two years I'd gotten to know Elliot well enough to know that while *I* may not have known what the hell he was doing, *he* usually did. For one thing, he was going to get a lot closer to Bangkok than I ever had. Maybe I was jealous. Maybe he was brave. Maybe I was chicken. Maybe the army would be good for him. I couldn't think of anything that could have been much worse than what he'd *been* doing. And, besides, he'd already done it. Signed up. Taken the oath. He couldn't have changed his mind at that point if he'd wanted to.

CHAPTER SEVEN

North Beach

*S*ix months later, around Christmas of 1962, Elliot
came home on leave. He'd just finished basic training and
some other hush-hush CIA sponsored school at Ft. Bragg and
was going to be on his way to Vietnam the morning of New
Year's Day.

His head was shaved. His ears stuck out. The leather
band around the edge of his green beret made a red, painful-
looking groove in his scalp. His face was tan. His nails were
clipped. He had a few crisp, new ribbons above his shirt
pocket and had already earned himself something of a reputation. The guys he'd been in boot camp with called him "Deacon Felton" or "The Deacon" or "Deak." He was the only
Mormon in the elite, newly created branch of the military they
called "Special Forces." None of the big Bible belt Baptist
bruisers who were his comrades in arms had ever met anyone
who belonged to the Church of Jesus Christ of Latter-Day
Saints, and Elliot talked to them fearlessly about the *Book of
Mormon.*

He told them the whole story of how this Moroni guy, this
sort of angelic fellow who glowed and walked a few feet off

the floor, told some New England dirt farmer by the name of Joseph Smith where to find some gold tablets hidden under a rock, along with a secret magic decoder device, and that the tablets explained how, shortly after the resurrection, Jesus Christ came to the United States and turned a bunch of naked savages into Christians. Elliot's army buddies took kindly to him the way people take kindly to the incurably insane. He used to do that with the real *Bible* in the cafeteria at Hillsdale High School. I remember this one thing he used to quote from *The Song of Songs*:

> *"Stay me with flagons,*
> *Comfort me with apples:*
> *For I am sick of love."*

People looked at him like he was nuts.

* ℊ ℊ *

We had dinner at his parents' house. It was New Year's Eve. I don't think Elliot's father knew about his wife's infidelity with the Lebanese real estate guy on the drain board in the kitchen, per se, but he knew *something*. Their marriage had deteriorated beyond recognition. They spoke to each other with icy niceness.

"Could you pass the pepper, please, dear?"

"Certainly, darling. Anything else? Salt? Parmesan? More salad?"

It made you want to throw spaghetti in their faces. They wouldn't have noticed if you had. They would have ignored it. They would have politely finished their desserts with noodles looped around their ears and spaghetti sauce dripping off the ends of their noses.

Elliot and I finally got the hell out of there and took what was left of a half-gallon of Gallo Hearty Burgundy with us up to San Francisco. To Chinatown. To North Beach. I was twenty. Elliot was nineteen. His uniform was so new you could smell it. It was the same smell as the polish on his boots. The creases in his pants were sharp as knives. He had a tentative smile twitching the corners of his mouth, like he couldn't make up his mind whether he was proud of the way he looked or embarrassed by it. It was the same way he looked when he used to wear his quilted smoking jacket. I half expected him to whip out his meerschaum pipe.

What Elliot had learned in the Special Forces so far was that every Asian over the age of eight wanted nothing more in life than to slit his throat while he was asleep. In Vietnam, for instance, according to what he told me he'd been told, there was a ten thousand dollar reward for every Green Beret any-one could get his or her hands on—just the hat, all by itself— ten grand for a hat.

Half the stuff Elliot told me I *still* have a hard time believ-ing. They had him imagining all kinds of whacko stuff. It was probably part of some sort of self-esteem program—like if just your hat is worth ten thousand dollars, the rest of you has got to be pretty valuable, too. I didn't think he would have fallen for it, though. I wasn't sure he *had* fallen for it; I never *could* tell whether he was acting or not. All I knew was that there we were, on Grant Avenue an hour before midnight on New Year's Eve, with noisemakers gyrating in our faces and confetti sprinkling our shoulders and firecrackers going off like gunfire at our feet and half the Asian population of San

Francisco jamming into us from all sides, and it suddenly didn't seem *unreasonable* that he'd gotten sort of jittery—which is not to say it still didn't seem pretty stupid.

I mean, what he hell did Elliot think? That someone was going to run up, grab his hat and go cash it in somewhere? He was scared, edgy, ultra-aware; a little paranoid, probably. The color had gone out of his cheeks. His eyes darted back and forth, and he backed up into some kind of karate stance, like he was maybe thinking about trying to take on all of China-town with his bare hands.

Then these two Caucasian guys in wingtips and three-piece suits came out of the noisy crowd, got on either side of Elliot and escorted him over into the alley behind City Lights. I couldn't hear what they were saying, but Elliot seemed to be agreeing with them. His head was bowed. His cheek twitched. He nodded and looked up at them and nodded again, and pretty soon the three of them walked up to Broad-way and shook hands. The wingtip guys disappeared back into the crowd.

Elliot marched like a toy soldier over toward the intersec-tion of Columbus and Broadway. The light turned red. There wasn't any traffic. The streets had been roped off. But he stopped anyway. I caught up to him.

"Ah, Elliot?"

"Yeah?"

"So, did we, like…know those guys?"

"No." He shrugged and took off across the crowded intersection.

"Hang on a second," I said, trotting along at his elbow. "Who were they?"

He sped up.

I grabbed his sleeve.

"Knock it off." He pulled his arm away and narrowed his eyes and bared his teeth like he was going to hiss at me again. I was thinking I might have to shoot him another quick wink. I guess just the thought crossing my mind must have calmed him down some. He glanced over his shoulder and said, "They're army intelligence."

"They didn't look that smart to me," I said.

Elliot smiled one of his twitchy smiles and stopped walking quite so fast. Then he told me in a halting, carefully worded, circuitous sort of way, that the Special Forces were so new and so elite and the training he'd just been through was such top secret hush-hush stuff that whenever any of them went out into the "civilian" population, plain clothes army intelligence officers followed them around.

"To what? Make sure nobody steals their hats?"

"Something like that, yeah," he said.

Then he clammed up on me again, like I wasn't qualified, somehow, to be let in on what went on among men on their way to some little nowhere country on the other side of the *National Geographic* world.

§ §

We ended up at the Jazz Workshop. Jimmy Witherspoon was there. I was too curious about what had just happened in Chinatown to care. I mean, come on, this was *me* he was talking to. I knew things the army *couldn't* have known. I knew all about him and Dru and about his mother and about his father. I'd seen him under his Indian blanket. We'd listened to Miles Davis. We'd listened to Yma Sumac! I'd heard him hoot like a howler monkey and growl like a jaguar. I'd seen him in his smoking jacket, I'd seen him almost wet his pants—so what was all this hush-hush army horseshit all of a sudden? What did he have up his sleeve? Maybe he'd caught Dru Davidson diddling some Vietnamese guy up by the Pulgas Water Temple. Or maybe he was a spy. But for who? Spain? Brazil? I couldn't figure it out.

We'd found seats by then. That was when I started noticing a girl in the row ahead of us—and whatever had been going on with Elliot took a back seat to the girl in the row in front of us. Her name was Virginia Good. Ginny. Ginny Good.

My eyes hadn't adjusted to the dark. She was fidgeting in her chair. Her voice trilled and broke at the top of a giggle. She cocked her head and her hair touched her shoulder. Her hair was brown, lighter and darker brown, and curly. It bounced up and down in thick spirals when she tilted her head back and laughed.

She had on a tight black dress, a black lace shawl and a string of pearls, but she still managed to look disheveled, somehow—like she'd come there fresh from riding a horse bareback along the edge of an ocean somewhere. Her shawl brushed my knee. When she talked she got her whole tiny, tough little body into it. The words tinkled like she was playing them on a piano. At one point, she got so adamant she had to jump out of her chair and stamp both feet on the floor like Jerry Lee Lewis. Great Balls of Fire!

"That's not *fair!*" she screamed.

Now, questions of fairness have always piqued my curiosity, I admit, but in fairness, what piqued my curiosity even more was that Virginia Good had the most perfect ass since

Donna McKechnie. I was instantaneously in love forever again.

The best I could figure it, Ginny was out on a date with two different guys at the same time. One of them was wearing thick, black-rimmed glasses. The other had a crew cut. They both had on narrow suits and ties, and although I'd still only seen her from the back, I presumed she must be pretty cute from the front, too—you have to be pretty cute to get two different guys to go out with you on New Year's Eve.

I had on a white, button-down shirt and a light green cardigan with imitation leather buttons and was feeling sort of adorable myself. I accidentally stepped on the end of Ginny's black lace shawl. Then I kept my foot there on purpose. The next time she moved, the shawl ended up around my ankles. Ha! That got the ball rolling. We had to fumble around at my feet, trying to get it untangled. Our heads kept bumping. By the time we'd gotten everything back where it belonged, it would have been rude not to have exchanged a few pleasantries.

The band was tuning up. Jimmy Witherspoon was clearing his throat. Elliot was slumped in his chair. I was eloquent. Charming. Shameless. Elliot covered his face with his ten thousand dollar hat. At some point in the conversation it became apparent that Virginia's dates were ticked. It was bad enough that they had each other to contend with, without some other asshole horning in. They joined forces against me and somehow got Jimmy Witherspoon on their side. I became the common enemy. Being the common enemy is a role I've always relished. With everyone ganged up on you, you don't have a lot to lose and if you win, hey. Besides, the guys she was out with were just a couple of snotty college kids, and as for Jimmy Witherspoon, he could go fuck himself —I wasn't old enough to get in there anyway. Somebody should have checked my ID.

The only thing that mattered was that Virginia liked me. I could tell. I had her laughing her ass off. She thought I was cute, too. I was. I was young. My heart was young. My veins filled with blood so fast I couldn't sit still. What did I have to gain? Plenty. What did I have to lose? Jack. I quoted long, surprisingly apt passages from Blake and Shakespeare and Allen Ginsberg —things I didn't know I knew, things I'd probably picked up by osmosis from Elliot.

I told her I was the smartest person in the world. I told her I knew everything there was to know. The guy with the crew cut asked me what he probably thought was a funny question. "How many pinheads can dance on the head of an angel?"

"Seven," I said.

Ginny laughed. I was on a roll.

Now, any fool knows that the last thing you want to do is *encourage* some twenty-year-old drunk from San Mateo ten minutes before midnight at a jazz club on New Year's Eve, but Virginia couldn't help but laugh. I was funny. The whole thing was funny. Jimmy Witherspoon was funny. The guys she was out with were funny.

Her dates kept encouraging me by getting more and more pissed off every time I made Ginny laugh —and by then she was laughing at just about *everything*. The more pissed off they got, the more eloquent I became and the more Ginny laughed.

Somewhere in there, Elliot stood up, took off his hat and introduced himself.

"Charmed, I'm sure." Virginia extended her hand.

"Your hand's so little," Elliot said.

"'Not even the rain has such small hands,'" I quoted.

"That's E. E. Cummings," the guy with the glasses chimed in.

"No shit," I said.

Then Elliot introduced me to Ginny and she introduced us to the two guys, and finally she introduced herself. Virginia. Ginny. Ginny Good. I stepped in and shook her hand. The boyfriends watched like cobras.

"I'm going to kiss you at midnight," I slurred into Virginia's ear while I was holding on to her hand. I thought I was whispering, but Jimmy Witherspoon glowered down at me from the front of the stage like he thought I might have been talking to him. Virginia made her eyes big and gulped.

Midnight came.

First, she had to kiss the guys she was with. It was only fair. After she'd bestowed scrupulously equal little pecks on each of their cheeks, it was my turn. Ha!

A spotlight lit up her face. It was the first time I'd gotten a good look at her and, wow, was she ever cute—tiny mouth, smirky, mischievous smile, confident body, clear, tan, healthy skin, a few freckles across the bridge of her nose—whoa, was she pretty. Her eyes sparkled an eerie, eerie, otherworldly blue.

The spotlight went out. My head swirled with snatches of drunk, beatnik poetry and after-images of tables and chairs and musical instruments and whisky-drinking blues lyrics and Ginny Good's pretty face and her eerie blue eyes.

At first it was just a tentative, sort of a who's going to call whose bluff kind of a kiss, with me mainly worried that I wasn't going to be able to get all the way through it without throwing up all over Jimmy Witherspoon's shoes. But then it turned into a big kiss. We both somehow managed to maneuver ourselves out of our chairs and were standing up, face-to-face, jamming closer and closer into each other.

She was small and strong. She felt like a dancer. Her hands were under my sweater, tugging at my shirt, and I had her dress pulled up to the tops of her nylons and felt the hem of her panties under the straps of a silky garter belt.

Then she was pounding on my chest and whispering into my ear, "We have to stop. We have to stop. My panties are getting *ruined!*"

"So are mine," I said.

The guys she was with were practically apoplectic by then, but what could they do? With Elliot sitting there, looking stern and menacing in his jaunty Green Beret and shiny black boots? Call the police? Get Army Intelligence? What?

Then Elliot stood up again, bent over in his stiff uniform, and kissed Ginny himself —brushed his lips across her forehead —and I think he might have been crying. I couldn't tell. I could never tell whether he was *ever* crying or not.

Virginia laughed like a four-year-old kid. She let her hair fall in front of her darling face, covered her tiny mouth with her tiny hand and said, "Oh, dear!"

* 𝓖 𝓖 *

The next morning, Elliot was the one who remembered her name. All I remembered was barfing his mother's spaghetti up and down Broadway the rest of the night and, vaguely, that I was in love.

I was picking him up to take him to the airport. It was late by the time I got to his house. He was out by the curb with his duffel bag, looking worried.

"Hey, remember that girl last night?" I asked him, after he'd stuffed his duffel bag into the back seat and had gotten into the car.

"Ginny?" He frowned. His mouth twitched.

"Yeah, right. Ginny what? Did she say?"

He didn't answer.

Then, on the Bayshore Freeway, a little ways past Coyote Point, almost to the airport exit, Elliot turned toward me and said, "Good."

"What's that supposed to mean?"

"That's her last name," he said. "Good. Virginia Good. She's in the San Francisco phone book. On 45th Avenue. I looked her up."

"Why?"

"I don't know. To see if she was there."

"Think I should call her?"

"I have no idea," he said.

"She was kissing me like a son of a bitch. Wasn't she? I had my hands all up her dress, didn't I? She was sort of nuts, too. Wasn't she? Didn't she have scars on her wrists from trying to kill herself or some kind of weird thing?"

Elliot made a little laughing noise out his nose. The muscles in his left cheek were twitching. He was grinding his teeth. He might have had tears in his eyes. He didn't answer—just looked at me and shrugged.

When he went through the gate at the airport, he looked at me and shrugged again in exactly the same way he had in the car. I don't remember whether we shook hands or not. We probably thought about it, but I don't think we did.

Later that same day, at around six o'clock in the evening, I found a listing for Virginia Good in the San Francisco phone book and gave her a call.

CHAPTER EIGHT

Coyote Point

"Helloooo...?"

That's Virginia answering the phone. I can hear it any time I want. Her voice is calm and husky and faintly musical, like a cello, and there's always the same inquisitive little pause there at the end that makes it sound like she's going to be happy to hear from me—but then in the same sad, soft, emphatic voice, she says, "I don't want to talk now," and hangs up.

Click.

I looked at the receiver. It was one of those heavy, black, expressionless rotary dial phones that used to be made out of something more like rubber than plastic. It was pointless to look at a disconnected phone, I knew that, but getting the phone hung up in my ear wasn't quite what I'd envisioned as the beginning of what I'd already made up my mind was going to be a lifelong undertaking. I pushed down the button to prove to myself that she had really hung up on me. When I let it go, there was a new dial tone.

I was just about to call her back when I made the brilliant determination that she couldn't have come up with a better way of answering the phone if she'd tried. That she hadn't tried was what made it so perfect. She didn't want to talk, period—not to me, not to anyone. I was at least on an equal footing with all the other guys I imagined must have been calling her cute ass up nonstop, morning, noon and night. Why she bothered to answer the phone at all threw me at first, but then I figured, hey, why not? Whoever it was was bound to call back, or if he didn't, someone else would. She was cool. Aloof. Self-contained. Utterly desirable. Perfectly unattainable. That sort of thing used to get me every time. And thanks to her hanging up on me, I had time to think things through. You don't just call someone like a Virginia Good up out of the blue. No. You make a plan. Maybe write her a letter instead. And it wasn't too late! She'd hung up on me. Ha! She couldn't possibly have known who I was. It was a reprieve. I felt like Dostoyevski.

So I wrote her a letter…and what a letter! It was inspired, it really was. Everything came together in that letter. I defined myself. I made myself up. I told her that I was a writer and that, as a New Year's resolution, I had decided to start keeping a journal and that, furthermore, since I met her on New Year's Eve, I had decided to make this so-called journal in the form of letters to her. I kept getting tears in my eyes it was such a good idea. Then, as long as I was writing the stuff anyway, I figured I might as well sign up for a night school writing class at the College of San Mateo.

ℊℊ

The class was taught by Gordon Lish. He's sort of famous now, too—or he was there for a while, anyway. He was fiction editor at *Esquire* in the seventies. Then he was an editor at Knopf, ran prestigious fiction seminars and made some kind of a stir in the publishing industry in the eighties by suing *Harper's Magazine.*. The books he edited were critically acclaimed stylistic bare bones masterpieces but never seemed to make much money—things by guys like Don DeLillo and Barry Hannah and Rick Bass and Raymond Carver and Harold Brodkey and Cynthia Ozick and Amy Hempel—and the five or six books he wrote himself enjoyed some critical success themselves but made even *less* money, which made it hard to show any actual damages when he sued *Harper's* for publishing an unauthorized handout from one of his seminars. I'm not sure how it all came about.

Somewhere along the line, Gordon Lish had taken to calling himself "Captain Fiction" and charging all kinds of money to go to his seminars, and I guess it ticked him off that *Harper's* went around giving away what he had to say for the price of a magazine. Nor am I altogether sure what he got out of the lawsuit, either, but I think he won. All I know for a fact is that in the spring of 1963 you could get him for free if you were under twenty-one and for seven bucks a semester if you weren't. I got him for free myself…well, for the first semester anyway (and he was worth every nickel of it, too). The next semester I had to pay the seven bucks.

The College of San Mateo was still over at Coyote Point back then. If you've never heard of it and don't feel like looking it up on a map, Coyote Point is this rocky bunch of red clay cliffs and eucalyptus trees jutting out into San Francisco Bay, just south of the airport. The classrooms were old army barracks left over from World War II. Gordon Lish stormed into one of the dilapidated Quonset huts with a leather satchel under one arm. He had his own literary magazine called *Genesis West* and hung out with guys like Ken Kesey and Gregory Corso. His hair was short and blond and thick; he was sort of short and blond and thick in general.

The satchel under his arm had loose papers and books sticking out around the edges, as if it couldn't begin to contain all the wisdom he was eager to impart. His face was flushed. He was out of breath. His gray wool sport coat was rumpled. His tie was loose at the neck of a faded blue work shirt. He seemed pretty image conscious. He wrote his name on the blackboard. Big initials. Chalk chips flying here and there. I'm not an expert graphologist, by any means, but the way he screeched the "G" and the "L" across the slate made it clear he wanted people to know he thought a lot of himself—and the way he scrawled the rest of his name showed that underneath all that initial bravado, he was as least as interested in making a buck as any self-respecting orthodontist might be. I thought that was a nice touch. If you want people to think you think a lot of yourself, you damn sure better have something to gain by it.

He thought the stuff I wrote had "merit." He liked finding people he thought might write serious fiction someday. He was interested in...

(Whoops. I have to leave stuff out here. I got in touch with Gordon Lish through his publisher to see if I could get his permission to quote a line or two from my copy of the forty-year-old mimeographed, coffee stained syllabus he passed out to the class. He said no. I couldn't use his quote. He declined to give me permission. Oh, well. It wasn't that great of a quote anyway.)

...No wonder none of his books ever made any money. Not making money was his criterion for writing serious fiction. I wish Danielle Steele had been teaching the class. Gordon Lish's dilemma was that on the one hand, he wanted to make big bucks, and on the other hand, making big bucks was anathema to the making of serious fiction. He seems to have solved it by charging all kinds of money to go to his seminars about how serious fiction shouldn't make any money.

I was the one who got him *started* in the seminar business, as a matter of fact. When the second semester was over, the College of San Mateo didn't renew his contract, so I called Lish up and talked him into continuing the class as a seminar. I had to be pretty persuasive, but he finally agreed. For a hundred bucks each—in the form of a check made payable to the Chrysalis West Foundation—three other of his former CSM students and I all went over to his house in Burlingame and read our serious, dreary, puerile fiction out loud to each other. That was his first fiction seminar. He's parlayed it into a money making bonanza over the years.

* 𝒢 𝒢 *

Back before I made Gordon Lish who he is today, the way we used to work it was that he would sit in my chair and I'd go up to his podium and read stuff about my idyllic childhood from the so-called journal I'd been sending to Ginny Good. He'd look up and beam sunbeams out his eyes at me and get all red in the face and tap the eraser end of a pencil on the desk whenever I got to something he wished he could have written himself.

It was when Gordon Lish *didn't* tap his eraser that I got skeptical. What the hell did he know, the fucking asshole? Here he was, pushing thirty, and still nothing but a two-bit part time teacher at the College of San Mateo. I think the College of San Mateo felt sort of sorry for him. That was probably why he got the job. He had a family to feed. He'd come there fresh from having been kicked out of Mills High School for telling kids they didn't have to hide under their desks during atom bomb attacks. The local papers took up his cause—he was Mario Savio before Mario Savio was Mario Savio—and the College of San Mateo took a stand for free speech and freedom of expression and gave him a part time job.

Personally, I think the real reason Gordon Lish got kicked out of Mills High School was for something as prosaic as not turning in lesson plans, but that wouldn't have gone very far toward calling yourself "Captain Fiction" and charging all kinds of money to hear what you have to say—so the story that got to the newspapers was that he got fired for telling his students that they didn't have to hide under their desks.

Despite his ambition (and no doubt in large part *because* of his ambition), however, he was a great teacher—not a good teacher, a *great* teacher. If he'd been a good teacher I probably would have written a book or two by now—but what Gordon Lish taught us was far more important than how to write a book or two here or there: the difference between Apollonian and Dionysian, for instance. Now, that's a great thing to have learned. Think of all the people who don't know the difference between Apollonian and Dionysian! I've long since forgotten the difference myself, but think of all the people who never knew the difference in the first place!

I think it had something to do with Nietzsche. The other thing I know about Nietzsche is that he was the guy who said what didn't kill him made him strong. Ha! He was also the guy who was incurably insane the last twenty years of his life. What didn't kill the son of a bitch drove him nuts. Which would you rather be? Dead or nuts? Now *that's* a question with two equally compelling answers, and ferreting out questions with equally compelling answers was what made Gordon Lish a great teacher. He even offered himself up as a sacrificial case in point. Nobody could tell for sure whether he was a total fucking asshole or whether he was so strong and selfless he didn't mind people *thinking* he was a total fucking asshole, if he thought someone might get some serious fiction out of it someday.

But the *real* best thing about Gordon Lish was that, when I got to know Ginny better, I could tell her that I was taking a class from a guy who had his own literary magazine and hung out with Ken Kesey, and maybe she would think that was slick, and maybe she would like me. That was the quintessential best thing. That was the only thing. All I wanted was for Ginny to like me. I would have done anything.

GG

I'd sent Ginny my brilliant letter at the beginning of January and had been dutifully sending her the entries I was making in the so-called journal every three days or so. Finally, sometime in March, I got a post card with a picture of Coit Tower on the front and a note on the back that said:

"p.s. I like getting mail."

That was it. That was all the note said. A postscript to nothing. She didn't even sign her name. She didn't need to sign her name. The ink was green. The stamp was upside down. Her handwriting was small and round and loopy, with a tail at the end of the last "g" in getting. I read the post card over and over, front and back, searching for secret signs and hidden meanings. The tower was obviously phallic, for example, and had to have had something to do with coitus, but all the post card really said was that she liked getting mail.

So what did I do? Send her more mail? No. I called her up again, that's what. And this time we actually talked for a while—well, until she interrupted and said, "I don't like talking on the phone. You know, *Jules and Jim*, disembodied voices, and all that."

"Yeah," I said, which of course, I *didn't* know, but I presumed she was trying to tell me that we should go out on a date. So I asked her if she wanted to go out on a date. And we did that. We went out on a date. It was a disaster.

She was living in a converted garage out in the Avenues by the Surf Theater. The Surf Theater was where she saw all her foreign movies. I had never seen a foreign movie in my life. Worse yet, I wore white socks, combed my hair every time I saw a mirror and sold shoes for a living. At Kinney's. In San Bruno. Ginny had never heard of San Bruno. She wasn't sure she'd ever heard of Kinney's, either, except she thought she might have gone to school with a girl whose father *owned* Kinney's Shoes, the whole chain, all the Kinney's Shoe Stores in the world.

Then my new car didn't start. I'd been counting on my new car to impress the pants off her on our big date. It was an off-white 1955 Lincoln with turquoise and cream-colored leather upholstery, power steering, power brakes, push button windows and a push button antenna. I'd just bought it. I'd traded in the pink '53 Ford convertible that had more than adequately served its purposes with Bonnie and Cyndi and the girls from the shoe store. This was the Lincoln's first real test. Nor can I say it completely flunked. It didn't start, I can say that, but who's to say not starting wasn't the best thing it could have done?

This is all getting too complicated. Okay, probably the best thing to do would be just to go back and *show* what the hell happened on this so-called date Ginny and I went out on. That's another thing Gordon Lish used to say: "Show it, don't tell it."

(Oh, fuck, I didn't ask Gordon Lish if I could have his permission to quote him on that. Maybe he thinks he's got some kind of copyright on the phrase, "Show, don't tell." He probably does. I wouldn't put it past him.)

I'm still not exactly sure what the hell that "show, don't tell" bullshit means, anyway—which may be the *real* reason I never wrote any books. Maybe it wasn't Gordon Lish's fault after all. Maybe he tried to tell me. Maybe I owe him an apology. Hey, yo! Gordo! Sorry, man. You're wrong about not letting me use your stupid quote, but you might be right about that show don't tell horseshit.

CHAPTER NINE

San Bruno

Downtown San Bruno was a picture post card of early sixties suburban America. The main street was crowded on either side with bars and restaurants and smoke shops and delis and stores—Lullaby Lane, Pet World, Rolling Pin Doughnuts, Woolworth's, you name it. Starting at the El Camino and going clear down to Artichoke Joe's, San Mateo Avenue was crammed with businesses all competing with each other—trying to get at the two bucks an hour I made selling shoes.

San Bruno Mountain loomed up beyond Artichoke Joe's. That's the hill you see when you take off from San Francisco International Airport—the one with the poured concrete letters stuck in the high grass saying:

"SOUTH SAN FRANCISCO THE INDUSTRIAL CITY."

I fit right in. I sold shoes at Kinney's. I liked it. I was good at it. Chicks dug the way I handled a shoehorn. I remember this one little high school chick, in particular. Norma Arce. She was really tiny—a few inches shy of five feet tall, but with wiry black hair sprayed into stiff briary patches that made her look taller. She had bright black eyes and a small flat nose, with nostrils like a porcelain Bambi. Her forehead wrinkled up like hand-drawn seagulls when she raised her bushy eyebrows.

She had already taken off her sandals and was sitting expectantly in the imitation leather chair when I came back with a stack of shoes for her to try on. I sat down on the padded shoe stool and walked it up closer to her. She inched one of her size four-and-a-half feet toward the gold pump I had poised between my legs. The skin below her knee creased into dark smiles. She wiggled her toes and giggled like it was going to tickle. I held the back of her heel, slipped her foot into the shoe and felt that snug little puff of warm air explode up the inside of my wrist.

"Did you paint your toenails yourself?" I asked, pointing to her other foot.

"Yeah." She smiled a shy, proud little gap-toothed smile. Then a frantic expression crept across her cute little face. She bent over. Her disproportionately large, dark-skinned breasts plumped up inside her black lace bra. "Why? Did I mess one up?"

"No, no. They're perfect. How do you do it, though?"

"Do what?"

"Paint your toenails," I said. "Do you do it standing up?"

"Yeah." The muscles in her forehead relaxed. "With my foot on the edge of the bathroom sink, usually—or on the top of the toilet seat. Sometimes I do it sitting down, too, but my legs get all cramped up on me when I do it like that."

"Do you put cotton between your toes?"

"You have to. Otherwise you mess it up." She reached inside the scoop neck of her lilac-colored blouse and straightened one of the straps of her bra.

"Have you ever had anyone paint your toenails?"

"Like did I get a pedicure? No."

"Did you ever want one?" I brushed my thumb along the edge of nail of her big toe—which really wasn't all that big.

"Sure. Are you kidding? I could just lay back and relax."

"Yeah, like eat pistachio nuts or Hershey's Kisses or something," I said.

"Did you ever paint a girl's toes?" She looked at me carefully, right into my eyes, and squinted like she was trying to make sure I was going to tell her the truth.

"No," I said. "But I never saw a girl's toes like yours before." I touched my fingernail against the hot pink nail of her cute little pinky toe.

"For real?" she asked.

"For really real," I said, staring directly at the bridge of her nose. "You want to know what's really amazing, though?"

"What?" She wet her lips with her tongue.

"I have a car the exact same color as your toenail polish."

"For real?" Her black eyes flashed. Her nostrils flared. Her bushy eyebrows came together. Her thick, liver-colored lips came apart. I could see her wet pink tongue glistening between rows of crooked white teeth.

"Yep," I said. "A '53 Ford convertible."

"*Exactly* the same color? Are you serious?"

"I am so serious. Why? You think I'm pulling your leg?" I tugged playfully at her Achilles tendon and smiled. Her skirt was short. Her legs were bare. She was wearing black lace panties that matched her bra. "Would I do something like that?"

She smiled back, even though she had to have seen through my slacks that my dick had gotten noticeably engorged during the course of our innocent conversation.

"I'd have to see it to believe it," she said.

"My mother calls it hot pink. What color do they call that nail polish?"

"Passionate Raspberry Parfait Au Lait." She splayed her tiny hand across her face and laughed and bent over again, farther this time, so far I thought I got a fleeting glimpse of the nipple of one of her breasts.

"Wow. That's kind of a mouthful." I imagined what it would feel like to have the thick, liver-colored nipples of her breasts come alive when I touched them with my tongue, when I held them and kissed them and sucked them into my mouth.

"The J. C. Penney lady said it was her favorite name of *all* the nail polish."

"It's the prettiest color nail polish I've ever seen," I said. "What's your name?"

"Norma."

"Norma what?"

"Arce," she said. "Like the cola, but spelled all the way out."

We drove up to the Chinese cemetery behind South City. She wanted the top down. That was fine with me. It was one of those warm, misty, tropical nights that happen once in a blue moon because of monsoons in Malaysia, maybe…but, wait. What about my date with Ginny?

GG

It was Saturday night. I stopped at Grossenbacher's to get Ginny a bouquet of flowers. Grossenbacher's was the florist shop down the street from Kinney's. According to an arc of Old English letters stenciled across the front window, it was officially Grossenbacher & Sons, but everyone just called it Grossenbacher's, and there was only one son—a guy named Pete. I used to get a kick out of acting like Pete was my buddy. I'd wave to him on his way into Carlo and Jimmy's, the Mexican coffee shop across the street where you sat at the counter on chrome and maroon Naugahyde bar stools.

"Hey, Pete!" I'd yell. "What's going on, buddy?" Then I'd watch him pretend like he was in a different dimension. Pete didn't want any buddies. Well, he did and he didn't; that was what I used to get a kick out of—watching him trying to make up his mind whether he wanted a buddy or not.

Pete wore thick reading glasses from Woolworth's, the kind he could peer out over the tops of when he was lost in thought, which was almost always, or when he had something to say, which was nearly never. I was probably the only person in town he ever really sat down and shot the shit with on a regular basis, and even I had ulterior motives.

Pete was close to sixty and bald as an egg but for a swath of close clipped salt and pepper hair around the sides of his head and a thick, salt and pepper mustache he kept trimmed the same shape as Stalin's mustache—probably just to piss off his father. His father was Mr. Grossenbacher. Nobody called Pete anything but Pete. He resented that. He resented it almost as much as he resented the sign on the front window. Sons? What sons? There was only Pete.

His father was in his late eighties and was still fiercely loyal to the royal family of Imperial Russia. It *should* have pissed him off that his only son had a mustache like Stalin's, but it didn't. His father was senile. He'd never even *heard* of Stalin. He lived in a world of his own, a world of caviar and lorgnettes and fringed epaulets and Faberge Eggs—but if his father *had* ever heard of Stalin, it would have pissed him off no end that his only son had a mustache like the mustache of such a man, and that gave Pete all the satisfaction a person could reasonably get out of the mere trimming of a mustache into a certain shape.

Pete could tell you the best way to get anywhere in a fifty mile radius of downtown San Bruno, taking into consideration not just distance, but commute patterns, highway construction and the likelihood of dead animals in the road. Giving directions was Pete's favorite thing to do. You couldn't help but get the feeling that the minute his father finally died Pete was going to turn the place into a Texaco station, get himself a star-shaped patch saying "Mr. Grossenbacher" stitched onto a pair of pinstripe coveralls and sit around giving directions to lost tourists all day.

I used to stop by and pick up flowers for Bonnie every once in awhile. Bonnie looked like Brigitte Bardot and had been my girlfriend on and off for a year or so. She used to go nuts when I brought her flowers. Which is what I mean about ulterior motives. Pete used to give me flowers for free, see— just things he was going to have to throw in the garbage anyway—and I'd maybe buy him a coffee over at Carlo and Jimmy's every now and then.

* 𝓰 𝓰 *

92

The store was closed, but I tapped on the window with my car keys and Pete let me in. I told him I was thinking about maybe picking up some flowers. He didn't say anything but just gathered up some left over snapdragons and freesia and chrysanthemums and baby's-breath, wrapped them in a sheet of green paper, snapped a few red rubber bands around the end and laid them on the counter.

I took out my money, like I always did. Pete said forget about it, I could buy him a coffee. Then I made the mistake of telling him they smelled good. The last thing Pete ever wanted to hear about was flowers.

"It's the freesia," he said. "The purple stuff."

"They're pretty."

"Flowers is flowers."

"I like how they all sort of go together."

"It ain't a professional job."

"Thanks, I guess."

"What do you mean, 'you guess?' You don't want 'em?"

"No, no. They're fine."

"So, what's that mean, 'You guess?'"

"It's a quote."

"Some quote. Who said this quote?"

"A guy named Beckett."

"Never heard of him."

"He's Irish. He wrote stuff in French then translated it back to English. Did you ever hear of *Waiting for Godot?* It's a play."

"I seen a play once," Pete said with a little nod and kind of a half frown which wrinkled his bald head. "At the Curran Theater…on Geary, between Mason and Taylor. A boat wrecks on a island and a old man lives there. Everybody works for him like a slave. If they don't do like he says, he hurts them with magic. It was a long time ago. Before they built the Bayshore. We went up El Camino. We could of gone Skyline. Skyline would have been quicker, but my father, he only knew just that one way how to get there." Pete stroked his mustache contentedly.

"I'll let you know how she liked these."

"You going to marry this girl?"

"I just met her."

"It's a new one? What happened to the other one?"

"Bonnie? She's still around."

"Why you want a new one, then?" Pete frowned again.

"I can't help it. I'm in love."

That stopped him. I don't think Pete had ever been in love.

"So, this new one, where does *she* live?" he asked.

"In San Francisco. Out in the Avenues…45th Avenue."

"Yeah?" he said and looked over the tops of his glasses and came suddenly alert. "You know the best way how to get there?"

Then, without waiting for an answer, he started telling me. I wrote the directions on a piece of paper. Pete adored it when a person wrote what he said down on a piece of paper. He beamed. He sparkled. He was beside himself with glee.

CHAPTER TEN

45th Avenue

It was foggy out in the Avenues. It's always foggy out in the Avenues. Wind blew drizzle into my face. My hair wouldn't stay combed right. I could feel it all pushed over to the wrong side and sticking up in back. I tried patting it down, but that just made it feel like it was sticking up all the more, so unless I wanted Ginny's first impression of me to be a cross between Alfalfa and Dagwood Bumstead, I figured I'd better get out my comb and try combing it—which wasn't really all that easy.

I had these flowers, see, and there wasn't a mirror anywhere. There was a shiny silver doorknocker, however. Ha! I put the flowers between my legs, squatted down a little and got out my comb. The doorknocker was like a mirror in a fun house. First I was nothing but chin, then I had the longest, saddest eyes I'd ever seen and a tall, tall forehead, like a Pharaoh, and when I finally got to my hair, it kept sticking up and up, higher and higher, like it wasn't ever going to stop.

Ginny pulled the door open. Her face was where the doorknocker used to be. I was looking right into her eyes. She was looking right into mine.

"Gadfrees! Gerry?"

"Hi," I said, still all scrunched down with this bunch of snapdragons and chrysanthemums sticking out from my crotch and a long, white comb hovering over my head. I must have looked like I was maybe trying to do the Limbo and give myself a benign lobotomy at the same time. "Here. I got you these." I took the flowers out from between my legs and pushed them toward her chest. She didn't take them. She just stood there.

She had on a torn red sweatshirt, a pair of worn out jeans with the cuffs rolled up and a pair of white, unlaced Ked's with no socks. Three yellow barrettes held her hair in an unruly pile on top of her head, and her face was so pretty and perky and pesky and smug that I barely heard her when she crinkled up her nose and cocked her head and asked, "Are you *supposed* to be here?"

"I thought I was, yeah. Wasn't I?"

"Gosh...*may*be," she said and took the flowers.

"You want to make it some other time?"

"Oh, dear! This is awful. Okay, I know what. Here. Take these back." She handed me the flowers again and I wished for the umteenth time that I'd never stopped off at Pete's. "We'll start all over. Come back in ten minutes."

I drove down to Ocean Beach and listened to the radio. I don't know for how long exactly, but I know it would have been for longer than ten minutes. Then I pulled the car up in front of her house again. That must have been when I left the lights on. I knocked on her door one more time. I didn't care what the hell my hair looked like.

"Come innnn..." She dragged out the word like she was singing some kind of a kid's song, like we were still pretending

I hadn't already been there. I tried opening the door. It was locked. I knocked again.

"It's open!"

"It's locked!"

"It sticks!"

It sounded like she'd said "instincts," like I was instinctively supposed to know some secret way of getting the son of a bitch open. "I think it's stuck," I said.

"Bash it!" she yelled.

I bashed into the door with my shoulder, but it still didn't budge. Then I turned the knob and bashed into it again and ended up in her hallway, sliding along like a surfer on a slippery little rug that almost sent me crashing into an umbrella rack and a stack of books on a little table under a mirror on the wall. I expected Ginny to be standing there with some big grin on her face, but she wasn't. She was in her bedroom with the door closed.

There was a sliver of light coming from under the closed door. A shadow passed through the light. I heard a drawer open. The shadow moved out of the light. A coat hanger rattled. A zipper zipped and unzipped. The slightest sound was magnified by my imagination. I could almost feel her putting things on and taking them off again. What sounded like a tube of lipstick tapped against what sounded like the top of a glass vanity table. An eyeliner brush popped out from an eyeliner bottle.

I put the flowers down, looked into the mirror, and was distracted by the daunting thought that she'd probably want to order drinks. What if the waiter wanted to see my ID? I was still only twenty. Ginny had just turned twenty-two. I was a little over a year younger than her. She didn't know it, but I did. I also knew that as soon as I got her out to my car, everything would be fine.

I had it all pictured. Once we got out to my car, she'd ease herself down into the understated luxury of those leather seats, and I'd maybe run the antenna up a ways and move the passenger seat up a bit...and when she heard the comforting hum of all those little electric motors moving things around, the last thing she'd be worrying about would be who was older than who. She might even sort of snuggle up against the side of my neck where I'd had the foresight to dab more of the Old Spice I kept in the glove compartment while I'd been listening to the radio down by the beach.

Ginny came out of her room wearing a red silk dress with tiny black buttons up the back. Her hair was thick and brown and curly. Bangs covered her forehead. She had to peek out from under them when she wanted to see. Her eyes were light, light blue...and green, and gray, and more amused than ever. What was so funny, I did not know. She took a long black coat out of the hall closet and handed it to me. My best guess was that she expected me to hold it for her. I held it for her. She slipped her arms into the sleeves of the coat and snuggled it around herself.

Ginny pulled the door closed behind us, turned toward the street and finally saw my gorgeous white Lincoln for the first time.

"Ooo, is that your car?" she asked in such a sweet little voice it almost sounded like she was cooing.

Overwhelming pride swelled inside me. "Yeah," I said.

"Why'd you leave the lights on?"

I ignored her question, calmly opened the passenger door, made my way around to the driver's side, got in, came up with

98

a mental image of how everything was still going to be all right, turned the key in the ignition, and actually expected the engine to start. But it didn't. I tried and tried, again and again. Pretty soon, all it did was click.

"Maybe we should call Triple-A," Ginny suggested.

"I don't have Triple-A." I shook my head.

"Oh," she said.

All the other things I didn't have rippled the surface of my fragile confidence like someone had thrown a pretty good-sized boulder into it. I didn't have anything. All the money I had in the world was wadded up in my pants' pocket, and I was three years in debt for this piece of shit car that sat there *clicking* at me—telling me things I already knew. I was a kid. I sold shoes for a living. My hair wouldn't stay combed right. I was out of my league, in over my head, barking up the wrong tree—click, click, click, you dumb cluck—but the amazing thing was that Ginny didn't seem to *mind* any of that. She seemed to sort of like it, in fact.

She probably felt like I did when I went out with Norma Arce. Ginny knew nothing could ever really *come* of it, but she was intrigued. I was cute. I liked her. I made her laugh. What harm could it do? I wasn't the sort of guy she'd ordinarily have anything to do with. That made me extraordinary. Ha!

We ended up taking Ginny's big black Buick Roadmaster—the kind that used to have those five little portholes on the sides. She had the seat up as far as it would go and still had to stretch some to reach the pedals. There were notes written in felt pen across the dashboard:

"TURN OFF LIGHTS!
LOCK DOORS!
REMEMBER KEYS!"

Ginny waved to the notes and laughed. "Don't pay attention to any of that. Mother wrote it. She thinks I have brain
damage."

* 𝓰 𝓰 *

We went to a restaurant called Ripley's. It was in North
Beach. You had to go down some narrow stairs. There were
red and white-checkered tablecloths on the tables and candles
in glass goblets and a fog of cigarette smoke hanging in the air.

When Virginia moved to San Francisco she went through
one of those underground gourmet guides and made up an
alphabetical list of restaurants to go to when she went out on
dates. Ripley's was next on the list. I gave the alphabet a
quick run through. Hey, at least it wasn't Vanessi's.

The guys she was used to going out with were "men"
from Harvard and Yale and Stanford—guys who could afford
to gamble the price of dinner at a fancy restaurant on the off
chance it might get them into her good graces. She'd been a
debutante. Her father grew up on an estate in Westchester
County. They had a summer cottage in Newport. Her grandmother dolled out toilet paper from a locked cupboard, one
square at a time. There was Frick money in the mix.

The maitre d' seemed to have sized us up based on his
impression of me rather than of her, however, and led us over
to a table by the kitchen door. That didn't last long. After
exchanging a few fidgety glances with a Filipino dishwasher,

Ginny stood up, took me by the sleeve of the burnt-orange Orlon sweater I was wearing—along with a really cool burlap-colored button-down shirt—and marched me over to an empty table against the far wall.

I lit a cigarette, propped my napkin into a small tent and blew cigarette smoke through a flap at the bottom. The maitre d' spotted us. He looked toward the table we had vacated, frowned and started walking toward us. Ginny shooed him away.

"He looks sort of mad."

"Mad, schmad. He works in a restaurant, for God's sake."

"I never went out to dinner much. The only place my parents ever took us was to Hedge's Wigwam. It was a cafeteria. Up on Woodward Avenue, down toward Detroit." I gave directions with my hands. "There was a wigwam on the roof."

"Is that why you've made your napkin into a teepee? Or has it become fashionable to order wine by smoke signals?"

"Sorry." I moved the napkin onto my lap.

"Don't be sorry, dodo. If you want to make teepees, make teepees. Recreate the whole battle of the Little Big Horn if you want, but if you're just nervous..."

"I'm not nervous," I said nervously, just shy of telling her I wasn't quite twenty-one yet, either.

"Have you ever read *The Confidence Man*?" she asked. "It's just confidence. That's all anything is. If you're confident, whatever you do's the right thing to do."

"...and if you're not?"

"Did you want to sit next to garbage cans?"

"No, but isn't it okay to just let things happen the way they happen?"

101

"Oh how very Zen and boring."

"I was confident New Year's."

"I barely remember New Year's."

"I kissed you. At midnight."

"You *did*?"

"Yeah. You kissed me back. You don't remember any of that?"

"Heavens, no. I have blackouts. I'm an alcoholic," she said brightly. "There was some sort of mix up, I know. I was supposed to go out with Ronnie and Charles showed up—or the other way around. I forget. It was all terribly confusing. We ended up all going together. That's the last thing I remember. Ronnie didn't tell me much the next day. And Charles *still* hasn't called. It's been *ages*."

"The other guy's still around?"

"Ronnie? Absolutely. Yes. Ronnie's not going anywhere."

"What does he think about...you know..." I moved my hands at the wrists, trying to think of exactly the right words. "...you going out with me?"

"He says I'm like the Mona Lisa."

"You're way cuter."

"Thank you, *dah*ling."

"I don't get the Mona Lisa thing," I said.

"Ronnie doesn't want to seem possessive. He says keeping me all to himself would be like keeping the Mona Lisa all to himself. Isn't that sweet?"

"I guess," I said and made a dismissive little gesture with my left hand. "But, to tell you the truth, it looked to me like they both wanted you all to themselves. The only thing that kept them from trying to kill me was Elliot."

"Who's Elliot?"

"My friend. The guy in the uniform? With the Green Beret?" I pointed to my head. "He's in Vietnam now. He's supposed to be some big pacifist. He wore a mask over his mouth for a while so he wouldn't accidentally kill any innocent gnats. Why he joined the army nobody knows."

"That sort of vaguely rings a bell. I think I remember him…your friend…Elliot. I remember thinking, 'How romantic! Marching off to war.' This is getting a trifle absurd," she said in a soft, determined voice and called confidently across the room, "Yoo-hoo! May we see a menu, please?"

One of the waiters showed up. Ginny ordered wine. The guy didn't ask to see my ID. She'd quietly taken over. It was like *My Fair Lady.* I was some uncivilized wretch she'd been given a once in a lifetime chance to study and refine.

When the wine arrived, she tasted it, smiled and said something to the waiter in French. I thought, uh-oh, she was going to send the wine *back* for some reason, like maybe just to show me it *could* be sent back, which only would have led to another chance for someone to ask to see my ID—but she didn't. She did everything just right. Even the maitre d' came by to see how things were going. Swimmingly, or some such thing, Ginny told him, also in French.

When it came time to order, I pointed to something cheap. The waiter nodded his guarded approval. Then she started rattling off a whole slew of other things and the waiter kept getting more and more enthusiastic.

"*Bon. Très bon. Magnifique!*"

Magnifique, my ass, all the money I had in the world would barely pay the bill and I'd just cashed my paycheck…well, fuck the car payment, this was worth it.

What I'd pointed to turned out to be duck. The only other time I ever ate a duck before was when my father shot one, and then I'd had to be careful I didn't chip a tooth on the birdshot still stuck in its flesh. The duck the waiter brought me had hot orange marmalade poured all over it, however, and I had no idea how I was supposed to eat the thing. If I tried to eat it with my fingers, it would have been like trying to eat a hot fudge sundae with my fingers, but if I tried using a knife and fork, the son of a bitch would have ended up in my lap—so I pretty much just made do with French bread dipped in hot orange marmalade sauce, and we took what was left of it and the rest of all the other stuff Ginny had ordered home with us in doggy bags.

* 𝒢 𝒢 *

Virginia slipped her arms out of her coat while I held it for her. A spark of electricity shot through my fingers. She kicked off her shoes and asked me to unbutton the back of her dress. I lifted her hair. There were freckles on her shoulder. And a mole. I told her about it.

"You have a mole on your shoulder."

"I know. I have one on my fanny, too. Ooo, rub right there." I dug my thumb under her scapula. "Harder. Feel the knots? My shrink says I have neurasthenia."

"Doesn't that hurt?"

"No, it feels yummy. Down more…right there. Oh!"

"I can't get any leverage."

"I'll put on my jammies."

She'd been saying odd little things like that all night, things that made her sound like a four-year-old kid. Jammies. Fanny.

Namby-pamby. Yummy. Mummy. Tummy. Tum. Tum-tum. Gads! Gadfrees! Dodo. Doo doo. Yow! Yowie, zow! Well, she went back and forth. At the restaurant she'd had to be efficient. With other guys she probably talked like a four-year-old all the time, but with me that wouldn't have been practical. We never would have made it to the restaurant, for one thing, and if we *had* somehow made it to the restaurant, we wouldn't ever have gotten waited on and never could have ordered wine. But now that we were back at her apartment she could finally be more herself again.

g g

Ginny disappeared back into her bedroom. I put the doggy bags into her otherwise almost empty refrigerator—a bottle of ketchup, a jar of dill pickles, a couple cartons of Chinese take-out, taco sauce. It crossed my mind that she went out on dates instead of going grocery shopping. The kitchen walls were shiny yellow enamel. Her mother had written all over them, too, only this time she'd had more room. The letters were gigantic:

"TURN OFF GAS!
TURN OFF LIGHTS!
LOCK DOORS!"

Back in the living room there were books and records stacked in lopsided piles everywhere. In one corner, there was a prayer shawl stretched over a plank of driftwood perched across a couple of cinder blocks. Ginny called it her shrine. On top of the shawl, there were five or six votive candles in bumpy red glass candleholders, a few pinecones, some sea-shells, feathers, dried flowers and three pictures the size of post cards. I didn't know it at the time, of course, but the pictures were of Virginia Woolf, Marcel Duchamp and Gurdjieff.

I sat down cross-legged on the rug. Ginny came out from her bedroom dressed in a long white flannel nightgown. The nightgown had tiny blue roses all over it. She was carrying a lit candle. She used it to light the rest of the candles on her shrine. Then she went into the kitchen, got a bottle of Beef-eater Gin and two pretty good-sized drinking glasses, turned on all four burners of the stove and turned out the bright kitchen light. She put the gin and the candles and the glasses down in front of me, then went over and sorted through one of the stacks of records. I filled our glasses and thought it was sort of slick that a girl named Ginny liked to drink gin.

"I feel like Bach," she said.

"You don't look like Bach."

She smiled the sort of smile the remark deserved. She liked me. I could tell. She put on *The Magnificat*, rigged up the record player to keep playing the same record over and over and, finally, plopped herself down in front of me.

The room was aglow with a combination of eerie blue flames from the stove in the kitchen and reddish flickering flames from the candles. Under her nightgown, I saw a pair of white cotton panties. Her hair hid her face. She peeked out from under her bangs. We drank her gin and talked and touched each other's hands, and the shadows of our hands flitted across the rug and flew across the walls like prehistoric birds. It was like we were telling ghost stories, like we were kids in a cave. I told her about the Leapies. The Leapies were little green florescent things I made up when I was a kid.

They looked like clothespins and never did anything but leap. That was all they ever wanted to do. They lived in heaven. I sang her the song:

"La la-la...all is calm, all is bright.
'Round yon virgin, mother and child,
Holy Infant, so tender and mild.
Sleep in heaven, Leapies.
Sleep in heaven, Leapies."

"How darling! Someone should make up a psychological test of how you *hear* things! What a good idea! Freudian hears! Don't you usually like what you hear better than what people say?"

"It's probably not a bad idea to know what was actually said sometimes, too."

"You sound like a lawyer."

"How'd you do that?" I touched the scar on the inside of her wrist. I didn't exactly want to get into a conversation about careers.

"With a broken bottle, I'm told. I was blacked out. Not very aesthetic, are they? Or effective. Tendons got in the way. You're supposed to cut up and down, not across. Live and learn, la la-la. From what I remember, it wasn't that exciting. Or noble. Warranted, maybe. Noble, no." She seemed to be talking to herself, nodding and shaking her head at the appropriate places. "I was at school. It was Christmas. I get funny around Christmas. I have since Daddy left. Roger *knew* that."

"Who's Roger?"

"My beau. Ex-beau. Roger Singmaster. I was at Sarah Lawrence. He was in grad school at Brown. His father's a partner in some big law firm. They live outside Philadelphia. His mother teaches French lit at Penn. Roger was going to be a banker. He'd been going to be a politician but decided bankers had more influence.

"He was charming and glib and confident, with intense dark black eyes and a shy, crooked smile—and the darlingest little cleft in his chin. We'd been dating for ages. We used to meet at a hotel across from Gramercy Park. It was all very tawdry. I had long luscious orgasms like melting Hershey Bars. Pigeons cooed on the windowsill. Mother adored him. We were supposed to get married. We were supposed to be in love. We *were* in love. Then I don't know what happened.

"He went home for Christmas. It's barely been a year. I stayed in the dorms. Everyone was gone. It was like Dickens. Empty hallways. Banging shutters—so I got drunk and took the train to Philadelphia and caused a big ruckus. His parents were conciliatory. His mother suggested I might simply have been taking up too much of Roger's time. His father talked about 'the long term.' I threw a brandy decanter through the dining room window.

"The next thing I remember is waking up in bandages, with Mother's voice on the phone, asking whether I thought she was going to be expected to pay for the rug in the Singmaster's guest room."

"What did he do? The Hershey Bar guy?"

"Roger? Nothing. Went back to Providence."

"You haven't talked to him?"

"He's dating some boring Bryn Mawr psych major."

"Then what?"

"Then what what?"

"What happened after you woke up in bandages?"

"Mother had me carted off to some loony bin in La Jolla. They told her I was schizophrenic. Now she worries I'm going to blow up half the block every time I boil an egg." She nodded toward the notes on the kitchen wall.

"I stayed with Auntie Rose in Laguna. Her house was full of Vedanta swamis. Do you know about Sri Ramakrishna? My cousin's a Vedanta nun. They have to be celibate, but all she ever thinks about is sex. Everybody goes around like Heloise and Abelard all day and all night. I wanted to be a Vedanta nun, but went to live with Daddy instead, and moved up here…and went back to school…"

"…and met me."

"…and here we are. I'm sweating like a sow."

"Want me to turn off the stove?"

"No. I like sweating." She fanned herself with the hem of her nightgown, and I felt warm, humid air wafting into my face and thought about how warm and moist it would be an inch or so inside the elastic of those girlish little white cotton panties.

* 𝑔 𝑔 *

We didn't say anything for a long time. Reflections of the candles flickered in her eyes. Blurred shadows crossed her face. Her face changed. Her hair turned long and silvery, and her eyes disappeared from their sockets, and her skin looked old and leathery, like a shrunken head. Then, right in the middle of the huge, scary fantasy I was having, Ginny took a deep, sharp, bone-chilling gasp of breath into her chest.

"Ahhh…" like that.

"What's the matter?" I blinked.

"Nothing." She couldn't quite put it into words, but whatever it was wasn't scary at all, it was *good*, really good, extra good, amazingly good. Then she seemed to be trying to say something else, but still the words wouldn't come to her. She shook her hair away from her face and covered her mouth mischievously and laughed and looked at me, wide-eyed, enthralled, delighted, and finally whispered, "Gadfrees! You were *glowing*! You were like a god! Your hair was long and blond, and your eyes were shining like flames, and you were floating off the floor!"

At first it felt like I just wasn't focusing right, but then it became clear that she really *had* changed—and this time what she'd changed *into* wasn't anything I could have described if we'd stared at each other forever. I blinked again and squinted and made a conscientious effort to try to see what the hell was really going on.

Virginia Good had somehow become someone or something I hadn't ever dreamed of before. Her looking like a shrunken head had been understandable, at least—afterimages, me being pretty drunk myself, and all that—but this…I didn't know what it was. A state of mind? The absence of a state of mind? I couldn't tell. Whatever it was, she was beautiful…utterly desirable and dangerous, like a bright, poison spider in a sparkling spider web—like a flower, a sublime, deadly flower.

"Do you know The Rose?" she asked in a dreamy, faraway, tiny little girlish voice. Then she recited it to me in the same dreamy voice:

"O rose...thou art sick. The invisible worm,...
That flies in the night...In the howling storm:...
Hath found out thy bed of crimson joy:...
And his dark...secret love...Does thy life destroy."

"What made you say that?" I asked.

"Gadfrees! I was reading your mind. Was I? I *was!*"

What she had turned into was spooky. Yeah, she was drunk off her ass, too, probably even more drunk than me, but there was more to it than that. Her eyes had changed. She was deranged. She had no conscience or guilt or guile. She was barely human. She was, like, mythological, surreal, fantastic, bewitching, like something or someone you might see in a painting—someone you'd fall in love with forever if you got the chance, someone you'd have to be in love with no matter what.

The burners on the stove had been on for hours. The room was an incubator. Unexplainable chemical reactions were exuding from under her flannel nightgown, animal smells, feral stuff, musk...and in one great big blazing insight, I came to the inescapable conclusion that if there was ever a time to consummate what was going on between us, that time had come. I had to get her out of that girlish nightgown...and what? Devour her? Eat her alive. Assimilate her. Get so close we couldn't tell each other apart. Know her. Get her inside me; get me inside her.

Nor was it just my boyish imagination. Ginny wanted whatever was going on between us to get itself consummated pretty soon, too. It was like something really important was at stake. The continuation of the species, maybe. Like if we didn't hurry up and fuck, baboons and orangutans were going to beat us out of our evolutionary place on the planet.

"You were looking like a shrunken head," I said.

"What?" She crinkled her nose and shook her hair.

"You looked like a shrunken head," I repeated stupidly.

"That's my soul. I have an old, shrunken soul."

"That's not true." I waved my hand dismissively. "I'm not glowing. I'm not floating off the floor. And you don't have an old, shrunken soul."

"I don't?"

"No. You have a beautiful soul. Everything about you is beautiful. I love you."

She blinked.

The spell was shattered.

Holy shit! What was I saying? What had I said? I love you? Had I said that? No. What self-respecting baboon would stop in the middle of ensuring the species its evolutionary place on the planet to say, "I love you?" Humanity's doomed. Orangutans rule.

"What does *that* mean?" Her eyes were huge. The question quivered with so many nuances of mirth and pity and hope and disbelief I couldn't have come up with an answer if there'd been one.

Then it didn't matter anymore. She climbed over into my lap, and the candles were sputtering almost out and flaming up out of pools of melted wax as we rocked back and forth, kissing each other and hugging each other and undressing each other all at the same time until she finally tossed what was left of her nightgown toward the kitchen and said, "I have little boobs."

"You're perfect," I babbled.

She took off her panties, and I got out of the rest of my clothes, and we half stumbled and half carried each other into her bedroom and got under the covers.

Then the phone rang. Then it stopped ringing. Then it rang again. Then it stopped again. Then it rang one more time. It was a special ring. She had to answer it. It was Ronnie, the guy with glasses from New Year's. Apparently, from what I was able to gather from Ginny's end of the conversation, Ronnie had just eaten a can of garbanzo beans and something having to do with eating a can of garbanzo beans meant he had to come over.

"Now?" I asked.

"It's an e*mer*gency," she said. Childlike mischief blazed in her eyes.

Hey, I had kind of an emergency going on at that point myself. But Ronnie's emergency took precedence. I started getting dressed. She didn't. She stayed in bed. Under the covers. Still sweating. Still exuding. No god damn baboon was going to beat *her* out of her place on the evolutionary ladder. It was a bit unbearable, if you ask me, but no matter what meant no matter what.

The garbanzo bean guy got there. I told Virginia I'd call her and left with as much dignity as I was able to muster, which, under the circumstances, wasn't much.

* 𝓖 𝓖 *

Then, motherfuck! My car still didn't start. I'd forgotten all about it. Son of a bitch! All the money I had in the world had gone to fill Ginny's refrigerator full of more doggy bags than I'd ever seen in one place before, and I *still* didn't have

Triple-A. I had to go back up and knock on her door again. The garbanzo bean guy had too come out and give me a push.

My gorgeous white Lincoln coughed and sputtered and spit and finally started. I waved to the garbanzo bean guy in my rear view mirror and was on my way back to San Mateo again, telling myself that going out with Virginia Good had been the stupidest idea I'd ever come up with in my whole entire life.

When I got up to Skyline, I remembered Pete's directions and it dawned on me that I'd forgotten all about the flowers. *She'd* forgotten all about the flowers. The garbanzo bean guy probably found them on the table in the hallway and gave them to her when he got back from giving me a push. Fuck the fucking flowers, I wasn't ever going to get a girl any god damn flowers again in my whole entire life if I lived to be a hundred and three.

When I finally got out of the fog and back onto the El Camino I started rethinking the whole thing. Maybe it hadn't been such a bad idea, after all. We'd hit it off for the most part, hadn't we? What the hell more did I want from a first date? We had our clothes off. We were in bed with each other. We were about as close as two people can get to fucking each other. I was god damn *glowing*, for Christ's sake. I was like a god. I was floating off the floor—until I remembered the part about saying, "I love you." That had been the stupidest thing I'd ever said in my whole entire life. I wasn't ever going to tell any girl I loved her again if I lived to be a hundred and three.

Yeah, well, on the other hand, I mean, who the fuck knows, you know? Besides, she was drunk. She had blackouts. She probably wouldn't remember a thing. Turning into my driveway was a relief. I looked on the bright side. At least my gorgeous white Lincoln had made it all the way home. I hadn't gotten pulled over for drunk driving. I sat in the driveway thinking that the best thing to do would be just to add it all up—everything that might have been good about it or bad about it, smart about it or stupid about it, forgettable or unforgettable, lucky or unlucky, all of it—just add it all up and stick the whole shebang into that gigantic equation wherein whatever happens is for the best.

* 𝒢 𝒢 *

I kept on writing Ginny letters. She wrote me letters back. We corresponded for another year or so. We talked on the phone and hung out with each other now and then. We got to be buddies. We saw Ingmar Bergman movies together. I took her over to Gordon Lish's house a couple times. Kesey showed up once—sporting a brand new red, white and blue cap in the shape of an American Flag on one of his front teeth. Ginny thought that was sort of slick, but for the most part between March of 1963 and March of 1964 I pretty much just bided my time.

She told me about different books to read and thought I might write a book about her someday. I *told* her I was going to write a book about her someday. She liked that. She wanted to be Zelda Fitzgerald; she probably *was* Zelda Fitzgerald. It's just too bad she never found anyone like Zelda Fitzgerald's husband to hang out with—someone who could capture her and captivate her and take her places and buy her things and keep her safe, someone who could love her forever no matter what. I tried, Lord knows. But I didn't succeed. Nobody did.

CHAPTER ELEVEN

Farmer's Market

*A*fter my ambivalent date with Ginny Good, I kept working at Kinney's in San Bruno until my gorgeous white Lincoln finally fell completely apart on the freeway and I had to get a job I could walk to. The job I got was at KayBee Toys in the Hillsdale Shopping Center. That was where I was working when Kennedy got shot.

Anyone who was over the age of six at the time remembers what he or she was doing the day Kennedy got shot. I was having lunch with Ralph Wood in Farmer's Market, the food court at Hillsdale Mall. We were over by the Mexican food concession. Ralph was drinking a cup of black coffee. I was scraping the last of a scrumptious side order of shell macaroni in tomato sauce into a warm, buttered tortilla when we heard the news. A pimply-faced kid in a SF Giants baseball cap at the table next to us turned the volume up on his transistor radio. Other radios went on. A crowd gathered around the portable TV at the Bavarian Hof Brau. Ralph and I just sat there.

Ralph was tall and skinny and ten years older than everyone. He looked like a bird. He was a thief. The bones around his temples stuck out. He cocked his head, trying to hear the news above the crackles of static coming from the kid's cheap black and yellow radio. "…earlier this morning, in Dallas, Texas…"

"Is he dead?" I asked.

"They don't know, man. Shut up and listen." He snapped at me, biting the words between his bad teeth like a vulture.

We weren't exactly friends. We just hung out with each other. My mother liked him. She was always trying to get him to eat. He never did. That used to hurt her feelings. Ralph had no chin and a long, thin nose that had been broken so many times there wasn't anything left inside to *break* anymore. It was like Playdoh—like if you squashed his nose over to one side it would stay there. He wore thick glasses with black rims. When they got broken, as they often did, he taped them together with black electrical tape or, in a pinch, with flesh colored Band-Aids.

The way he slicked back his hair was the last straw. His hair was black and spiky and always seemed to be trying to stick up in a ridge across the top of his scalp. He *was* a bird; an angry, intense, scavenger bird of some sort—a raven, say, or a buzzard—with watery, magnified, red-rimmed eyes that always seemed about to pop out of their sockets. This was especially true when you got him on the subject of Henry Miller. Ralph loved Henry Miller. He worshipped and adored Henry Miller. He had stolen every book Henry Miller ever wrote, some of them hundreds of times over. I don't think Ralph actually *read* any of the books; I think he just liked what he'd *heard* about Henry Miller—that he fucked a lot of cool chicks and didn't take any shit off of anyone.

Well, I take it back. Ralph may have skimmed a copy of *The Books in My Life,* but only to find out what *other* books were worth stealing. What Ralph liked about books was giving them to people for presents. He used to break into people's houses and leave stolen books all over the place. My mother caught him at it one Christmas Eve. She woke up and found Ralph crouched in the living room, arranging hard cover copies of *Death on the Installment Plan, Naked Lunch* and *To the End of the World* in a semicircle around the darkened tree—scared the Bejesus out of the both of them.

Ralph wasn't a healthy person. He didn't *want* to be a healthy person. He cultivated ill health. He *wanted* to look like a bird. He wanted to look like the guys who wrote the books in Henry Miller's life. He wanted to look like Celine and Beckett and Burroughs and Bukowski and Blaise Cendrars. He never ate and never slept but just wandered the aisles of all night grocery stores, slipping paperback copies of *Tropic of Cancer* into the deep pockets of a floor length herringbone coat.

Well, either that or he drove around in his faded tan Corvair, getting into fights. Ralph got into at least one fight every two or three weeks, year in and year out. He picked fights on purpose, for no apparent reason. He went out of his way. He'd drive up and down the Peninsula at three in the morning, just to pick a fight with someone he'd heard was a good fighter—Spike in Millbrae, or Tony Rapaglia up in South City, or Jojo Chaplinski down in East San Jose.

And Ralph *wasn't* a good fighter. He was a bad fighter. He had good form; that was about it. He was too tall and too skinny and too unhealthy to be a good fighter. With him it was philosophical. He'd go screeching up to wherever the guy lived and blow the weak horn of his faded tan Corvair and shine his spotlight into the guy's windows and yell his name and get out of the car and stand on the guy's lawn, bobbing and weaving like a cross between Ichabod Crane and the Marquis of Queensbury—until Spike or Tony or Jojo came out and popped him one in the mouth. Then Ralph would prop himself up on one elbow, feel around in the grass until he found his freshly broken glasses, fit the pieces painfully down over the bridge of his freshly broken nose, shake his head admiringly and compliment the guy.

"Good punch, good punch," he'd say, and that would be the end of it; well, unil the next time.

Which is what I mean about philosophy. Ralph didn't exactly enjoy getting the crap kicked out of him every two or three weeks; it was *necessary*. He simply wanted to have whatever bad could possibly happen to him to just hurry up and happen and get itself the hell over with. Years later, he got strung out on morphine for the same reason. He wanted to become the biggest junkie in Northern California so he could go over to England and take the same cure William Burroughs took. He stole morphine from Veterinary Hospitals up and down the El Camino and succeeded in becoming a pretty good-sized junkie, but he never made it over to England, never took the cure. The last time I saw Ralph, he had imaginary flukes in his veins. He was sitting on his couch, busily stabbing a needle into his forearm, trying to kill them, one at a time, trying to impale one of the wiggly little critters on the end of the needle long enough to squash the life out of it between the yellow nails of his thumb and forefinger.

Everything I know about him after that is apocryphal. I heard from Dick Joseph, for instance, that Ralph's father died and he got back to Ohio just in time to sabotage the casket. His father's body fell out onto the steps of the church. Ralph sued the funeral home and the casket company. Next I heard he was in the Ohio State Penitentiary for insurance fraud. Then I heard he was dead.

I had a hard time believing the one about him being dead. He would have been a hard guy to kill. What could have killed him? A gun? A knife? He was made entirely out of chicken gristle, for God's sake. A bullet would have bounced off. A knife would have bent. Cancer, maybe. Cancer can kill anyone; or maybe I just have a hard time believing anyone's dead.

But, back when black coffee was still his drug of choice, Ralph Wood was just the guy you wanted to be hanging out with when you heard the news that Kennedy got shot. Not because he could put it into perspective, no, anyone could put it into perspective—what Ralph knew was how to *capitalize* on it. He was deep in thought, biting the inside of his left cheek.

"You know what this means?" He looked over the rims of his glasses at me and slicked down his quivering coxcomb.

"Johnson's President? Jackie's a widow? John-John's an orphan?"

"No, man. Jesus." His eyes popped farther out of their sockets. "Get serious. It means it's going to be a good time to pick up chicks, that's what."

"You think?" I said.

"Sure. Chicks are gonna be sad that Kennedy got shot, man. Sad chicks get all vulnerable and shit. They want someone to come along and comfort them."

So we went off to do that. We walked over into the Emporium and strolled up and down the wide ceramic aisles between the cosmetics' department and the lingerie section stopping sad, vulnerable chicks to see if they might want to be comforted. We didn't actually succeed in picking up a single sad, vulnerable chick, but we did *try.* Ralph thought Henry Miller would have done the same thing under the circumstances. Guys are idiots. Chicks are idiots. Henry Miller's an idiot. How the human race continues to thrive is beyond my ability to comprehend.

CHAPTER TWELVE

Clayton Street

Kennedy got shot in November of 1963. Then came my Christmas with the Mafia girl. My Christmas with the Mafia girl lasted until March of 1964. I don't remember her name. I always just think of her as the Mafia girl. She wasn't even Italian; she was tall and thin and droll and Irish, with lots of freckles everywhere, even on her lips. She had short red hair I could mess up whenever I felt like messing it up. I liked that about her. Apropos of nothing, I'd just reach over and mess up her hair. Ha! Sometimes I messed it up with both hands, as hard as I could. She liked it—the harder I messed up her hair the better she liked it, but the funny thing was that her hair never really got messed up at all, no matter what we did. I tried everything.

She had green eyes…bony thighs…narrow feet. She licked her lips before she kissed me and kept her eyes open. There was a smell about her, too, a smell I still conjur up unexpectedly sometimes: baby powder and diapers and her sister's expensive perfume, all mixed together with the taste of tangerine lipstick—Marnie! Ha! Marnie McCracken.

Marnie came into Kay-Bee's to buy presents for her sister's kids with a fistful of fifty-dollar bills her brother-in-law had given her. I carried the presents out to her car for her. That was my job. One of the presents was a tricycle. We came into some slight contact with each other while we were trying to get the tricycle box jammed into the back seat. She was driving her brother-in-law's black two-door '62 Chrysler Imperial. He hadn't gotten around to trading it in on a new one yet.

Minuscule sparks of static electricity crackled between the hairs on our arms. We caught each other's eye and smiled. One of her breasts brushed my cheek. My elbow poked into her bony ribs. I said something about the weather. She looked bored for a second, then her expression softened. She shrugged her shoulders and looked right into my eyes like she was trying to tell me to shut the fuck up and stick my hand up her dress. It was a compelling expression. She might have used it a time or two before back in New Jersey—or maybe she practiced it in front of a mirror.

"Hey," she said. "What's this mean? 'Some assembly required?'"

"You have to put the thing together," I said. "Screw in some screws."

"Fuck," she said. "They probably don't even have a screwdriver." She shaded her eyes from the setting sun and wet her tangerine lipstick with her tongue.

"Who?"

"Oh, my sister and her husband. He thinks he's Johnny Potatoes. If a light bulb burns out, he calls in an electrician."

"I might have a screwdriver."

"You might?"

"No, I do. Definitely. There's one in the stock room. I could bring it over."

"When are you off work?"

"Right around now." I looked at my watch. "I'd have to go punch out."

"Go punch out," she said. Then she shot me that same shut the fuck up and stick your hand up my dress look and lowered herself sort of sideways down into the driver's seat with her legs spread apart and waited there with the door wide open.

Marnie was staying in a big house up in the hills, almost to Belmont, around where Elliot used to live, with her older sister and her sister's husband and their two kids. They were all originally from New Jersey, but Marnie had only been in California a couple weeks. She had a little bit of a Joisey accent; I made fun of it, but only very gently. She complained that there wasn't any snow and liked it that I was from Michigan. That was what we had in common—the lack of snow. She was looking for a job as a cosmetologist, but in the meantime, she helped take care of her sister's two boys.

After we got the tricycle put together out in the garage, I stayed for dinner. The four of us played Monopoly. Her sister's husband was the Mafia guy. I didn't know he was even Italian. I thought he was Jewish. I had hotels on Connecticut, Oriental and Vermont before anyone else had anything on anything. He was pissed off that I was kicking his ass.

"You from here?" he asked.

"No. Michigan."

"Detroit?"

"Near there, yeah—a place you probably never heard of."

"Try me." He flexed the muscles under his eyes.

"Huntington Woods," I said. I knew a lot Jews lived in Huntington Woods.

"Never heard of it." He rolled the dice.

"Seven," I said. "Connecticut. Ha! Pay me."

I found out later that it was more than just that I was kicking his ass in Monopoly that was pissing the guy off; I found out later that he was trying to fix Marnie up with a guy he knew back in Jersey, some other Mafia guy. I never seem to know it when people hate my guts. I think we're getting along great, and the fact is, it's all they can do to keep from popping me in the mouth.

* 𝓖 𝓖 *

But the only really pertinent thing about my Christmas with the Mafia girl was that it coincided with Ginny's Christmas with her Negro poet. His name was Jim Moss. All I really know about him is what Ginny told me, but that was plenty. She told me *everything.*

Sometime in October, she moved out of her place on 45th Avenue and into Jim Moss's apartment up by U.C. Hospital. They lived together until she got too nuts around the end of January of 1964. Ginny always went increasingly crazy around the holidays. It had to do with her father taking off the day before Christmas when she was five. Well, either that or the influence of the planet Neptune in her astrological chart—and getting drunk a lot didn't help. From November until March, Virginia Good drank too much and when she did, she often went completely nuts.

The Christmas of her Negro poet was no exception. They fought; physically, mentally, emotionally, spiritually —you name it. They fought about her being rich and him being poor, about him being black and her being white. His grand-

126

mother had been born a slave. Her grandfather had *owned* slaves. She called him every nigger name in the book; he called her every kind of honky slut cunt bitch name he could think of. They fought about poetry and music and art and what to have for dinner. Then there was always all that making up to do. They wore each other out.

She broke his windows. He threw the contents of her shrine through the broken window and down into the street— Virginia Woolf, Gurjieff, DuChamp, the whole works. She tried to kill herself by turning on the oven and all the gas jets on the top of the stove, playing Bach's *Mass in B-Minor* on the record player and reading *The Confessions of Saint Augustine* at the kitchen table. That *really* pissed Jim Moss off—the last thing he wanted was some dead-ass white chick reading St. Augustine when a couple of Irish cops came around to see what all the shouting had been about.

He kicked her out in increments, beginning in the middle of January. She stayed with her sister Sandy for awhile, then moved into a flat on Clayton, four or five blocks up from Haight Street. She and Jim Moss continued to see one another and continued to like each other despite their irreconcilable differences. It lasted until March of 1964. I was there when it finally ended—well, almost finally ended, I guess would be more accutate. I'll get to all that.

Ginny called me up. She was hiding out. She was sick. She needed to be rescued. Her voice was low and mysterious. I told her I'd bring her things to make her feel better. It wasn't a date. I brought her tea. I changed out of the shirt that smelled like the Mafia girl, put some Lipton tea bags and one of my mother's fancy tea cups into a paper bag, walked up to the El Camino, caught a Greyhound bus to Seventh and Market, hopped on a Haight Street bus and got off at Clayton.

* 𝒢 𝒢 *

Haight-Ashbury was like downtown San Bruno—there may even have been a Kinney's Shoe's nestled among the Asian and Palestinian mom and pop grocery stores, florist shops, restaurants and bars. There was a bowling alley and a movie theater and plenty of parking everywhere. The streets were clean. The only stoplight was at the corner of Haight and Masonic. Usually no more than two or three cars at a time ever had to wait for the light to change.

Clayton Street was crowded with tall, skinny Victorian flats, going ever more steeply up toward the address Ginny had given me. In the valley by Frederick Street, I stopped to pick some wild flowers, daisies and bachelor buttons and whatever else happened to be growing there. I remembered I'd said I wasn't ever going to get a girl any god damn flowers again, but that had been a long time ago.

Across the valley and up toward Parnassus Heights, lighted houses glittered through wisps of fog among dark hills. A dog barked. Telephone wires crackled. Golden Gate Park was a rectangle of black. The panhandle was bordered by streams of headlights from the traffic going up Fell and down Oak. The spires of Saint Ignatius Church were lit up in the background. It was peaceful and serene and unreal, like a picture on one of those big glossy San Francisco calendars.

Another block or so up the hill, I came to a huge brown-shingled house with ivy growing all over it. The porch light was on. The address I'd written on a scrap of newspaper was

128

nailed in brass numbers into the shingles. I combed my hair, looking at my reflection in the window before I rang the bell.

A guy named Bud answered the door. He was from Madison, Wisconsin and had a spindly goatee. Lots of people lived there. Ginny had found the place in an ad on a bulletin board at San Francisco State. The people who lived there were communists. It was a co-op. None of the cups or saucers or plates or knives or spoons matched any of the other cups or saucers or plates or knives or spoons. Nobody seemed to know who, if anyone, had actually rented the place.

Ginny was sitting on a rug in the middle of the floor in her room, wearing a plain white flannel nightgown—no little blue flowers. There were lit votive candles in a semicircle in front of her and books scattered around—open books, closed books, fiction, nonfiction, kid's books, school books, books of all kinds. Her room had a sort of bay window balcony that looked out over the front porch. I worried that she might have seen me combing my hair, but the shades were pulled down. I gave her the flowers. She laid them on her new shrine, which was made up all of Vedanta stuff this time: sticks of incense and a fat Vivekananda book, surrounded by pictures of Jesus, Buddha, Sri Ramakrishna and the Reverend Mother. I made us tea in the community kitchen. We talked and talked—primarily about her Negro poet.

She was trying to ditch him. He was stalking her. She showed me pictures of the guy. He didn't look full of shit. That's the first thing I notice about a person. Even in pictures you can tell whether somebody's full of shit or not. He had on a cap in one of the pictures, but it wasn't a full of shit cap. It was a cap like my grandfather used to wear, the kind of cap Henry Miller used to wear. I liked the look of the guy. He was all twinkly and smart looking. You could tell he and Ginny had liked each other when they hadn't been fighting.

Ginny got out an old green Webcor tape recorder with "Property of Sarah Lawrence College" stenciled in black letters on the cover and played me a tape she and Jim Moss had made. It was a conversation they'd had when they were first getting to know one another. He did most of the talking, but it was clear that Virginia was there, hanging on his every word. His vocal cords got thicker and thicker as the tape wound slowly from one reel to the other. My own vocal cords swelled some, just listening to the way Ginny had been listening to the guy.

His voice was beautiful. The tape was pretty much a monologue. Ginny didn't have much to say. It was mostly him talking about jazz, about how jazz and sex and seduction are all the same thing. He interspersed the monologue with nuances of different musical instruments he had the uncanny knack of reproducing with his voice, like a scat singer: clarinets, a saxophone, brushes on a snare drum. Of course it was all just sweet talk to get into her pants, but it was *good* sweet talk, really sweet sweet talk, and it sure was *working*. You could tell that too.

"Jazz means fuck," Ginny's voice said.

"Yeah? Where'd you hear that, sugar?"

"In music history."

"You're pretty educated, ain't you, baby?"

I could almost see them. They were in her apartment on 45th Avenue. She would have been in one of her flannel nightgowns; he would have been sitting across from her. There would have been a bottle of Beefeater Gin on the floor between them. The tape recorder would have been off to one side. She would have had nothing on under her nightgown but a pair of white cotton panties. Her hair would have been hiding her face. I could almost hear it in the tape when his thick black index finger brushed the inside of her upper thigh. I could almost feel her squirm, could almost see his hand moving slowly, deliberately, up toward her pretty face, touching the tiny, erect little nipples of her breasts, pushing her hair out of her eyes, touching her cheek, holding his hand under her chin, touching her mouth, leaning toward her, kissing her eyes.

"How about we turn this off now?" Jim Moss said.

"Uh-huh," she said.

Sure, I was jealous. What do you think? You'd be jealous too. The guy's voice was mesmerizing, mellifluous. He was saying things I wish to this day I could say. He was a poet. And, yeah, absolutely, of course I knew he fucked her brains out the minute I heard the tape recorder click off. Hell yes, I was jealous—but it was still that delicious kind of jealousy where nothing's any skin off anyone's nose yet. It wasn't a date. I was her buddy. We'd been hanging out. Going to movies. Talking on the phone. Writing letters. I had brought her tea.

I heard the whole story, how she moved in with him, how it deteriorated, how they fought, how she got drunk and blacked out and broke his windows…that it had been Christmas, that she'd tried to kill herself, that they'd worn each other out, that it had been the same with all the men she'd ever known.

We kept talking. I told her about the Mafia girl. She was jealous. She thanked me for things. The tea. The flowers. She was fragile and tough and spoiled and endlessly entertaining. Her hair fell in her face. Her eyes peeked out from under her bangs. I touched the inside of her thigh. She squirmed. I unbuttoned her nightgown and touched her little nipples and held her hands and ran my finger across the scars on her wrists. We laughed and got tears in our eyes, but mainly we just talked…talked and talked. We talked until the sun came up and kept on talking.

Around nine, I got us coffee. Some of the communists were in the kitchen. One of them was hunched over a spiral notebook, writing down the particulars of that morning's bowel movement. He'd been recording his bowel movements every day since he graduated from the University of Washington a few years back—color, shape, consistency, et cetera.

The rest of the communists had some idiosyncracies as well, but for the most part they all seemed pretty normal. They were all just kids going to school, letting their whiskers grow, reading Karl Marx…and Lenin and Trotksy and Paul Goodman, wearing clothes that didn't quite fit right or go together well—due, no doubt, to the relatively recent absence of mothers in their lives. They made coffee by pouring boiling water through folded chemistry paper stuck inside a glass beaker. I thought that was pretty slick.

What they all seemed to have in common was Bob Dylan. They listened to Bob Dylan all the time, morning, noon and night. They had the same two albums everywhere—Bob Dylan in a sheepskin coat holding his guitar and Bob Dylan in the same sheepskin coat with his girlfriend's head on his shoulder. It was a hard rain that was 'a gonna fall. They all seemed to know that. They were expecting it, counting on it, waiting for it, hoping. I may have had a vague inkling that a shower or two was on the way myself by then.

"Oh, where have you been, my blue-eyed son?
Where have you been, my darling young one?"

When I got back to her room, Ginny was on the phone with Jim Moss.

"Well, no, actually. It's not a good time. I have a friend over." She looked up at me, then held the receiver out so I could hear what Jim Moss was saying.

"Tell him get stepping. Say I'm coming by."

"He says I should tell you to leave," Ginny said, without covering the receiver.

"Do you want me to leave?" I asked.

"No."

"Say I'll kick his motherfuckin' ass!"

"I don't want to do that," Ginny said. Her voice was sad and emphatic, like a cello, and somehow, from that point on, in the space of about a tenth of a second, she was my girl-friend, and I was her boyfriend. One minute I was the Mafia girl's boyfriend and she was my girlfriend and the next minute she *wasn't* my girlfriend, Ginny was. That was that. It was like getting run over by a truck.

"It ain't no use to sit and wonder why, babe
It don't matter anyhow.
And it ain't no use to sit and wonder why, babe
If you don't know by now."

CHAPTER THIRTEEN

Stockton Street

$\mathcal{T}$he day after Ginny and I spent the night talking our heads off on Clayton Street, I ditched Marnie McCracken, abandoned my job at the toy store and moved up to The Navarre Guest House on Stockton Street next to the south end of the tunnel between Union Square and North Beach—just down the hill from the historical plaque marking the spot where Sam Spade's partner, Miles Archer, was shot and killed. I washed dishes and waited on tables in exchange for room and board.

When I wasn't working or over at Ginny's, I wandered around downtown San Francisco—North Beach, City Lights, Chinatown, Macy's, the Emporium, the St. Francis, the cable car turnaround at Powell and Market, the Tenderloin, Maiden Lane, Lefty O'Doul's, the burgeoning topless joints, you name it. A few of the guys I used to know in San Mateo came up now and then—Thulin, Ralph, John White, Murph. In fact, the first time Ralph Wood ever smoked dope was in the elevator at The Navarre Guest House. There ought to be a plaque.

Thulin got us the dope from some beatniks in North Beach; Thulin got everyone his or her first dope. Ralph and I ended up on the floor of the elevator, laughing ourselves silly. We couldn't stop. Even when it wasn't funny anymore, it was funny that it wasn't funny anymore.

John White had been one of Elliot's friends at Hillsdale before I got there. He was an actor. He was always playing some different *character* or other, always taking on new roles—Lee Marvin in *The Killers*, Rod Steiger in *The Pawnbroker*. He was always anyone but himself.

Oh, and as for Murph, he's my brother-in-law. He ended up marrying my sister Nicki. They met at Ralph Wood's apartment in San Mateo. I told her I didn't want her hanging out over there. She hung out over there anyway.

* 𝒢 𝒢 *

But the main thing about the Navarre Guest House was that it was where Ginny and I finally got around to consummating having become boyfriend and girlfriend—in the squalid little roach-infested room they gave me in exchange for washing dishes. It wasn't nearly so romantic as it would have been with all those candles blazing back at her apartment on 45th Avenue, but it was where we were.

The room had a single small window looking out at a box canyon of dirty brick walls. The mattress still had the impression of the dead body of the disabled World War II Vet who'd lived there for decades before I moved in. He'd been an alcoholic. There were cigarette burns and whisky circles on the windowsill. The smell of his deadness mixed with the smell of thriving nests of cockroaches in the walls.

She sat on the edge of the bed wearing a pair of faded, tight-ass Levi's. They buttoned up the front and were loose at the waist. I unbuttoned them one button at a time while she pulled her white gauze Mexican peasant blouse off over her head. She unclasped her bra and tossed it and her blouse over toward the chair on the other side of the room. I pulled her pants and her panties off all at the same time. She got under the covers. I got undressed and got under the covers with her. We tried to make ourselves comfortable and got as romantic as we could get around the edges of the indentation the dead guy's body had made in the mattress, but we weren't able to get very comfortable or very romantic, either one.

At that point it was more philosophical than anything else—like Ralph Wood picking a fight with Jo Jo Chaplinski— something we just had to do and get the hell over with. We were in a big rush. She had a date with Tom Piper. We had to hurry. We hurried. We got it the hell over with.

Then the phone rang. Tom was in the lobby. Ginny freshened up in the bathroom down the hall. I walked with her to the elevator. Every Wednesday she and Tom went to the symphony. Tom was one of her suitors from San Francisco State. Their relationship was Platonic. She had all sorts of suitors. She was charming and cute and smart and had a really extra cute ass, as I've said.

Hank Harrison was another of her suitors from school. He had a big nose and little eyes and never fit in. Later on, when everyone else was wearing buckskin jackets, Hank would be the guy in the seersucker suit. He was sort of semifamous in the sixties and seventies—first as manager of the Grateful Dead, back when they were still some little jug band down in Palo Alto calling themselves the Warlocks, then as the founder of LSD Rescue, which according to Hank, became the Haight-Ashbury Free Medical Clinic. He wrote a book or two, too. Now the only thing famous about Hank Harrison is that he's Courtney Love's father.

I can't begin to remember all the guys who had the hots for Ginny back then. The guy with the spindly goatee who had answered the door at the house on Clayton Street the first night I went over there was another one—that Bud guy. He was also a Baha'i. Ginny liked *spiritual* guys.

Ron Silverstein was another one. He was an older guy with a bunch of doctorates who taught philosophy at St. Mary's. Oh, and he had also converted from Judaism to Catholicism because it was so god damn *mystical*. Ginny liked that *a lot*. He had her all talked into thinking she was Heloise and he was Abelard. She was a pushover for all that dark, secret, forbidden love nonsense…and there were still all her so-called ex-boyfriends hanging around: Jim Moss and the garbanzo bean guy and Charles and that whole college kid contingent. What the fuck she was doing with me, nobody knew.

All I distinctly recollect of the next few months is Ginny reading *The Alexandria Quartet* out loud to me on the roof of the house on Clayton Street while I rubbed Coppertone into the perfect small of her muscular back. Ginny thought she was Justine. Tom Piper was Nessim. I forget who I was—Laurence Durrell, I guess. She had high hopes for me. She loved finding herself in the characters of books and thought I was going to make her one some day. I loved rubbing her back while she read to me. That was the only education I ever got. It was the only education I ever wanted. The backrubs never stayed confined strictly to her back.

Toward the end of June, Ginny started getting antsy about me *saying* I was going to be a writer. I mean, here she was, the belle of the ball, with all these substantial guys chasing after her, and it got harder and harder for her to explain why she'd chosen to be with me. Who could she say I was? *What* could she say I was? A dishwasher? A waiter? A former cart boy at a toy store? An ex-shoe salesman at Kinney's? No. She had to think I was a writer. That was what I'd *said* I was, after all. That was what I'd *told* her I was. She was all set to be Zelda Fitzgerald. I wasn't doing my part. I had to get a move on.

* 𝒢 𝒢 *

Somewhere around in there I made it easier for Ginny to convince herself that I was at least *going* to be a writer someday by taking off to go get things to write about. Around the first of July or so, I hitchhiked down to Mexico, over to New Orleans and up through Mississippi to New York, thinking I might find some stuff to write about along the way...so I could hurry up and write some god damn books and get rich and famous like Scott Fitzgerald so she could be Zelda to her heart's content.

In Tijuana, I got thrown in jail along with some guy I'd gotten a ride from. We'd left his car on the US side and had walked across the border. He had a lot of money and a nice car—a little yellow Porsche. He was worried his car might get stolen or he might get robbed. A cab driver was showing him a stack of dirty pictures. Plain clothes Mexican police arrested both of us. I was just standing there, not doing a damn thing. I didn't even get to see any of the pictures. We ended up in the Tijuana jail. There was feces all over the floor.

A drunk Marine from Camp Pendelton grabbed a drunk Mexican by the back of his shirt, picked him up from one of the benches and threw him into the shit on the floor. Then the drunk Mexican got up and grabbed the drunk Marine by the back of his uniform and threw *him* into the shit on the floor. That happened a few more times. They were both so drunk it looked like it was in slow motion. As soon as the Mexican got comfortable on the bench, just as he was about to pass happily into oblivion, the Marine managed to pick him up by the back of his shirt and throw him down into the shit again. I leaned against a wall and watched.

After a while one of the guards let me out and walked with me down to an interview room. There were kids sticking their hands out toward me from between the bars of their cells— big-eyed Mexican kids who looked like they hadn't done anything wrong, either. A Police Lieutenant threw my comb into a trashcan and turned me loose. I walked back across the border, found the guy's car, got his wallet from under the seat, went back to the Tijuana jail and bailed him out. He was grateful. I could have left him there. I had his car keys. I had his wallet. I could have taken them both and split. I didn't. Whether that was worth writing about or not, I didn't know.

I liked being on my own, being free—having no money and only what clothes I was wearing, standing in a hot desert as it was starting to cool off, with no cars coming from either direction and a huge orange moon rising above the horizon. The sun went down. The moon came up. A prairie dog barked. Nobody expected anything. I had no one to worry about but myself.

In Yuma, Arizona, I shoveled horseshit from one pile of horseshit to another pile of horseshit to make some money to get something to eat. In Texas, a trucker put his hand on my dick. I was asleep. I'd been having a dream about this cute little Mexican chick at the diner where I'd spent most of the money I'd made shoveling horseshit. She was going to come with me to New Orleans, but didn't. Whether that was worth writing about or not, I didn't know. Maybe so.

In Jackson, Mississippi, some guys in a red pickup thought I was a freedom rider. I wasn't. They were members of an organization called "Americans for the Preservation of the White Race." One of them held a shotgun under my chin. He held it steadily, like he'd done it before. I told them in my best Southern drawl that I was on my way up to Memphis, looking for work. I was all for Negroes being able to eat at white restaurants and drink from white drinking fountains and go to school with white kids and not get themselves lynched every five seconds, sure, but the way I figured it was that Martin Luther King and Ralph Abernathy were doing a fine job of fixing all that. I simply did not see how getting my head blown off would have helped much. The guys in the pickup dropped me off at the north end of town. That might have been worth writing about, but I doubted it.

In New York, some guy dropped me off near the World's Fair. I took a look at the big brass sculpture of that empty world that was supposed to be the symbol of it all and noticed a lot of pigeons pecking at the cement. Their feathers were iridescent in the sun. It was hot and humid.

I stopped off at Washington Square, got whacked on the shoe by a cop for lying on a bench, and heard Bob Dylan singing in the basement of a brick building. People were lined up going down a stairwell. You had to pay money to get in. I didn't have any money. A guy on the sidewalk told me Dylan stole everything he did off of Woody Guthrie. I told the guy, "No shit." I knew all about Bob Dylan from the communists on Clayton Street. I wondered what was going on back in San Francisco. I missed Ginny. Was that worth writing about? Fuck if I knew. Fuck if I know. Who knows what's worth writing about? Not me. That's for sure.

The next morning, I called Ginny collect from a Chock Full O' Nuts that was next to an advertisement for *How to Succeed in Business Without Really Trying* in which Donna McKechnie's name appeared in small print. I thought about giving Donna a call, but that would have been stupid, so I called Ginny instead.

"I've been somewhat...promiscuous," Ginny said in that inimitable way she had of making it sound like it wasn't *her* but some naughty next door neighbor girl who'd been fucking everybody and his brother while I'd been gone. She *was* schizophrenic. She and the naughty neighbor girl did *everything* together. And if it wasn't that little slut, it was someone else. Ginny was never alone. She always had imaginary playmates. She talked to herself in different voices and read books out loud to herself—wait, wait, here's what I mean. Here's another part of another letter:

How absolutely wonderful I feel today. Alone. Sitting in intense chaos with piles of poetry books all over and getting very hung up on T. S. Eliot—my God—here we are, me and Dylan and T. S. and Edna and Emily and Wallace. We are having a PARTY! We are! Have you read, beside all the serious decay poems, Practical Cats? The neighbors must think I'm off again because they've (cats) got to be read aloud—so they are being—and there are parts which if aloud must be allowed to be loud so they are being and then when they are, and at some more subdued parts, laughter is provoked so must be evoked—Loud—hee, hee, HA

HA HA—like that. So what the neighbors hear is cats, loud and huge laughing cats. I love and am good.

Loud—hee, hee, HA HA HA—like that. Ha! She used to laugh so hard sometimes she *squealed.*. She peed her pants. Then it was so funny that she peed her pants she squealed again and peed her pants some more. Fuck. Where was I? She'd been "somewhat" promiscuous.

"Somewhat?" I asked.

"Fairly."

"Like, who with?"

"Oh, dear. Just Jim, I guess."

"Jim Moss? I thought you didn't want anything to do with him anymore?"

"I thought so, too. Oh yeah, and Bud. I forgot."

"The guy who lives there? I thought that was a bad idea?"

"It probably was. Oh, and Ron Silverstein, of course."

"What do you mean, of course?"

"Well, that was pretty inevitable, don't you think?"

"Who else?"

"I'm not sure. I was blacked out some."

GG

I hitchhiked back to San Francisco as fast as I could hitchhike. I had visions of the love of my life up on the sunroof with Jim Moss—his shiny black hands rubbing squirts of Coppertone down the small of her back and up the sides of her sturdy rib cage.

"Oh, yeah, and Bud."

142

Bud's goatee tickling the tips of her pretty nipples got me through Kansas.

"Oh, and Ron Silverstein, of course."

Visceral visions of her and Ron Silverstein grabbing at each other like animals, tearing each other's clothes off, like Heloise and Abelard finally released from their vows, got me through the Rocky Mountains in no time flat.

"I was blacked out some."

Holy shit. That could have meant most anything. I had visions of Ginny and a bunch of Vedanta swamis and Buddhist monks and Catholic priests all in one great big huge sweaty, heaving, mystical pile of naked flesh frolicking up and down the aisles of Grace Cathedral that sped me the rest of the way to San Francisco.

* 𝒢 𝒢 *

While I'd been in New York, my parents had moved up to Oregon, to Ashland, Oregon—where I am now, where I've finally quit playing golf long enough to sit down with my little stack of letters and things and say this stuff.

Ginny wasn't in San Francisco when I got back. She was visiting her aunt in Laguna Beach. No one was around when I got back. I was on my own. Sometime during the next week or so I got a job in the Industrial Relations Department of the State of California, rented an apartment on Bush Street and got married to a woman named Sabine. It was a fake marriage. A newspaper vendor I knew from the Navarre Guest House introduced us. Sabine was from Austria on a tourist visa and needed to get married in order to stay in the country. I needed to get married in order to stay out of the army. They were drafting people right and left by then. Staying out of the draft was a full time job. I did all kinds of things—getting married was just the beginning.

I called Ginny at her aunt's house in Laguna Beach and asked her if she thought it would be okay if I got married. She said, "Sure." Ginny didn't want me going to Vietnam any more than I wanted to go to Vietnam.

The ceremony was at City Hall. The newspaper vendor was our witness. Sabine kept his change machine in her purse during the ceremony. I kissed her on the cheek when the judge said I should. She was pretty cute, too, but it was all strictly business. Nobody wanted to go to Vietnam. Well, except for Elliot, I guess, and he had reasons of his own. He had reasons of his own for everything he ever did. Reasons I never understood. Reasons to this day I don't understand. Reasons I'll never understand.

CHAPTER FOURTEEN

Pacific Heights

*J*n September I moved into a huge Queen Anne mansion on the corner of California and Octavia in Pacific Heights. The owner had converted her private residence into eleven separate apartments. Her name was Carrie B. Rousseau. She had lots of cats. Her apartment was on the first floor. When she opened the door all you saw were cats—on couches, in chairs, rubbing lovingly around her ankles, everywhere. The place reeked of unchanged kitty litter.

She didn't charge much rent—forty-five bucks a month, which even back then wasn't much—and the place was completely furnished with all kinds of antique Japanese silk screens, English China and Chinese rugs that Mrs. Rousseau and her husband had picked up on trips to Europe and Asia before World War I. Maybe it was because of the cats that she didn't charge much rent. She and her husband had both been architects. They'd had a hand in the rebuilding of San Francisco after the 1906 earthquake and fire. He was dead. She was lonely. She may also have been slightly nuts.

I remember sitting with her out in what used to be her living room. It had been turned into a parlor. There were

couches and floor lamps and end tables and table lamps. Anyone who lived in the building was welcome to sit around
down there, but not many people did. Mrs. Rousseau and I
talked about as much as we didn't talk. She ended most of her
sentences by saying, "Don't you know." It wasn't a question.
I'm not sure what it was, but she looked right at me when she
said it.

Her eyes were still blue and sparkly, and the way she put
on makeup was probably the same way she'd put on makeup
the day she got married—circles of rouge, puffs of flesh-col-
ored powder. She looked so innocent, so sweet, her mouth
painted into a pert little pucker of bright red lipstick like Betty
Boop.

"I went down to Grant Avenue this afternoon, don't you
know," she said one night. "I had to order a funeral arrange-
ment from Podesta Baldocchi, don't you know. Another day,
another funeral…they're dying like flies, don't you know."
Her voice trailed off. She reminded me of my grandmother.

Mrs. Rousseau knew a song my grandmother used to sing
to me: *Hello, Central, Give me Heaven (Because My Mother's There)*.
I used to lean my head against the prickly arm of my grandmother's maroon overstuffed chair while she soaked her feet
in Epsom Salts and sang songs from the olden days to me.

When I found out Mrs. Rousseau knew the words to the
Hello, Central song, I got all excited. She wouldn't sing it, no.
She didn't like to sing. "I have a terrible singing voice, don't
you know," she said. But I got her to say the words out loud
to me. It was a real tearjerker of a song…all about a kid calling the operator after his mother had died, probably not long
after the telephone was invented. "Central" was what they
used to call the operator. The kid says, "Hello central, give me

heaven, for I know my mother's there. You will find her with the angels, over on the golden stair." Then at the end he says, "Kiss me mama, it's your darling. Kiss me through the telephone." I forget what the operator said. What could she say?

After Mrs. Rousseau died, I read in the *Chronicle* that some quasi-religious New Age cult bought the place. They were going to turn it into an ashram or a monastery or a cloister of some sort, but then they tried to back out of the deal. They claimed the house was haunted by the ghost of Carrie B. Rousseau and the everlasting souls of dozens of dead cats. I'm sure it was, too. It more than likely still is.

Mine was the smallest apartment in the building. There was a breakfast nook in the tiny kitchen and a bedroom and a big closet—that was it. The door off the kitchen opened out onto a patio, half a block down from the Hayes Street Hill. There was a park up there. I was happy. I was making money. I was writing stuff. I was reading stuff. I was living in an opulent mansion full of silk screens and Chinese rugs and English China for forty-five bucks a month, and the love of my life stayed with me most every night. What more I could ask for, I did not know.

* 𝒢𝒢 *

Then it started getting close to Christmas again. I'd heard about Ginny and her Christmases, but I'd never actually been privy to the whole phenomenon in any kind of day-to-day way. I didn't believe much I hadn't seen for myself. I still don't. Ginny and her Christmases you had to see to believe. I saw. I believed. I believe.

The first indication I got was that one night, probably around the middle of November, she came crashing through the kitchen door, laughing, out of breath, drunk off her ass, and told me not to let anybody come into the apartment.

"Lock the door," she said. "Don't open it, no matter what." She jabbed a finger at my chest and ran into the bedroom. I closed the door behind her.

Not long afterwards, four or five huffing, puffing policemen showed up. I opened the door a crack but kept my foot behind it.

"We need to talk to the girl who came in here," one of the cops said.

"No girl came in here," I said.

By the expression on his face, the cop knew I was lying, but then he seemed to be trying to think what it was that Ginny had actually done wrong. Yell? Run? Hide? Laugh? Were those things against the law? He couldn't exactly put his finger on it, but whatever it was, he'd better not catch her doing it again.

Ginny was ambivalent toward policemen. It had something to do with getting raped by that cop after she stole the bulldozer back in high school. One of the things that characterized her Christmases was that when she got drunk she pissed off cops for no apparent reason. She used to play with them, to toy with them, to ruffle their feathers. She'd see a cop across a street, wave to him, call out to him in that same confident voice she'd used to get the waiter's attention at Ripley's, "Yoo-hoo, Mr. Policeman!" That was it. That was all she ever said.

Then she'd laugh and take off running...and when the cop saw her running, he chased her. She didn't know why.

He didn't know why. Nobody knew why, but when other cops saw her being chased by a cop, they all stopped whatever they were doing and chased her, too. It was a game, like cop tag. They hardly ever caught her, and even when they did, they didn't know what to *do* with her. What *could* they do? Arrest her? For what? Waving? Laughing? Running? She was like the Pied Piper of cops. She ran and ran. They chased her and chased her.

This was my first crack at getting her from November to March in one piece. Other guys had had their chances. Roger Singmaster had had his turn. She ended up in a loony bin in La Jolla with bandages on her wrists. Ronnie and the college kids had their turn. Jim Moss had his turn. None of them had made it past February. I was determined to make it forever. I thought I was up to it. I wasn't. Nobody was.

It always started with just a drink or two. During the rest of the year she was fine with a drink or two. She just got giggly and cuddly and talked too loud and went to sleep, but once she started drinking around Christmas, she simply never stopped. Even after she was blacked out, she kept getting more blacked out. It was an amazing thing to see. When she was blacked out, she didn't have any fear or shame or guilt or pretense, which opened her up to all the sin and sickness and misery and sadness in the world, to all the joy and beauty and charm and affection and love. She felt too much, knew too much, absorbed too much all at once. She ran into traffic. She rolled around in gutters, laughing and crying simultaneously.

It was really just your basic vicious circle. She'd drink a bottle of gin, black out, know everything, love everyone, be loved, pass out, wake up the next day, drink Fizzrin, hear what had happened the night before, feel contrite, know nothing, love no one, be unloved, take sole responsibility for all the sin and sickness and sadness in the world, feel empty, want to die, drink a bottle of gin, black out, know everything…on and on, over and over, at least once a week from November to March.

Some years she went into mental hospitals. Other years she managed to get through the whole rigmarole with whatever guy she was with. Not many lasted more than one Christmas. I lasted five. That's the all-time record. I'm not bragging. It wasn't exactly something to brag about—well, you know, unless you think beating your head against a brick wall is something to brag about.

It breaks my heart sometimes still after all these years to know what Ginny would have been if she hadn't been such a schizophrenic drunk. She would have been a god damn icon. She would have had followers, worshipers, acolytes, an entourage. She would have given Zelda Fitzgerald and Anais Nin and Isadora Duncan and Josephine Baker a run for their money in the memorable chick department. She was the first hippie, for one thing. I've mentioned that. Yeah, well, she was. I have proof. Documentary evidence. You could look it up.

There's a picture of her in the school paper at San Francisco State: *The Gater.* The picture was taken in the spring of 1963. Ginny's dancing on the lawn across from the library; her hair's kind of in her face, but you can still tell it's her. Jim Moss is in the background, egging her on. And the first time the word "hippie" was used to describe the sort of person who we all know now as a "hippie" was in the caption to that picture. She may even have had some flowers in her hair— which, in my book, makes Ginny the first hippie. Merriam

Webster may wish to quibble, but hey, she's got her own damn book. In *my* book, Ginny Good is the first hippie. Ha!

It wasn't just the picture, either. She was an icon in all kinds of other ways, too. She ironed her hair and put cucumber slices on her eyelids at night. She ate alfalfa sprouts and Northridge Farms Honey Wheatberry Bread and tofu and great vats of zucchini, parsley and green beans, all on the personal recommendation of Dr. Henry Beiler himself. He hung out with Ginny's aunt and the Vedanta Swamis in Laguna Beach and literally wrote the book on hippie food. Check it out. *Food is Your Best Medicine*, the book was called. While everyone else was still drinking Nehi Grape, Ginny Good was guzzling frothy concoctions of Tiger's Milk, Brewer's Yeast and Blackstrap Molasses. While everyone else was just beginning to catch on to the idea of eating Big Macs and Round Table Pizza, Ginny Good was the first one on her block to cook brown rice to perfection.

Nor did it end there. She was the hippiest little hippie chick who ever lived. She defined the whole idea in about a billion different ways. Later on, she carted boxes of her old clothes down to the Digger's store so other chicks could become hippie chicks too, then so did they, and so on and so on. It wasn't just a matter of appearances, either. Ginny was all up into astrology, astral projection, past lives, psychic this and New Age that, the I-Ching, Eastern Philosophy, Paul Reps, Alan Watts, Fritz Perls, R. D. Laing, Arthur Koestler, Wilhelm Reich and Sam Lewis—Sufi Sam. Whoa, I haven't thought about *him* in a while!

Ginny and Sufi Sam liked each other. We used to hang out at his house over by Precita Park. She was one of his favorites, one of his devotees, an acolyte, a disciple. Sufi Sam gave her a special disciple name, a devotee name, an acolyte name: Mumtaz. Ha! She went around calling herself that for years. Mumtaz was the gorgeous mogul chick in whose memory the Taj Mahal was built. Sufi Sam thought Ginny was some kind of budding Sufi saint herself.

He didn't think as much of me as he did of her, but he thought enough of me to have me help him fiddle with a translation he was working on of some of the poetry of Jalaluddin Rumi. I tried to get him to make it more modern. Sufi Sam gave me a funny look and said that would be stupid. Who was I to disagree? I still have part of one of the translations I worked on in my little stack of letters and things. It sounded like Ginny to me:

> *"I am light, you are my moon, don't go to heaven without me.*
> *The thorn is safe from the fire in the shelter of the rose's face:*
> *You are the rose, I your thorn;*
> *Don't go into the rose garden without me."*

She might have been the first hippie in a billion ways, but Ginny Good drew the line at not shaving her armpits. Part of being the definitive hippie chick was not doing things all the other hippie chicks did—and she had the most perfect armpits ever. Strong arms. Muscular shoulders. When she stretched her arms over her head, the veins in her armpits showed up like veins in leaves. She was beautiful—a beautiful living creature. Fuck.

She was just a regular chick, too. She got her feelings hurt and had sibling rivalries and liked to drink coffee and read the pink section in the *Chronicle* and go to movies. She wanted to make something of herself. She wanted to have kids, to get a house, to cook, to sew, to plant vegetables, to sing in a choir, to sit on a porch swing somewhere and watch the sun go down. She wanted to make something of me. She wanted to get me rich and famous and educated so we could do all those things with each other. I didn't get rich. I didn't get famous. I didn't get educated. We didn't do those things with each other. We did other things, different things.

CHAPTER FIFTEEN

Boulder Creek

Christmas of 1964, we spent at Ginny's father's house in Boulder Creek. Sandy was there, too, with a guy named Joel Pugh. There's a long story behind Sandy and Joel—he was sort of bald is all I know. You could find out the rest of the story on some of the Charlie Manson true crime websites, I suppose. Ginny liked going to Boulder Creek. I'll let her describe it. Here's a long letter she wrote from there probably in around 1967 or so, maybe even 1968. It was fall is all I know (oh, and any time you get to the part where she says, "ect., ect., ect.," that was the way she wrote it...it's pronounced the same way it's spelled, too, by the way):

Dear Gerry: Your letter was far from stupid...on the contrary it shocked, pleased and enlightened me far more than previous epistles. However, I shall not comment too much on it because I'm happy...tra la. In fact, I think I am more ME—the real (definition: real = a more or less consistent identity or state with it's most consistent ingredient equaling feeling wise, a state of well being, not complacency—with love and an intense feeling for beauty) me now. Reasons for it (the real me emerging) being: (a) Grandmum's death, (b) Mother's acceptance of me whoever I might be, and mostly (c) Boulder Creek's PEACE.

No one here is demanding an identity from me (e.g. and plus I am therefore not demanding one of myself). There is no noise. Quiet! AHH! Pieces dig peace. Need it. The "real" identity is unfettered by anyone's expectations and the result is, oh glory, NUMEROUS *occasions of ecstasy in different forms—all calm because there is no one here to step on moments or for me to have to tell them to. Talk! Ug.*

Last night I almost really dissolved into the light. My arms went first, then legs, then somewhat trunk and head. It said a peaceful environment is NECESSARY. *The light did. Daddy is lovely. He's going to give me anything—even a jog to Europe. Maybe I'll go. A Great Pyrenees! Can you imagine? If I go to Europe, you can take care of him and he will love you and you can take soft ethereal journeys in his warm white furries and remember sometimes me. Things are getting better all the time. I'm reading the latest Hesse—Beneath the Wheel.. Icky, so-so, but I like him anyway.*

There is something sad. The woods are dying. No water runs in the streams and everything is dry and brittle. There was ONE *leaf that still had its colors—sitting in the harsh crisp dusty others. A month ago you or I would have disdained and UGHed it, so paltry it would have been in the others' glory. It would have been then less than an ordinary leaf. Now, while far from gorgeous, it is pretty. And is a martyr—a humble testimony to the grandness that was—a slightly moribund but brave clinging remnant of a wondrous and glorious civilization! Oh little leaf! (I started out perfectly seriously.) And it's true anyway!*

Please go to the library and pick up a copy of Gurdjieff's All & Everything: Beelzebub's Tales to his Grandson. Skip his intro called Getting That's Going or something and jump into the story. You are in for a GRAND SURPRISE. *It's nothing like the Ouspensky crud. Also Childhood's End is neat.*

Grandmother's funeral was quite nice. Requiems played all day. And beside her picture burned two lovely angel candles and there was a book of Kipling and Br'er Rabbit.. Death! Did you write to your Grandmother? You'll be sorry. She will HAUNT you. I will HAUNT you. You will be HAUNTED to the end of your days on this Earth!

Oh, and, yes, I almost forgot! A pussy willow contains infinite treasures and cosmoses and games! Yesterday I played and played with pussy willows—I kept breaking open those furry peters and there were caterpillars and hamsters and all manner of soft creatures who could be blown away into dandelions and stars and worlds and philosophic lessons.

I think I'll go out into the woods now. You should do the same sometime. It saddens me that you have to have your ass whipped (how's THAT!) to go out to where you think, 'Why haven't I done this more often?' And to where you learn fresh things—wood music, drum beats, daddy long legs, trunk monsters, ect., ect., ect. Get yo Lil Ass On Out To Them Woods and Dig Almighty Everlovin Mother Nature. (I've been associating with a rock group lately.) Oops, I'm sorry.

OH OH! Guess what just happened! I was deep in the woods. I went out there right after I told you to. And ran into a hornets nest and they chased me screaming all the miles home—in my hair and all over me and now I am just bumps—hurting, stinging bumps. Poison oak and bees—and I was eulogizing nature at the time and an hour before that I said to God, 'Oh, it's such paradise. It's too perfect. I know you'll punish me, but how?' NOW I KNOW and am more scared of bees than ever. It was like a cartoon, only I had no lake to jump into."

(Picture of stick figure girl being chased by bees)

And I had miles to go and made it in lickety-split and was screaming and brushing them off and I was even laughing because that incessant objective part was watching the hilarity and I brought some in the house and ran to Daddy and SAT DOWN on his stool to give him an account of it all while they were still in my shirt and hair!! 'Til I realized and ran to the shower and tore off clothes and jumped in and then heard them in the bathroom and BUZZZZZ couldn't come out for fear.

And in the woods, running with them on and chasing me I took a wrong turn and bumped into a wall which gave them an advantage and I was thinking Oh, no—maybe I'll die here and they will find me all stung out and they were BZZZZING in my ears (I even bit one) and I've never run so fast or hysterically or long like that in my life, not to mention the screaming up hill and down. They stopped chasing me just as the beloved house came into view.

It's not the next day now. It's the same bee sting night. I decided to tell you about it now. Good night. And may Allah protect you from the stings and arrows of outrageous yellow jackets.

It's the next morning and the mailman will be here any minute. Now bumps itch like hell. I wish you could have come here.

Ginny's father was around my age at the time. The age I am now. Old. After Ginny's mother divorced him, her father remarried, had another kid, and ended up living in a big gray house on a golf course in Boulder Creek. He was a kind, generous, thoughtful guy. His name was George, George F. Good, as I've said, and he really did look quite a bit like Harry Truman. I mentioned it to him that Christmas, the Christmas of 1964.

"How many times do you get told you look like Harry Truman?" I asked.

George F. Good was fiddling with his stamp collection, but stopped for a second and looked up at me and said very slowly and precisely, as was his wont, "I'll tell you a story about Harry Truman." Then he went back to fiddling with his stamps but continued the story. "Harry Truman was reading letters that had been sent to him at the White House. Bess was with him in the room at the time. Bess was his wife."

"I knew that," I said. "He had a daughter who played the piano, too"

"Margaret, yes…who was actually better known for her singing…which reminds me of another story, but first things first." George F. Good looked at a stamp through a magnifying glass and went on with his original story. "The letters he was reading were apparently not as congratulatory as he might have liked them to be. Most in fact were crude and critical. Harry Truman turned to Bess and said, 'Why is it only sons-of-bitches know how to lick a stamp?' I always found that story quite telling." He put the magnifying glass down and looked up at me again.

"That's a telling story, all right," I said. "What's the other one?"

"Ah," he said and smiled. His teeth were small. He waved his chubby hand through the air. "It's more or less along the lines of an aside."

"I've got nothing against asides," I said.

"The music critic from the Washington Post wrote a review of Margaret's abilities as a singer. He said she wasn't very good." George F. Good made a face. "The next day Harry Truman wrote the music critic a letter which said in part, 'Someday I hope to meet you. When that happens, you'll need a new nose."

"That's kind of a cool thing for a president to say," I said.

"He was a father, first and foremost—was the point I took from the story."

"Hey, Ginny's a really good singer, you know. Like, in case nobody ever mentioned that to you before."

He smiled. He thought I was amusing. I was. He thought I seemed to like his daughter pretty well, too. I did. On a shelf above his desk, there was a picture of him taken when he was around twenty-two—the same age I was then. He was in his last year at Princeton, reading a newspaper that had a picture of Charles Lindbergh landing in Paris on the front page. A few years after our conversation, George F. Good got overwhelmed with grief and fearful for his safety when he heard that Sandy had been living with the so-called Manson Family, and not long after that, he died.

* 𝓰 𝓰 *

But back then, during the Christmas of 1964, he didn't know what to do about Ginny anymore than I did. We took the family golf cart down to a little combination gas station and grocery store. On the way back, I told him his daughter was pretty seriously nuts. Everybody knew she was nuts, but nobody wanted to talk about it. He nodded and sighed and thanked me for telling him.

Christmas morning he gave her a hundred shares of stock in a company called Dental Supply, which at the time was worth five thousand dollars—which at the time was a lot of money. There were strings attached, however. That's not a figure of speech—in keeping with the spirit of the holidays, there were three pieces of red thread attached with Scotch tape to the bottom of one of the stock certificates. Her father thought that would be a gentle, nonjudgmental way of saying that if she had to be hospitalized, she could use the money from the shares to pay for it, and if she didn't have to be hospitalized, she could use the money for whatever else she might

159

want to use it for. It was like an incentive, a bribe to stay sane. He didn't know what else to do. There wasn't much else he *could* do.

He also gave her a diamond and ruby encrusted watch that had belonged to his mother. It was a pin, actually—a watch pin—which Ginny promptly lost that New Year's Eve. The watch had been in the family for over a hundred years; it took Ginny less than a week to lose it forever.

CHAPTER SIXTEEN

Clift Hotel

$\mathcal{G}$ inny lost the watch pin in North Beach. We'd gone up there to be at the Jazz Workshop at midnight. It was the two-year anniversary of the night we met—which brings me to a point at which I don't have to rely quite so completely on what's left of my piecemeal memory. Ha! Yippee! I have a little green diary of stuff I wrote about during the first nine days of 1965. The diary begins with a list of Ginny's New Year's Resolutions. They're in her handwriting and no doubt speak for themselves:

Gerry will: 1) Persistently, unrelentingly, write at least 3 pages every day, 2) Tell the truth each day about the above, 3) Eat like a hog and become fatter, 4) Get the scholarship to Stanford by next year, (this means writing stories, attending State and applying to Stanford), 5) Take me to a swank hotel once a month and out for dinner and to a culturally and intellectually stimulating event, 6) Keep his apartment clean and neat at least 5 days a week; this resolution may be waived only in the event that Gerry is immersed in writing—at which time slobdom is permitted, 7) Make money—lots of it, 8) Not be sexually narcissistic except if he is

absolutely compelled by frustration for a period of seven (7) days, and 9)
Read at least one book a week.

Hey, wait a minute, how come Ginny's New Year's Resolutions were all things *I* was supposed to do? What the hell
was *she* was supposed to do? I don't think either of us ever
knew. Oh, well. Then comes a little preamble in my handwriting—which I barely *recognize* anymore. Who was this kid?
And after that, the day-to-day diary begins:

Perhaps the most ominous prospective New Year's Eve I've ever
experienced began with Ginny on the threshold of acute nuttiness. She
was to have gone out to dinner with Tom and his mother—a situation
that was scary for various reasons, guilt about her relationship with Tom
in his mother's eyes, how she gets around Christmas, etc. She in short
didn't go and came over to my house (in a very beautiful but depressed
state). We checked into the Clift Hotel, had a bottle of champagne and
went out to a dinner of filet mignon and shish kebab at Omar
Khayyam's. From there we went by cable car to North Beach to be at the
Jazz Workshop (where we had met two years ago) at midnight. Some-
where in the wild, mad confetti crowd, Ginny lost her new beautiful watch
and was sick all night.

Friday, January 1: Ginny and I woke up in our huge bed between
sweet yellow sheets, puttered around with TV and finally slept again 'til
12:40 in the afternoon. I got a small bottle of good champagne and we
drank it in front of the city from the edge of the bed. We went to lunch at
David's (lox, pickled herring, sauerbraten, blintzes and pastry) that we
took with us to the movie <u>Goldfinger</u> that evening. Afterwards, we
cleaned my apartment and went happily to bed.

January 2: Ginny was to stay in bed all day for her cold. I read to her and rubbed her back while she rested. I made a police report for her lost watch and called about apartments for us to rent. At 4:00 she went to the doctor's and from there we again had drinks at Omar Khayyam's. I let Ginny drink. I was happy and confident and she was loving me. Ginny's drinking resulted in a horribly painful psychotic episode in which she smashed my typewriter and gouged a long slice of skin from my back. I was stupid and sorry for letting her drink (like I was daring her psychotic counterpart to emerge amidst all this love, as though love was a weapon to overcome Ginny's demons). It didn't work. I cried very softly, she harder.

January 3. Sunday: I knew it was morning when Ginny kissed me, her cheek on my shoulder. She seemed better but embarrassed and shaky. I cleaned the kitchen and bought groceries. She stayed in bed but any favorable responses to food or reading or back rubs grew less and less spontaneous as the day went by. Finally she was a sick girl again— strangely sick and mostly weak, tired, nervous—aftermath from last night I guess. She went to Tom's and watched television.

January 4: I went quickly dressing and not shaving late to work today—extra talkative for some reason. At noon Sabine called. She wanted me to meet her that night. I took my clothes to the laundry and cleaners, then went to Sabine's. We talked. I got drunk and pretty sick. Ginny came over and made me feel much better.

January 5: There was no hangover today and I ran excitedly on cof- fee and nervous energy, manic as hell. At noon I seduced Ginny, then laughingly took her home (to Tom's). After work I took a bus downtown and walked in the windy rain for an hour with no coat, trying to get my typewriter fixed. Finally I traded it for an electric. Picked up my laun-

dry, came home, called Ginny late and started writing. After I'd written a bit, I called Ginny again. She was sick-drunk and on her way over here. We laughed. I dictated to her and she typed. She got out of her nuttiness quickly and was loving me for typing. I got aroused, realized I couldn't work any more. I was tired and went to bed. We made love nicely, pretty much all for me. I think it's less enjoyable if Ginny doesn't have an orgasm.

January 6: Pretty uneventful. I came home at noon, washed my face and got in the mail all nine Beethoven Symphonies. Ginny was here. We looked witty and irritably at each other. She said I kiss either like a fairy or too femininely, so I kissed her coarsely—she probably thought I was reacting and therefore it was phony (as perhaps it was a bit, but not that much). I don't like her to ask me questions like, "What are you thinking?" when I'm doing something to her which might be construed as a vent for some kind of queer tendencies. They're not, but if I say so, she'll wonder why then did it cross my mind. When I got home, I took a long bath and finished Herzog. Beautifully done—writing and ideas.

January 7: I couldn't get out of Bed (capital letters, like God) this morning. I slept 'til one-thirty. Missed an appointment at noon to bring some clothes over to Sabine's and was slightly disappointed to find that at so late in the afternoon, Ginny hadn't missed receiving a call. My stove doesn't work. I paid my rent and bought a shoeshine kit from the Fuller Brush man. I worked ten hours straight writing Ginny's Luft paper while listening to all nine of the symphonies. When singing burst out in the last one—after eight without any—it scared the crap out of me.

January 8: Friday: Was an hour late for work. At noon I took some clothes over to Sabine's in order to set up our phony apartment. After work I got the gasman to fix my stove and talked with Mrs. Rous-

seau for a long time. She might be able to let me rent one of the huge beautiful apartments for Ginny and me. I worked on as much more of the Luft paper as I could without having the proper Jung quote. Ginny called me from the Hub Tavern. She had walked out on the symphony and was more angry-drunk than nutty. She came over. We had drinks in the big room and we painfully made love—apologizing and making up later calmly, truly.

January 9: Saturday: Elliot came bouncing up to the window in front of which Ginny and I were having a salami, cheese and French bread breakfast. He had been to the zoo. We talked, listened to some stories Elliot told about Vietnam and Thailand and then the three of us went to Stow Lake in Golden Gate Park. Ginny and Elliot paddled themselves around in a paddleboat for a while, just the two of them. I was quiet and a bit uncomfortable. Ginny was a marvelous hostess and Elliot was interestingly nerve jangling—to me at any rate. We took Ginny to her Doc. Elliot and I tonight had another episode of mutual irritation. He asked my permission (half just to make me squirm and half seriously) to take Ginny to Squaw Valley next weekend. That, in the frail state Ginny, myself and ourselves are in, was not the right thing to have asked for reasons I'm not going to go into.

At that point, the diary skips a month—in fact, the only other entry in the whole thing is that on February 17, Ginny went to the hospital to get an abortion. It was before they were legal. We had to go through all kinds of rigmarole.

Reading these diary entries reminds me what kids the three of us were, doing things kids have been doing forever—falling in love, irritating each other, running into predictable complications, figuring them out as best we could. We're still figuring things out as best we can. Well, some of us are. I am. Fuck.

Which brings me back to Elliot "bouncing" up to our window. Everything up to now has led to Elliot bouncing up to our window that Saturday, and everything from now on is going to lead to what Ginny and Elliot and Melanie and I all tried to do with each other back in the summer of 1972. Keep that date in mind. Saturday, January 9, 1965. That was the first time Elliot flat-out tried to steal Ginny away from me. That was the beginning of everything. Could he take her to Squaw Valley? Ha! No. He couldn't. He could stick Squaw Valley up his ass.

CHAPTER SEVENTEEN

Vietnam

$\mathcal{E}$lliot Felton had been infatuated with Virginia Good since the night we both met her on New Year's Eve. If he hadn't been on his way to Vietnam the next day, he would have called her himself. He remembered her name. I didn't. He'd looked her up in the phone book the night before I took him to the airport. He'd been infatuated with her the whole time he'd been gone. He thought he was in love with her. Now that he was back and the two of them had paddled in a paddleboat for an hour or so, he *knew* he was in love with her.

We talked about it one night, just the two of us, Elliot and I. He never came right out and said he was in love with her, he just was. There was nothing he could do about it. He knew it. I knew it. Ginny knew it. It was as close to a fact as anything like that can get. It lurked under the surface of everything the three of us ever did, separately or together, like the creature in *The Creature from the Black Lagoon*. It was like we knew the creature was there and we *didn't* know the creature was there—like we were in the audience and could *see* the creature swimming around, hiding among all that lush, creepy vegetation, but we also went obliviously about our business, doing our everyday dog-paddling at the surface of the lagoon with our bare legs dangling.

Elliot's discharge hadn't officially come through yet, but for all intents and purposes he'd completed his military service. He'd done everything that had been expected of him and more. He had all kinds of new medals—an Army Commendation Medal and a Good Conduct Medal—and a bunch of new ribbons above the pocket of his uniform. One of the medals had a silver oak leaf hooked up to it. He was a god damn bona fide war hero. He showed me the certificates that went with the medals. They were all typed up neat as you please on a clunky old Courier ten-pitch typewriter.

𝒢𝒢

The day after he got back from Vietnam, Elliot bought a conservative blue suit and a conservative brown suit and five white shirts and five narrow ties and a pair of black wingtips and a pair of brown wingtips from Roos-Atkins. The next week he went to work at Dean Witter's on Montgomery Street as an assistant to a stockbroker his mother was dating. Elliot had learned a thing or two in the military. He had a plan. He knew exactly what he wanted to do with the rest of his life.

He also knew stuff not many people were in a position to know at the time. He'd been at the front lines of a war everyone in the country was getting curiouser and curiouser about. According to him, the U.S. Army had no business in Southeast Asia, period. The war was a racket. The South Vietnamese Government was nothing but a bunch of money-grubbing thugs. Elliot knew who killed that Diem guy, for example, and why—to get him the hell out of the way so the USA could run the war its way, that's why.

He told me flat-out to stay out of the draft no matter what I had to do, but by then I'd pretty much figured that out all on my own. The way Elliot saw it was that the only thing the people in Vietnam wanted was to feed their families—to grow their rice, to fix their fishing nets, to ride their bicycles—and that Ho Chi Minh was one tough son of a bitch who wouldn't ever make any concessions to anyone about anything. The war would go on forever. Ho Chi Minh couldn't lose. He wouldn't lose. He didn't. Ha!

Most of the time Elliot was in Vietnam, however, he was actually in Thailand—smoking Thai sticks and living in rickety houses on bright sandy beaches with well-paid Thai chicks. It sounded like a kind of polygamous religious community, like paradise, like heaven on earth, like something Brigham Young might have dreamed up. Elliot fit right in. I was probably a little jealous.

It didn't help matters much that Ginny was enthralled by the stories he told. She'd never known a bona fide war hero before. Elliot and his buddies had it made. They shared everything and ate mangos off trees. It was utterly ephemeral and serene and lavishly financed by the bottomless pockets of the U. S. taxpayers.

That was where Elliot's plan came in. It was his single-minded intention to recreate that same sort of camaraderie up in Marin County or down by Big Sur. He wanted to get a bunch of people together, to live with them, to build things together, to cook, to clean, to write and paint and sculpt and play music and make movies, to sell stuff, to share everything. But the first thing he had to do was to get money—lots of it—

and the way to get money was to have patience. That was the biggest thing Elliot learned while he'd been in the military. Patience. He was calmer than he'd been before, more sure of himself, confident, quiet—a grownup, an adult.

* 𝒢 𝒢 *

"We had a sort of…mascot," Elliot said one night in that halting, fidgety way he talked when he talked to Ginny and me at the same time.

The three of us were sitting out in Mrs. Rousseau's parlor. It must have been a week or so after he'd been back. Ginny's legs were lying over the arm of one of Mrs. Rousseau's over-stuffed chairs. She had on a pair of Levi's and a faded green t-shirt with no bra. She was fiddling with the ends of her hair with one hand and steadying a good-sized glass of wine on her chest with the other hand. I was at one end of a loveseat. Ginny was still conflicted about whether to have an abortion or not—she and her father's lawyer were trying to sort things out—and we were still in the throes of the worst of the Christmas whacko stuff. She was getting drunk and going completely crazy every few days. There was barely time to catch our breaths between bouts.

"His name was Jin." Elliot got an enigmatic hitch in his voice and looked over toward Ginny.

"Gads!" Ginny said. "Really?" She removed her legs from the arm of the chair, put her bare feet down onto the rug, reached over toward the gallon jug of Red Mountain on the floor and filled her glass again. She was well on her way to getting drunk. That she overused the word "really" was a sure sign.

170

"Yeah. He was like you in other ways, too. But old."

"I have an old soul," Ginny said. She shook her bangs out from in front of her eyes and took another sip of wine.

"So did he." Elliot smiled—a little too sweetly if you ask me. He'd been getting awfully familiar. At least he wasn't wearing his fancy green hat and his spiffy uniform with all the ribbons and medals. He'd come by after work that night, dressed in a suit, the blue one. Ginny was eating it up. "But he had the leathery old face to go with it," Elliot said. By which, of course, he meant to point out that Ginny did not have a leathery old face, but that she had a pretty, young face. They were totally flirting their asses off with each other. Elliot looked down, like he was shy. Then he looked up again, right at Ginny, and said, "He used to tell our futures in movements—like a dance."

"What do you mean, like a fortune teller?" I asked.

"It felt like that, yeah," Elliot said softly.

"So he did a dance, and you guys knew the future? Cool," I said. I was skeptical, sure, but I also just wanted to keep interrupting so he wouldn't launch into one of his god damn spellbinding war stories Ginny found so enthralling. I never knew what she was going to do, what kind of ruckus she might cause.

"Well," Elliot said. "First he'd throw a handful of sticks on the ground..."

"That's the I-Ching!" Ginny said excitedly.

"He didn't call it that. He didn't call it anything. He didn't speak English. He just did it. He held the sticks in one hand, like Pick-Up-Stix. Then he put them up to one ear and shook them and looked like he was trying to listen to them. Then he listened to the sticks with his other ear and threw them onto the ground." Elliot moved his hand abruptly, like he was throwing a handful of sticks onto the Chinese rug in Mrs. Rousseau's parlor—it startled us, Ginny and me.

"Yeah, we all sort of jumped, too." Elliot smiled again. "Then Jin got down on his hands and knees and looked for a long time at the way the sticks ended up in the dirt. That was when he picked out whose future it was going to be that he was going to tell. It was always just one guy. Then he'd start dancing. It was more like a pantomime, like Marcel Marceau, maybe, but barefoot and dressed in a raggedy shirt and wearing a rope for a belt. When he got to the end, the guy he'd picked out knew what was going to happen to him. One of the guys…" Elliot stopped.

"What?" Ginny asked. "One of the guys, what?" She frowned. She was starting to get antsy, loud, impatient, insistent. None of those were good signs.

"One of the guys knew he was going to die." He looked right at her again.

"Oh," she said quietly.

"When Jin had finished, he and the guy put their arms around each other and got tears in their eyes. Nobody else knew why. A few days later, back in country again, the guy was gutted. He looked like a fish. There wasn't any warning, just a swoosh. I was right behind him. You could see what he had for breakfast." Elliot blew a little laugh out his nose. "He was the one who taught me patience."

"The dead guy?" I asked.

"No, silly. Jin, right?"

"Yeah," Elliot said.

"How?"

"The same way, I guess," Elliot said. "I don't know, I just knew, you know?"

"Yeah," Ginny said.

I rolled my eyes.

"He threw his sticks and danced his dance, and I knew everything was going to be fine, no matter what. It was like I'd passed the only test I'd ever have to take—like, phew." He wiped his forehead. "Thank God that's over with, you know?"

Ginny nodded. She was enthralled.

I rolled my eyes higher.

Elliot brightened up a bit and kept on talking. "That was when I knew what I wanted to do, too. How I wanted to live. Quietly. Peacefully. With people I can share everything with. I can't explain it."

"Try," Ginny said. She was on the edge of her chair, reaching haphazardly toward the Red Mountain, which she was guzzling in big gulps by then.

"It all just sort of *came* to me during the same...detail. The same time the guy in front of me was killed. What Jin had told me with his dance just, like, descended, you know? I was enveloped in calmness, certainty. Patience. Peace."

"A peace which passeth understanding." I shook my head and made a little clucking noise like a squirrel.

"Shut up." Ginny frowned. "Quit saying really, really stupid stuff."

Two reallys right in a row, wow—that was a very bad sign.

"Okay," I said. I felt like Pontius Pilate. I couldn't tell by her eyes whether she was completely blacked out by then or not, but she was pretty close if she wasn't.

"I can't explain it," Elliot said. "It was just a feeling. You had to be there."

"Take me there," Ginny said. Elliot seemed to know the effect he was having on her. We'd already had our chat. He knew that she was pregnant, that she was going to have my kid, for Christ's sake. I'd told him about Christmas, that she went nuts when she got drunk, that I didn't want him rocking any boats. I'd already told him to stick Squaw Valley up his ass. But he couldn't help himself, I guess—any more than she could.

"I can't," he said in that conflicted way he had of trying to talk about things he couldn't talk about.

"You *have* to." Ginny said.

Elliot looked at me. I didn't give him a clue. He was on his own. They were on their own. We were on our own. It was going to play itself out.

"We were waiting for a...helicopter." Elliot seemed to have trouble thinking of the proper civilian words to call some of the things he was talking about.

"We had Teddy. Bear, we called him. We had Bear's body. There wasn't anything to do but wait. I went into a kind of trance. I was sitting down, leaning against a pile of rubble from a...house, a hooch that had been torched a few months back. Grass had already grown up. The whole country's a jungle. Things grow..."

"Like weeds," Ginny said.

"I am the grass, I cover all," I said.

Elliot kept talking. "Stalks of—yeah—weeds, I guess. Grass. I don't know. A sort of ragweed looking thing with little cauliflower faces was swaying back and forth between my legs." He moved his head slowly from side to side. Elliot was on the edge of his own chair by then as he continued telling the story:

"Then a shadow went over my face. I looked up into the sky. The shadow was coming from a cloud crossing in front of the sun. Pieces of the cloud evaporated around its edges, but the cloud just kept coming and coming. It just didn't stop. It was unstoppable. I looked down again...and saw a little no account spider that had made a web between a couple blades of the tall grass. I was just watching him. He didn't seem to know. He was just building his web, patiently adding another strand. He started at the top and strang it all the way down to the bottom."

"Strang?" I asked.

"Shhh." Ginny waved her arm vaguely in my direction.

"Then I saw another spider," Elliot said, completely ignoring everything but Ginny. "One about the same size as the first one...and all of a sudden they were, like, *glaring* at each other. They had transparent bodies and long, almost invisible legs. They *ran* at each other then. Not for any reason that I could see, but they ran from opposite ends of the web straight at each other, and when they came together they were slashing their legs at each other like swords or switchblades. They were trying to kill each other, trying to bite each other with their tiny, tiny, mean little teeth...and I got sadder than I ever knew I could get. It had to do with Bear, with Jin, with the future, with me, with the country, my country, their country, my friends, my father, my mother, their friends, their families, their kids, the whole world. It felt like everything was like that. Mean, you know? Cruel. Fighting just to fight. Everything was fighting. Grass was fighting with grass. Flowers were fighting with flowers. The world was a brutal, bad, vicious, vicious place to be."

"Gadfrees," Ginny said.

"It got better, though." Elliot smiled his twitchy smile. "The sun came out from behind the cloud then...and the spiders weren't fighting anymore. They were dancing!" His face got bright the way it had when he'd wanted to dance me around like a rag doll backstage at Hillsdale High School. He was almost laughing out loud. "The two spiders turned in circles on their tiptoes, holding each other's hands above their heads, and parted slowly, longingly, like they were going to miss each other, then darted in opposite directions across flashes of light from the sun shining on their web. I started laughing. I couldn't help it. I felt like an idiot, but it was funny. The way everything was all of a sudden *dancing* with everything else—the spiders and the grass and the flowers and the clouds. I mean, one minute everything's fighting with everything, then everything's all of a sudden *dancing* together. It was ridiculous. Absurd. Laughable. Insane. I closed my eyes. I wanted it all to just stay that way. Nice. Dancing. I was happy. I had tears in my eyes. Just before I closed my eyes, whatever I looked at twinkled...and when I opened my eyes again, everything was—clear. Defined. Done. Understood. It felt like I knew and had always known...and *would* always know what the world is like without me in it. I can't explain it. The spiders weren't fighting or dancing, either one—they weren't even spiders. That's the thing I can't explain. Flowers weren't flowers. Grass wasn't grass. Clouds weren't clouds. The sun wasn't even the sun. Then I couldn't remember what they were when they weren't spiders. I couldn't figure out what they'd been doing when they weren't fighting or dancing."

"Gosh," Ginny said.

"Yeah," Elliot said.

"I don't get it," I said.

"There's nothing to get," he said. "That's the point. It was just a feeling. Laughing. Crying. Both. Neither. It was so stupid and tragic and sad and funny at the same time that I had about ten different kinds of tears in my eyes. How can you forget what you'd always know? How can you remember not being somewhere?"

None of us said anything. Not even Ginny. We all knew what he'd been talking about, whether we could explain it didn't matter. We were friends, somehow, the three of us. We were going to do things with each other, share things. I can't explain it. None of us could, not in a million years.

CHAPTER EIGHTEEN

Ocean Beach

*N*ot long after our chat in Mrs. Rousseau's parlor—
and a week or so before Ginny finally just went ahead and *had*
the abortion—Elliot's father killed himself. I don't even
remember his name. I always just called him Mr. Felton. His
father killing himself knocked Elliot for a loop, another loop.
He was always getting knocked for loops.

Elliot's parents had finalized their divorce before Elliot
got back. There had been lawyers and private investigators
digging through twenty years of dirt with a backhoe. His
father knew all about the Lebanese real estate guy by then—
and the Nicaraguan plumber and the Irish roofing and siding
salesman and the Italian maitre d' at Westlake Joe's. They
were separated when she took up with the stockbroker, but
I'm sure *he* was on Mr. Felton's list of guys who'd fucked his
wife, as well.

Elliot's mother got the car and the house and everything
in it, right down to whatever was left of the bottle of lemon
scented Joy under the kitchen sink. His father got nothing but
the furniture that had been *his* mother's furniture before the
marriage. Mr. Felton also got nothing but sadder and sadder

with each passing day. He was too sad to work and had to take early retirement. He was too sad to do anything. He didn't have a house or a car or a wife or a job, and he had always been the kind of guy who only knew who he was by what he had. Now he had nothing. Now he was nobody. Even *I* felt a little sorry for the guy, and I'd always thought he was exactly the kind of brittle, authoritarian asshole who deserved to get shattered.

❊ 𝒢 𝒢 ❊

When Elliot got out of the military, his father was living in a two bedroom duplex out in the Avenues, a block from Ocean Beach. After he got the job at Dean Witter's, Elliot moved in with his dad and took the N-Judah downtown before dawn every day in order to get to work by six in the morning.

The first time he caught his father crying, they pretended it wasn't happening. Then they got used to it. They had no choice. His father cried all the time. He stood by the living room window and looked out at the fog with long tears rolling down his face. Elliot felt like they had traded places. When Elliot had cried when he'd been a kid, his father used to take off his belt and give him something to cry about. Now Elliot understood why. It drove a person nuts after awhile. He wanted to grab his father by the shirt, to shake him, to slap him, to take off his belt and give his father something to cry about...but Elliot knew it hadn't really done *him* a lot of good, so he didn't. Later he mentioned that maybe he should have.

Besides look at the fog and cry, Mr. Felton went surf fishing and read *Anna Karenina*. One morning, toward the end of the book, Elliot found his father on the back porch with his head blown half off. He was holding the shotgun like an Easter lily. His body was stiff. His shoulders were stuck to the planks of the back porch with dried blood and brains. They had to be pried loose with a fancy chrome-plated crowbar the coroner kept handy for such occasions.

Elliot kept the apartment and took up surf fishing. He quit his job. His plans went awry. He never took his new suits out of the closet again. His mother paid the rent. She was selling real estate by then. Elliot finished *Anna Karenina* from where his father had left off. The fringed bookmark that had belonged to Elliot's grandmother was still marking the place. There were only around twenty pages left. When he was done reading it, Elliot started the book all over from the beginning.

On particularly blustery days, Elliot put on his father's rain gear, trudged down to Ocean Beach with his father's fishing rod and his father's fishing tackle, leaned into gale force winds blowing salt spray into his face and fished his guts out. Sometimes Elliot even caught a fish—usually some bony, bottom-dwelling scavenger fish, not fit for human consumption—but once he caught a pretty good-sized sea bass and invited Ginny and me over for dinner.

* *GG* *

His duplex was like walking into 1942. It was an oasis of middle-class Mormon restraint. Elliot's grandmother's furniture was arranged the way Mr. Felton had it arranged before he killed himself. There were rugs with fringe at the ends and crocheted doilies on the arms of overstuffed chairs and fringe hanging from dim yellow lampshades. Dust puffed up when Ginny and I sat on the couch. We watched it disperse up through the dim light being shed by one of the lamps and settle back down onto the ornate walnut end table. She was subdued. So was I. So was Elliot. We were all pretty much just going through the motions.

His father's old room was stern. There were government memorabilia on a mahogany chest of drawers—pictures of his father standing next to J. Edgar Hoover and General MacArthur and a picture of a young Mr. Felton in a crowd of people behind President Eisenhower. In the closet there were four pairs of black wingtips, each with a separate set of shoe-trees.

The thing Elliot couldn't seem to get over was that his father had managed to get through the ordeal of being held captive in a Japanese prisoner of war camp for more than a year. Elliot thought that if a person had survived that, he could survive anything. Not true, it turns out. His father couldn't take not having a car or a house or a job—or the inescapable conclusion that his wife did not love him.

Elliot still made art out of anything he touched. Walking into Elliot's bedroom in the duplex was like walking into the sky. There was no furniture. He slept on a pile of pillows and down comforters on the floor and there were great heaving gobs of urethane foam all over the walls and ceiling that Elliot had airbrushed different shades of white and foggy shades of gray, like huge cumulus clouds.

Ginny and I went into the dining room and sat down at the table. Elliot had built a centerpiece out of pinecones and seashells and driftwood. We were ill at ease. He served baked sea bass on one of his grandmother's silver serving trays. He would have looked more at home in his quilted smoking jacket, tugging at his meerschaum pipe, but he looked at home enough. It was sad. I don't know why. It just was.

When we were through with dinner, which amounted to not much more than the three of us picking the bones out of the sea bass and leaving most of the meat on our plates, we drank a bottle of wine and talked about Tolstoy. Elliot showed us a picture of his father that had been taken a couple of days after he'd been liberated from the prison camp. He just stood there holding it, looking at it. His father was nothing but skin and bones. Elliot went over by the window and looked out at the fog. It was too sad for words. Ginny and I didn't know what to say. We didn't say anything. Then we said we'd better be going. Elliot didn't say anything. We left. And Elliot pretty much dropped out of the picture for another couple of years or so.

* g g *

Ginny and I were having troubles of our own at the time. It would not have been practical to have a kid; it would have been cool, but it would not have been practical. She and her father's lawyer talked on the phone a lot. He arranged for her to get a letter from her shrink who arranged to get another letter from another shrink—which was what you had to do to get an abortion back then—and Ginny went into the hospital and had an abortion in the middle of February. I waited in the lobby. It didn't take long.

At the beginning of March, Ginny and I moved into the biggest apartment in Mrs. Rousseau's building. It was huge, with all kinds of Queen Anne windows and nooks and crannies and more of her fancy furniture, but it still only cost a hundred and fifty bucks a month. We lived there less than three weeks.

Ginny went off on one of her irresistibly deranged, drunk, blacked-out binges sometime toward the end of the month. Her Christmas troubles were winding down, but she still had another humdinger of a fling left in her. She ended up at a pizza parlor on Fillmore Street and picked up some guys in one of the local fledgling rock-and-roll bands who used to hang out there—some of the Charlatans is my best guess, but it could have been Jefferson Airplane guys. I think the pizza parlor was the one that got turned into a rock-and-roll club called The Matrix a year or so later. It could have been most anyone, though. Sopwith Camel? Sons of Champlin? Moby Grape? I don't know. A bunch of fledgling rock-and-roll guys used to hang out on Fillmore Street.

All I know is that at around two in the morning there was a lot of noise coming from the kitchen. There arose a clatter. I got up to see what was the matter. Ginny and two scruffy guys were drinking wine, smoking dope and yucking it up at our new kitchen table. I kicked them out. Ginny threw a fit—a bigger fit than usual. She broke two of the big bay windows overlooking California Street, wrecked one of Mrs. Rousseau's Japanese silk screens and smashed my new electric typewriter.

We had to move out. Ginny stayed with Tom Piper. I went up to my parents' house in Oregon. The only reason I was able to put up with Virginia as long as I did was that I always had somewhere to go to get the hell away from her when she went completely crazy for too long. That's how I have the little stack of letters I still have. She wrote to me while I was up in Oregon.

In early May of 1965, I hitchhiked back down to San Francisco. The Christmas stuff was pretty much over—well, you know, until the *next* Christmas. She was the picture of health, happiness and good cheer. While I'd been in Oregon, Ginny had taken acid with one or another of her rock-and-roll buddies. I was jealous. The last thing I wanted was my god damn girlfriend taking LSD with some scruffy rock-and-roll asshole—especially when I hadn't taken acid with anyone, and even more especially when it was all she could *talk* about.

I absolutely *HAD* to take acid. It wasn't just a matter of popping a pill, either; no, no, you had to *prepare*. There was a whole catechism. You had to read *Doors of Perception, Joyous Cosmology, King Solomon's Ring,* and a bunch of other books: *The Hobbit, The Lord of the Rings, Zen Flesh, Zen Bones*—I can't begin to remember them all. There was a whole bibliography. Then you had to *go* somewhere, to the ocean or the woods, and finally, on top of everything else, it had to just, like, *happen..* Jesus. It sounded like a lot of trouble to go to just to get stoned, but, hey, I'd never taken acid before. Who was I to say? She had. Like I said—with one of her scruffy rock-and-roll buddies. La dee da.

We picked the woods.

We went to La Honda.

CHAPTER NINETEEN

La Honda

$\mathcal{I}$n the spring of 1965, La Honda was a sleepy little backwoods mountain town halfway between San Francisco and Santa Cruz. Except for the main, two-lane, blacktop highway, there was nothing but one-way dirt roads leading to secluded houses.

We rented a cabin. We had our pick from among six of the boxy, dilapidated, one-room structures. We took the one farthest away from the rental office that doubled as a grocery store. Across the street there was a vast, inviting, redwood forest. Ginny took the key to the cabin while I bought stuff to eat later. Her black Buick was the only car in the lot. I knocked on the cabin door. She let me in. Overhanging fir trees filtered what little sunlight came through the dusty windows. There was a hooked rug on the floor. I put the groceries on the stand beside the bed. We each took a single small speckled orange pill.

It was late afternoon. The sun was about to go down. Nothing happened for a while. The bed in the cabin was soft and springy. We lay down next to each other. She put her head on my chest. I put my arm around her. She was contrite. We didn't talk. The first thing I noticed was a tingling little itch in my throat, but deeper, like somewhere down inside the autonomic nervous system of my esophagus. We got up and sat on the edge of the bed and looked at each other. She must have been feeling the same tingling itch. Then not much else happened for another little while.

* 𝒢 𝒢 *

We went outside. When we got to the edge of the steamy blacktop road, we stopped, looked and listened—then we held hands and ran as fast as we could across the street and deep into the redwood forest. It was still warm, the tail end of a day that had gotten up into the mid-eighties or so. Insects had started to become more noticeable, I noticed. That was about it. Flies and gnats had always left little vapor trails in the air, but the vapor trails I was beginning to see seemed to be lasting slightly *longer* than usual.

The itch in my esophagus had extended to my chest and was working its way down into the pit of my stomach. The last of the sun's rays showed spiders' webs covering everything. That wasn't particularly unusual, either. In the woods, just before the sun goes down, spiders' webs *do* cover everything. But these spider webs were *thicker* than usual. They were, like, replicating themselves as I watched—and pretty soon the whole forest floor was half an inch deep with spider webs, sparkling like snow. *That* was unusual. The floor of a forest on a warm day in May doesn't sparkle like snow. Something was definitely going on.

The tingling itch had settled in my groin. I could taste the fillings in my teeth. A fly circled my head, but slowly—so slowly, he almost stopped in midair. His huge hairy body was luminous green. The veins in his wings had black insect blood coursing through them. Then he flew away, leaving a bright, phosphorescent green stream of light behind him in the air. The stream of light stayed in the fly's wake until it began to sort of…melt. Another bright fresh trail from a smaller insect cut through the air and stayed there, then another and another. Insects were leaving bright vapor trails everywhere—pretty soon the whole volume of plain old-fashioned, otherwise empty midair was all scribbled up like a giant Etch-A-Sketch.

I wanted to tell someone what I was seeing, but who? Ginny? Where was she? Was she seeing stuff like that, too? The questions didn't stay in my mind long enough for me to actually go seek her out and find her and ask her. But then I looked down at the ferns by my feet and forgot all about Ginny. I couldn't move.

My legs were surrounded by delicate, brittle, lacy structures that would be utterly destroyed if I so much as moved a muscle. I crouched down carefully—and whoa! A big shiny deep maroon carpenter ant was climbing up one of the stems of the fern, bearing the heavy burden of some ant version of an albino watermelon on his back, juggling it from one side to the other while he tried to walk. The ant was following the filigree of an emerald green fern frond to its logical conclusion.

He felt things out with his feelers, stopped, turned around too quickly, and tripped over a glistening follicle of silky hair growing from the fern. It was like there was a tiny silky hair factory deep inside the body of the plant churning out tiny silky hairs for the express purpose of tripping wayward carpenter ants, making life all that much more difficult for the poor struggling buggers—and it dawned on me that that was why plants were *called* plants, because they were *factories*, turning sunlight into green cells shaped like emeralds, turning emerald-shaped cells into silky hairs no thicker than the filaments of a spider's web.

The carpenter ant regained his balance and continued on. He looked drunk, disoriented, confused. The weight he was carrying was too huge. He couldn't see straight, he could barely walk, but he had to keep trying to get to wherever it was that he was going. He was wobbling from one side to the other, catching his balance, taking another tack, frantically trying to get God knows where. I wanted to help him out, steer him in the right direction, but I couldn't figure out where the hell he wanted to go any more than *he* could figure out where the hell he wanted to go.

I looked at the ground under the fern plant. A huge volcano was erupting a steady stream of shiny maroon carpenter ants. Next to the anthill there was a decayed pinecone crawling with even *more* carpenter ants. That must have been where the ant on the fern frond was trying to go. He needed to find his way to that pinecone…but why? I picked it up. The ants clambered off like they were jumping from a burning building. One of them landed among the thick hairs on the back of my hand.

I had a factory inside me! The factory inside me was making thick hair follicles, one at a time. *I* was a plant! Cells like molten iron were stretched into strands of iridescent hair ten times stronger than steel—and that was just one of the products from just one of the factories. I had all kinds of factories in me, making all sorts of different things, all at the same time. How could you possibly keep that kind of complexity straight in your brain? How could anyone? It went on forever, asleep or awake, nonstop, every minute of every day and every minute of every night; from the instant you're conceived it goes on and on, mindlessly, thoughtlessly, second after second, tick-tock, tick-tock, to the day you die—and even after *that* it goes on. New factories take over, the factories of death, putrefaction, decay and rebirth.

The ant that had landed in the hair on the back of my hand made its way like Tarzan, swinging from one hair follicle to another like they were vines in a jungle. Then he took one last mighty swing and jumped off into thin air. But even thin air wasn't just thin air; it was something into which an ant could hurl himself without getting hurt—and if an ant could do it, why couldn't I? I could. It would be easy. I'd end up unscathed. I could climb to the top of a redwood tree and fall, just let go.

That was when I noticed my thumb. It was huge. I used my thumbnail—this thick, slightly nicotine-stained, translucent tool with which I had miraculously come equipped—to peel away one of the outer scales of the decayed pinecone in a conscientious effort to find out what in God's name the ant on that fern frond might have been looking for. It had to be something pretty good, whatever it was.

The thick, hard, dusty brown scale I was trying to rip away from the body of the pinecone was straining with every fiber of its being to remain attached. It was making tiny creaking noises, little squeaks and squeals like I was tearing it out from its mother's womb, but I didn't care. I was transfixed. I was obsessed. I had to find out what the fuck was going on in there. I needed to know why that ant from the fern frond wanted so desperately to find his way back to the pinecone.

What was so important? What did he want? What the hell was happening in there? I had to know.

Then—CRACK!

The scale broke off at its root, deep inside the body of pinecone.

And—POUF!

There was an explosion. Thousands of microscopic little paratroopers landed on my forearm and attacked a pretty good-sized army of quivering hair follicles. The bravest of the paratroopers aimed for my eyes. I ducked just in time and felt a sprinkling of vicious, single-minded, suicidal commandos settle into the thick brambles of one of my eyebrows. A short-lived battle ensued. Who won or lost didn't matter. The dead buried their dead; the living went on about their business.

I resumed the task of tearing apart the pinecone. By this time I was sweating. It was mortal combat. Man against nature; survival of the fittest. I was a human being, after all. A pinecone was no match for a human being, for God's sake. Ha! Wasn't it God, in his infinite wisdom, who made mankind to lord it over all of nature? Yes. It was. Surely a lowly rotting pinecone must have had better sense than to think it could trifle with a MAN.

By then I had forgotten *why* I was taking the pinecone apart; by then I was just doing it because I was doing it. I tore another three or four scales off the pinecone indiscriminately, brutally, ruthlessly, like I didn't give a shit how many babies I was ripping from their mothers' wombs or how many brave armies of microscopic paratroopers I was exterminating. I was a machine, a heartless, mindless, brutal killing machine. Nothing could stop me. I tore off another layer.

And—YEOW!

The hugest, meanest, most menacing, sharp-nosed, big-toothed, hairy-legged, black—SPIDER!

LEAPED out at me!

From its LAIR!

It was grimacing its fangs at me like straight razors, threatening to slash slits in my bare eyeballs. It was intent on eating my brain, boring through my skull with all eighty-five moving parts of its salivating mouth and feasting on the deepest recesses of the warm, sticky gray matter of my mind. I threw the pinecone away, jumped back and yelled.

"AAAHHHAAAH..."

"What?" I heard Ginny ask. There was a frown of apprehension in her voice. What could I answer? I'd been attacked. "What happened?" She sounded far away.

"Nothing," I said. Her mind, I presumed, was in as fragile a state as mine. I didn't know how to tell her without upsetting her that a spider had leaped at me from the inside of a pinecone and had tried to bore through my skull and eat my brain.

"Why did you yell?"

"I saw a spider."

"Oh," she said. "I saw moss."

* 𝑔 𝑔 *

I made my way gingerly over to where Ginny was seeing moss. It was past dusk by then. The sun was long gone. It was almost dark. We were like ghosts. All we could see of each other was the long-sleeved cotton pullover shirts we were wearing. Hers was baggy and gray. Mine was yellow;

there were three small buttons at its throat. I never bothered to button any of them. It was too dark to see our pants.

"Let's take off our clothes," Ginny said.

"How will we ever find them again?" I was still a little worried about that spider—a trifle paranoid, perhaps. She'd been seeing moss and wasn't worried at all.

"Let's make them into *scare*crows."

"All the crows are asleep. Who would we scare?"

"Wraiths," she said in a spooky voice. "Ring Wraiths. The black riders."

"Ring Wraiths won't be scared by a couple T-shirts on a tree."

"Yes they will. Come on."

Ginny pulled her shirt off over her head and draped it onto a bush. She steadied herself with her hand on my shoulder while she took off her shoes and her socks and her pants and her panties. She was serious. My shirt was the brightest. I took it off and spread it across the bush to give us the best chance of ever finding our clothes again, then steadied myself with *my* hand on *her* shoulder.

There was barely a hint of daylight left in the sky. Vague, looming shadows that had been nothing but giant redwoods felt more sentient now—like they might have been a little put off by our presence. Usually they had the forest all to themselves at night. God only knew what they did then. They reminded me of those Ent guys from the Tolkien books, like any minute one of the big, hulking things was going to open his eyes and start talking to us in a really deep voice.

The Hobbit and *The Lord of the Rings* trilogy had been mostly what we'd been reading since I got back—well, except for all that cosmic consciousness crap Ginny was making me read.

The Tolkien books were by far my favorites. They were like *The Alexandria Quartet*, but easier to understand. Ginny had a hard time deciding which character she was. Justine had been easy. Who else could she possibly be? But in the Tolkien books, she went back and forth among Arwen, Eowyn and Galadriel. She wanted to be all three. I was Strider, of course—Aragorn.

The forest had become otherworldly; I couldn't tell where it ended and my imagination began. The redwoods around us *sounded* like they were talking, snickering among themselves at the two foolish naked humans who'd taken a notion to cavort in their forest—or was that a gust of wind whispering through their ancient branches high, high above our wee little selves? Unseen ferns and bushes brushed my bare hand. They could have been Elves. We might have been in Rivendell.

There didn't seem to be a moon anywhere and what stars we could see, we could see but fleetingly behind the swaying branches of the trees—a twinkle here and there, that was it. We took a few steps deeper into the forest and touched each other's hands. Then we stopped and put our arms around each other and hugged each other in the dark.

We were both still a little shaky. The night I'd kicked the scruffy rock-and-roll assholes out of Mrs. Rousseau's apartment hadn't been all that long ago—and a lot more had happened since then. I'd been gone. I'd come back. She'd been filling me in, little by little, but she'd definitely gotten herself fucked a significant number of times while I'd been in Oregon—by the guy with whom she first took acid, for one.

I'd wanted to hear the whole story—I always wanted to hear the whole story—what he was like, what *it* was like, where he fucked her, how he fucked her, everything. She told me as best she could, as much as she could remember, especially the part about taking acid. It was scary stuff—and now *we'd* taken acid, and we were out in the woods with no clothes on, and there were the dark riders of Mordor and brain-eating spiders and goblins and giant talking trees to worry about.

Hugged is too strong a word. We just stood really close together with the tips of the hairs on our bodies brushing against each other. Tiny hairs on the front of my body brushed against tiny hairs on the front of her body, but our skin didn't come into contact. Some of the hair on my chest knew the feel of the nipple of one of her breasts, and the tingling itch that had settled in my groin seemed to swell some. I couldn't be sure. It wasn't distinctly sexual. It was more like a flower opening up in the morning sun. We were sharing each other's warmth, sharing each other's metabolism, feeling the energy our bodies created by being alive.

We stayed like that for a long time, enveloped in utter affection and the mutual warmth generated by the humanity of each other's separate being. Now was not the time to try to talk, but if she wanted to know what I'd meant when I'd said, "I love you," that night on the floor of her apartment on 45th Avenue with all those candles blazing, this was it. Love—the thing itself, unexplained, unspoken.

"Let's explore," she said and took my hand.

* 𝒢 𝒢 *

We walked deeper into the woods, feeling our way more than seeing our way, until we found the burnt-out stump of a huge ancient redwood tree and climbed down inside. It was like a cave down there, like one of the underground forts I used to dig when I was a kid. The opening was small, but once we got inside there was plenty of room for both of us to move around. The walls were damp and sinewy and cool to the touch. It was absolutely pitch dark black. There was no moon or stars. It was blacker than black. There was no light at all, not the slightest illumination coming from any conceivable source whatsoever—and yet we started to *glow.* We could *see* each other. We were glowing in the dark, brighter and brighter.

Now, whatever else I may be, I've always at least been *logical.* I don't accept stuff on faith. I don't believe anything I haven't seen with my own eyes—and even the things I *have* seen that seem to stretch credulity, I can usually figure out some set of circumstances that explains them…well, you know, to my own satisfaction, at least. But this! Not only was it incredible, it was *unexplainable.* And yet I saw it. We were luminous. Deep down inside that utterly dark, burnt-out old stump of an ancient redwood tree, Ginny and I generated our own light, and it grew stronger, brighter. We were angels or fairies or lightning bugs or ghosts.

She couldn't believe it or explain it either, but we both saw what we saw, and in exactly the same way. We couldn't have made it up if we'd tried. Our hands *danced* together. Her small pale glowing greenish-white hand knew when to move away and when to move closer to my glowing greenish-white hand. Our hands were puppets. We put on a whole Punch and Judy show with our glowing hands. Our hands left phosphorescent trails, like the insects had left in the air.

It was like that Kirilian stuff. Our whole bodies glowed. The auras of our small glowing bodies commingled. We were like Tinkerbell, like two Tinkerbells—a boy Tinkerbell and a girl Tinkerbell, naked, cavorting, dancing together deep inside the root system of a redwood tree that had been there since before Columbus discovered America, since before Leif Eriksson discovered America, since before Guinevere and Lancelot and King Arthur cavorted in Camelot, since before Mohammed ascended from the temple mount into heaven, probably since around the time Jesus calmed the storm and fed the multitudes and walked on the Sea of Galilee.

We'd been thrown into a storybook, somehow—a real storybook, a history book, a book of revelation and reevaluation, a visceral combination of fact and fiction and fantasy. We weren't making this stuff up. It was happening. There were elves and dwarves and sprites and wizards and leprechauns and druids drinking magic elixir in the forest above us. They were dancing around a gigantic bonfire shooting sparks at the stars in the Andromeda galaxy. Or maybe we were in heaven, maybe this was how we would be if we were in heaven together. We'd been given a glimpse. These were our immortal souls. We were momentarily in heaven on earth.

GG

After we had somehow finally managed to extricate our immortal souls from the cavern under that huge redwood stump, we made our way back toward the highway. There was no bonfire. There were no trolls. We could see better than we could see before. More stars had come out. There was a sliver of moon. We found our clothes. I started to put on my shirt. Ginny wrinkled up her nose. I got the key out of my pants' pocket and we gathered our clothes into bundles in our arms. We crept through the bushes by the road, peeked out to make sure no cars were coming, then ran lickety-split across the still warm blacktop and slipped unseen through the door of our cozy cabin.

When we got inside I locked the door and lit the dim lamp next to the bag of groceries on the table beside the bed. Ginny dumped her clothes onto a chair at the foot of the bed and did a pirouette over toward the bed like she was free at last. I put my clothes on top of her clothes. We sat on the edge of the soft, springy bed. She reached over toward the bag of groceries. I ran the palm of my hand up her stomach and closed my fingers around one of her breasts. Her little nipple was hard. I leaned over and touched it with my tongue. She stopped reaching for the groceries. I sucked her tough, perky little nipple into my mouth.

"Aren't you *star*ving?" she asked.

"Mm-hmm." I nodded my head but didn't stop what I was doing.

I heard the bag rustling. I smelled oranges. God, they smelled good. Then I got a whiff of the big kosher dill pickle I'd picked out from the big kosher dill pickle jar by the cash register, and suddenly I was so starving to death I was going to die. My brain had burned every calorie my blood had in it to burn. I looked up. Ginny was taking the peel off one of the oranges.

"Wait, wait," I said. "I want to see."

We moved into the middle of the bed facing each other, with our legs crossed under us, and took the orange apart together. Once we got the skin off, we took the orange apart membrane-by-membrane. It was like taking apart the Taj Mahal. We were awestruck by the magnificent structures, things no architect ever dreamed of building, chambers and antechambers, rooms and anterooms and inner sanctums and nurseries with little baby orange seeds rocking in elaborate cradles.

"God," Ginny said.

"Yeah," I said.

Then we ate them. Ha! We ate the chambers and the antechambers, the rooms and the anterooms and the inner sanctums and the nurseries and spit the babies out into the palms of our hands and tossed them into an ashtray.

Orange juice dribbled down our chins and onto our chests. We licked orange juice off each other's lips and kissed each other's mouths and ate the little pieces of orange pulp on each other's tongues. When we were through with the first orange, we ate the second orange the same way.

Then we started in on the pickle. We slowly bent that giant green kosher dill pickle until its skin ruptured. Then we watched each tiny pickle seed emerge slowly, painstakingly, from the body of the former cucumber as if it were being born, as if the pickle were giving birth to one baby pickle seed after another—twins, triplets, quadruplets—creating slimy, succulent afterbirth, which Ginny and I stuffed voraciously into our mouths. We crushed newborn baby pickle seeds between our teeth and looked into each other's eyes and knew exactly what we were doing as we chewed them and swallowed them in churning gobs mixed with sulfuric saliva, which seared and burned into newborn baby pickle seed brains all the way down to our churning sulfurous stomachs to fuel the factories inside us.

"Blows the mind," Ginny said.

I didn't want to hear that. I didn't want to try to talk, period; but I especially didn't want to hear that particular phrase. It got me all screwed up. Our recent abortion was already on my mind—all those innocent orange seeds in their nurseries and the pickle seeds being so miraculously born and so viciously killed didn't help—but what really screwed me up was that it didn't sound like anything Ginny would have said on her own.

"Blows the mind."

She didn't talk like that. It sounded like something she'd heard, something she was repeating, something the guy she'd taken acid with the first time had said.

"Blows the mind."

The phrase kept reverberating. Had it been after he fucked her that he'd said it? Before? During? Was she on her hands and knees in front of him when he said it? Was he squeezing the cheeks of her perfect ass when he said it? Was he pulling her cunt onto his cock when he said it? Were the juices from her pussy puddling up around his dick when he said it? Was he watching his cock fuck her?

"Are you okay?" I heard Ginny ask.

"Yeah. I'm fine."

"We're all icky and sticky," she said.

"No, we're not. We're okay."

"Yes we *are*, dodo. *Look* at us!" She laughed. We looked at each other. She was glistening with dried pickle juice and orange pulp. I was too. "Come on, let's get in the shower." She stood up and took me by my hands.

Jealousy was an aphrodisiac. Jealousy had always been an aphrodisiac, even when I wasn't stoned on acid—I'd been jealous of Ginny and other guys since the night Elliot and I met her; I'd been jealous of her two dates; I'd been jealous of her boyfriend in high school, the one who dumped her after she got raped by a cop; I'd been jealous of the cop; I'd been jealous of the garbanzo bean guy who had to come over to 45th Avenue that night my car didn't start; I'd been jealous of the Hershey Bar guy in that tawdry hotel across from Gramercy Park; I'd been jealous of Jim Moss sticking his big black dick in her; I'd been jealous of Ron Goldstein and Bud and the guys she couldn't remember; I'd been jealous of Tom, I'd been jealous of Elliot—but acid intensified everything. I was more jealous than I had ever imagined I could be. I was going to die of jealousy. I was going to explode from jealousy.

I followed Ginny into the shower. Drops of water on her skin sparkled like diamonds. I kissed her shoulder. She tasted like salt. I soaped up my hands and washed her breasts and washed her belly and slinked down onto my knees in the shower and washed between her legs and dropped the soap and rinsed her off with the sparkling streams of water streaming down her stomach. My taste buds turned what she usually tasted like and the residue from the little bar of motel soap into their constituent molecules and came up with exotic perfumes and tastes I'd never tasted before. I opened her pussy up with my fingers and licked her hard little clit. She tasted like vanilla—like lemon, and cinnamon, and lilacs, and apples—and there was still a hint of the juice from the dill pickle and the oranges, too.

I stood up and turned her around and fucked her a little, like a dolphin, maybe, or a slippery little sea otter. When we got out of the shower, I picked her up in my arms and carried her across the room and laid her down onto the bed and spread her legs apart and stuck my dick in her right away, hard, no preliminaries—and fucked her on the bed like a whore, like a slut, like a two-bit bitch who'd fuck anyone anywhere. I fucked her like her boyfriend in high school. I fucked her like the cop. I fucked her like all the guys she'd ever fucked. Then I turned her over and fucked her some more. I fucked her like the guy she took acid with the first time fucked her, and I kept on fucking her. We worked our way down to the floor, and I fucked her like a dog, like a goat, like a lamb, like a squealing little pink pig. The hooked rug cut wrinkles into her pretty kneecaps.

g g

Later, lying on my back with the dead weight of Ginny's tough, succulent little body on top of me in the small soft springy bed again, after the aphrodisiac of my jealousy had worn off some, my imagination was finally able just to go wherever it wanted to go. Whether my eyes were open or shut, it didn't matter—Byzantine frescoes were interrupted by glimpses of green grinning imps flowing in and out of my racing consciousness.

Some of the images were more elevated than others. There was a little Disney animation, some Tolkien and Dr. Seuss, but there were all kinds of humane, religious looking things, too—stuff that guys like Bosch and Brueghel might have painted.

All in all, I was pretty pleased with the way my imagination handled itself. Mayan and Egyptian and Sufi motifs crawled across the walls like our cozy little cabin was some kind of non-denominational Sistine Chapel. They went on and on, flowing through me, each more exquisite than the last. I really sort of had to go with the flow. I had no choice. The minute I tried to stop and appreciate one or another of these fleeting miracles for much longer than no time at all, they got all jumbled up in my brain—but there was a phrase that kept repeating itself, a mantra I kept hearing: "Leave them alone and they will come home, wagging their tails behind them."

I had no idea what was going on with Ginny. Whatever it was, it wasn't something I wanted to try to talk about. By the time I would have asked a question, too many answers would have come and gone, all at once, doubting themselves at every turn, up and down a whole huge hall of mirrors in my mind.

It was best not to ask. It was best not to try to talk. It was best not to *try*, period—to do nothing, to relax, to let go, to leave all the little factories I had going on inside me alone, just to let them do their own thing, to let them be, to stay the hell out of their way.

* *GG* *

The next morning we went back out into the forest again. I couldn't for the life of me find that fern plant, or the ant-hill—and I didn't even *try* to find the pinecone or that huge, mean, menacing spider who'd tried to eat my brain. There were a few flies flying around, but they weren't leaving any vapor trails.

The tree stump, we found. We made a special point of finding it, but the tree stump was nothing but a big burnt-out old stump of an ancient redwood tree. We looked inside and saw the cavern we'd been in, but there was no longer a story-book world of any sort going on down there. It was just dirty looking—and dark and damp and uninviting—certainly not the sort of place that could by any stretch of the imagination be mistaken for heaven on earth.

CHAPTER TWENTY

Shrader Street

*A*cid changed everything—politics, relationships, fashion, religion, war, peace, freedom, diet, philosophy, soap operas, you name it. The normal things you used to just *do* from day to day—get up, brush your teeth, eat a bowl of Wheaties, go to work at some flunky job—all that changed once you dropped your first little orange speckled hit of LSD or ate your first sugar cube or drank your first Dixie Cup of Kool-Aid. Your hair grew long. You couldn't look into a bowl of Wheaties without imagining where the wheat grew, who planted it, how it got cultivated and turned into flakes and put into orange boxes...and who cut the trees to make the boxes and who drove the trucks...and that was before you even got to the milk and the sugar and all the grass the cow must have eaten, not to mention what the fuck exactly *was* it that went into the making of a champion? You wore necklaces and bright-colored clothes; the gray hooded sweatshirt you used to put on without thinking about it one way or another became an elfin cloak.

One of the changes *I* noticed was that Ginny didn't seem to give a shit whether I wrote books or not anymore—so I didn't. That was a relief. I barely read books anymore. It was all I could do to look at the pictures on psychedelic posters or in *Zap Comix*. Reading was too linear. Words were too cumbersome. Even the individual letters out of which words were constructed just got way too squiggly and artificial looking to *mean* anything anymore. Nothing made the kind of sense it used to make.

Ginny still read books. She read books all the time, meaty stuff and fluff—but she had never read books in a very linear way, anyway—she didn't do much of anything in a very linear way. Taking acid had nothing to do with it.

* ♫ ♫ *

When we got back from La Honda, Ginny and I rented a two-bedroom apartment—410 Shrader Street, Apartment 3. It was a few buildings up from Oak, a block and a half down from Haight Street, three blocks from Ashbury.

When we went to see about the apartment, the guy who managed the building had a monkey on his shoulder. He was an old Russian guy, probably in his early seventies. He'd been a circus performer—a daring young man on a flying trapeze. His last name was Forkel. His first name was Vela, but I never thought of him as anyone but Mr. Forkel. He reminded me of Vladimir Nabokov—well, of pictures I'd seen of Nabokov on dust jackets. Nabokov had worked in a circus, too. Nabokov also lived up here in Ashland, Oregon for a while. In the fifties, I think. He used to catch butterflies in the woods at the end of the ally behind my mother's house.

Mr. Forkel and his wife lived in the front apartment. It had bay windows looking out onto Shrader Street. After I rang the bell, the first thing Ginny and I saw was the monkey. He popped his head up under Mr. and Mrs. Forkel's white lace curtains and gave us a sour look. Ginny gave him a sour look back. He grimaced at her and scratched his head. She scratched her head and stuck out her tongue at him. That was when Mr. Forkel's wife pulled the curtains aside and saw us standing there. Pretty soon Mr. Forkel let us into the hall-way—him and his monkey.

The monkey crouched on Mr. Forkel's shoulder. Its fur had a greenish tinge. It scratched its tiny, dirty, human-look-ing fingernails through its owner's sparse gray hair like it was looking for ticks. The monkey offered Ginny a piece of lint with a mawkish grin, showing off the bright blue veins on the insides of its lips. She took the lint from the monkey's fingers. They frowned at each other.

Mr. Forkel called the monkey Houdini. "Hang on a sec-ond," he said. "Let me get rid of Houdini, here."

"Is that its name? I mean *his* name?" Ginny asked, cover-ing her mouth as if she may inadvertently have hurt the mon-key's feelings.

"No. She's a girl. I call her Houdini to keep her con-fused." He had only a slight accent. He scooted the monkey into his and his wife's apartment, and we followed him down the long hallway to the rear apartment on the right-hand side.

"You got the garden out back. It goes with this apart-ment." Mr. Forkel opened one of the window shades. Dirty white curtains billowed out. The cross ventilation seemed okay. I liked the idea of having a garden. We could grow things, rhubarb, tomatoes, like my grandpa used to grow. The curtains, we could wash—we could spiff the place up in all kinds of other ways, too, paint the walls, maybe.

"It's how much, again?" I asked.

"Two twenty-seven fifty. Two bedrooms. Furnished. The owner didn't raise the rent after the last tenants moved out. They weren't here long."

"Why the fifty cents?" I asked.

"Owner's Chinese. It's a Hong Kong corporation."

Mr. Forkel went back to his apartment. Ginny and I walked around awhile, into the kitchen, into the bathroom. We tried the faucets, flushed the toilet. We sat on the couch. The refrigerator clicked on. We heard a siren. A bus stopped. There was the sound of compressed air when the bus door opened and another hiss of compressed air when the bus door closed. The bus drove away. We heard the voice of a kid yelling. The refrigerator clicked off.

We went into the back bedroom. Clotheslines on rusted pulleys were strung between the backs of the buildings. Facing the street, the buildings were the ornate, multicolored Victorians San Francisco's famous for, but in back they were dull blocks of wooden planks, painted pastel blue or peach or yellow. Falling-down fences heaped with mounds of thriving ivy separated the yards between the buildings. Two of the yards had been cemented over. Weeds grew out of cracks in the cement. In one there was a yellow dog dish, another had a vegetable garden. Between the buildings, the golden spires of St. Ignatius Church glinted and clouded over, in and out of the sun and patches of fog. We took it.

That was where we lived from May of 1965 to the spring of 1968—well, on and off; it's all kind of a jumble. That thing they used to say—"If you remember the sixties you weren't there."—that's not exactly a meaningless cliché. I moved out now and then. I went up to Oregon, came back, got my own place for a while, moved in with Ginny again. We had other roommates sometimes. Brenda Creswell was one. All I remember about her was that she played the same Judy Collins record over and over on some cheap-ass record player that hadn't had a new needle since she'd moved to San Francisco from Nebraska.

Mary Kramer was another roommate. She was stable, down to earth—a nurse. The only unconventional thing about Mary was that she was Pigpen's girlfriend. They were a miracle of contrasts. I remember getting up one morning and finding them at the kitchen table. Mary had just finished a nutritious, well-balanced breakfast and was dressed for work in her prim white uniform. Pigpen was wearing his black leather hat that was coming apart at the seams. Purple carbuncles pocked his unshaven jowls and poked up around the edges of his scraggly mustache. His jacket was coming apart at the seams; he was sort of coming apart at the seams, in general. I think Mary might have been trying to reform him, to clean him up, to nurture him, to give him some stability, to keep him from drinking himself to death. It wasn't working. As soon as she left, Pigpen poured whiskey into a cup of black coffee.

All kinds of people used to hang out at our apartment on Shrader Street. We got our acid from Superspade. He got it from Owsley. It was to the apartment on Shrader Street that Hank Harrison brought little Courtney over for us to baby-sit—that day we took acid and her little towhead two-year-old glow lit up the place. Steve Gaskin used to drop by now and then. He was trying to get Ginny and Brenda to start up a commune with him out in the sticks somewhere.

⊱ 𝒢𝒢 ⊰

Ginny went into the U. C. Hospital psycho ward during most of the Christmas difficulties of 1965—from November until the end of February. I hid under her bed a couple of times, spent the night, then snuck out when visiting hours started the next day. When it turned spring, things quieted down again.

During the summer of 1966, we mellowed out, lived our lives. I worked at little jobs. Ginny continued taking classes at San Francisco State, although going nuts around Christmas kept getting in the way of accumulating enough credits to graduate. I explained things to her teachers. A few of them gave her a passing grade based on the work she'd already done, but most didn't; they couldn't, they said.

New hippies showed up in Haight-Ashbury every day. They just *appeared*—like crocuses in the spring. One day a guy would be a straight-laced claims adjuster, taking the bus down to Montgomery Street every morning, and the next day he'd be all decked out in hippie threads, leaning against the front of the Psychedelic Shop, asking for spare change. It was by their eyes that you could tell they were hippies. That was the key. It wasn't their clothes or their hair or their beads or their bare feet—it was their eyes. If you'd taken acid it was in your eyes. You were a hippie. If you hadn't, it wasn't, you weren't. They danced around like dervishes, smiling the smiles they'd seen other hippies smiling, wearing clothes they'd seen other hippies wearing, smoking joints they'd been given instead of spare change. Most of them didn't have places to stay, but they found places to stay. They were kids. People took them in like strays. Ginny and I were getting old and wise and weary.

* 𝒢𝒢 *

By the fall of 1966, our apartment on Shrader Street had become a crash pad for all the people we knew who didn't live in Haight-Ashbury—Thulin practically lived there, that fucker. He and Wanda got married there. Holy smokes, was *that* ever a surprise. Well, he and Wanda got married in Golden Gate Park, actually, but we all came back to Shrader Street when the wedding was over.

I've mentioned Thulin, right? One-Eyed Jon? The guy who gave Ralph Wood his first marijuana that time in the elevator of the Navarre Guest House? He had just the one eye, see. That was why we called him One-Eyed Jon. He ended up on the cover of *Rolling Stone* as one of the acid cowboys of Taos, New Mexico, but back then Thulin's main claim to fame was chicks. He fucked more chicks than you could shake a stick at. I think it had something to do with his eye. When I met him over at Ralph Wood's place by the railroad tracks in San Mateo, the first thing I asked Thulin was about his eye.

"What's wrong with your eye?" I nodded toward it.

"This?" He reached up, plucked out his left eye, held it between his fingers and looked at it with his other eye. Then he flipped the eye over in his hand, got his thumb behind it and acted like he was going to shoot it at me like a marble. "Nothing, man." He smiled. "It's glass. It's a glass eye."

My own left eye squinted sympathetically as Thulin popped the eye back into its socket, and I felt a wave of empathy toward him. He pulled the same stunt on chicks. It worked like a charm. He'd meet a new chick, take out his eye and pretend to shoot it at her like a marble—always with the same goat-like grin and with his face glowing with simple-minded mischief and irresistible charm—and she'd melt.

It must have aroused them in some visceral way, reaching down into some forgotten sexual, psychological mechanism left over from when men gave women the choicest tidbits of freshly killed animals as tokens of affection and desire. What-ever it was, Thulin fucked more chicks than anyone I ever knew. That was what the whole Haight Street thing was all about to him. That was what it was all about to lots of people, including, no doubt, all the chicks who were getting them-selves fucked.

I remember Thulin trying to explain the whole hippie thing to Mr. and Mrs. Forkel. Ha! If he could explain it to them, he could explain it to anyone. He couldn't, of course, but that didn't keep him from trying.

* 𝒢 𝒢 *

There was a tarnished silver samovar and a tray of tall glasses on an end table in Mr. and Mrs. Forkel's apartment, along with pictures in silver frames, pictures of circuses and pictures of old people, their parents probably, daguerreotypes maybe, and pictures of Mr. and Mrs. Forkel when they were around our age. Young.

In one of the pictures, Mr. Forkel was on a platform high up inside a circus tent. He was wearing a white body suit. His wife was beside him, wearing a tutu and sitting on the bar of a trapeze. She was smiling. He was stern and athletic looking.

Thulin and I sat down on a couple brocade-upholstered chairs across from them. Mr. and Mrs. Forkel were sitting with their hands folded in their laps on their brocade-upholstered couch. After it had brewed long enough, Mrs. Forkel got up and poured us a glass of tea. "A glass tea," she called it. Her accent was thicker than her husband's. She sat back down on the couch and folded her hands in her lap again.

Mr. Forkel wanted to know if we could tell them what was happening in the neighborhood. He said this exact sentence, I swear, word for word: "Something's happening here but we don't know what it is."

"You sound pretty hip already," Thulin said.

"That's eet," Mrs. Forkel said. "Heep! I hear thees word many times."

"It's from jazz," I said.

"Hep cats. I know of hep cats. *Le Jazz hot*," Mr. Forkel said.

"Yeah, well some bunch of beatniks turned it into the word 'hip' and pretty soon the newspapers were calling people hippies."

"It is going like this everywhere on? And why the hair long? The beads around the neck of the boys? The asking of spare change? Who has so much spare change? I'm telling you the truth, just going to the Cala, we see...such things, in the parking lot, on the sidewalk, everywhere. Do we, Vela?"

"We see a lot of things."

"It's like a revolution," I told them.

"We have seen a revolution," Mr. Forkel said. "We have lived through a revolution. This is...silliness." He waved the gnarled fingers of his right hand.

"Yeah, it must look a little silly, I admit. It's not very political. It's more, like, personal, individual. It probably started with a kid named Bob Dylan."

"Who this boy is? What his mother is thinking?"

"Dylan, my ass." Thulin frowned. "It started with Woody Guthrie, man. No, Kerouac. Or Henry Miller. Burroughs! Or Gandhi, maybe. Walt Whitman? Or Jesus, maybe—peace and love, turn your other cheek and all that. Yeah, yeah, it started with Jesus and them, that's what I think."

"Kennedy getting shot had something to do with it, too, Jon."

"Yeah," Thulin said. "God damn Kennedy, man. He went around giving us this big glowing picture of how things were going to be, you know? Like, how there was going to be such peace and prosperity—then went and got himself shot and left us stuck with LBJ and Curtis LeMay. People were pissed. They started making a stink. Mario Savio stirred up stuff at Berkeley. Lay your body down on the gears of the machine and all that. Then Kesey came up from Stanford, and him and Cassady went around passing out free acid to everyone who could swallow and they got Timothy Leary to drop out of Harvard, along with what's-his-name, that Herb Alpert guy—and got a bunch of bands together, The Airplane, man, Quicksilver, The Dead, and the Mime Troupe got the Diggers in on it, Emmet Grogan and them, giving away free food and free clothes and free places to crash."

"What is it, then?" Mr. Forkel asked. "This 'acid' that they give away?"

"LSD, man! Lysergic acid di-thalidomide."

"I don't think it's thalidomide, Jon."

"Di-something, man. Totally blows your mind, whatever you call it."

"It's a drug, I take it?" Mr. Forkel said.

"It's a hallucinogenic. It makes you see things that aren't there," I said.

"Why do you want to see things that aren't there?"

"You don't *want* to, man. You just do," Thulin said.

"Imaginary things," I said. "You know how dreams are? Like how things keep changing from one thing into another all the time? It's like that. It's like your imagination sort of gets superimposed onto things and turns them into things they're not, you know? It's not that easy to explain."

"Sounds like schizophrenia."

"It probably is. Sort of. It's like, you know Dostoyevsky?"

"Unfortunately, he died before I was born."

"Well, you know how Dostoyevsky used to have seizures, right?"

"Epilepsy. Yes. In Russian it is another word."

"Well, he used to say he wouldn't trade what happens to him during one of his epileptic fits, not for anything. I think acid might be sort of like that."

"And this is what has caused the children to let their hair grow long, wear jingle bells and dress up like wild Indians?"

"Plus there's this whole war thing," Thulin said, holding his forearms out in front of him, letting his hands do some of his talking. He looked like a fireman carrying a kid from a burning building, like he was holding the knowledge of the ages in his arms, like it was his job to save them from their ignorance, to inform Mr. and Mrs. Forkel of modern day reality. "I mean, who's gettin' anything out of that, you know?

Innocent bystanders, that's who, and all they're gettin' is killed. We spend billions of dollars to stock the black market in Saigon. We could buy the whole country for what it's costing. We could turn it into Disneyland. Disneyland East."

"Nobody cares about the war in Vietnam," I said.

"What do you mean, man? Like who?"

"Like anyone with any brains, that's who."

"So, what's all these demonstrations about?"

"Politics. Anyone who joins anything's an idiot—that's all you need to know. You want to change the world? Be good. Don't fight. Eat your vegetables."

"Thank you Krishnamurti," Thulin said.

"Where'd you hear about Krishnamurti?" I frowned.

"Ah, some chick, man. I don't know." He waved his hand.

"Are they going stop? Or it goes more on?" Mrs. Forkel asked.

"I don't know. There are more people coming out here all the time."

"Yeah, man. More chicks." Thulin widened his eye. "All that's really going on is chicks, more new chicks every day, coming in from everywhere."

"I think they have too life good. No pay the rent. Free food for eat. Free clothes to wearing. Free to sleep places..."

"Free love," Thulin said, and his good eye got extra wide.

"Oh my God." Mrs. Forkel removed her hands momentarily from her lap and held them to the sides of her face, covering her ears with her fingers.

"It's a phase," I said. "It'll go away."

"I don't know." Mr. Forkel shook his head sadly. "Will it ever be Russia again? No. Never."

"But that was a real revolution. This is just silliness," I said.

"I hope you know," Mrs. Forkel said.

CHAPTER TWENTY-ONE

Foghorn Fish-and-Chips

Wait. I can't keep anything straight. I was talking about Thulin getting married. Okay, so, not long after Thulin described the definitive history of the rise and imminent fall of Haight-Ashbury to poor bewildered Mr. and Mrs. Forkel— which must have been somewhere around October of 1966— he got married. Ha! That was a surprise. He wasn't exactly the marrying kind.

Thulin still lived at Ralph's place in San Mateo, but he'd been coming to the Haight pretty regularly for the last six months to pick up chicks. Ginny and I had an extra bedroom we let him use now and then. We had a weird affection for Thulin. He'd get us dope, amuse us with his eye and totally crack us up when he got carried away with starry-eyed lust for some new chick or other. We really couldn't help but let them use the extra room when the need arose. Usually it never lasted longer than a day, often no longer than an hour or so, but Wanda was different.

Ginny and I were with him up on Haight Street the day he found her. We got to see the whole romance from beginning to end. Wanda was fresh up from San Carlos High School and didn't have a nickel to her name. Thulin spotted her standing on the sidewalk in front of Foghorn Fish-and-Chips. He stopped dead in his tracks.

"Oh, my *God.*" Ginny rolled her eyes. "You are such a rake, such a roué, such a snake—when are you ever going to leave these little girls *alone?*"

"Tomorrow," Thulin said, staring straight at Wanda.

She wasn't in line, but was lurking off to one side, looking longingly at the twin vats of boiling oil, salivating at the smell of deep fried fish and batter and malt vinegar and thick-cut, brown-skinned, French fried Russet potatoes still bubbling around the edges. Thulin kept his eye on her as she watched the English guy take a new batch of fries from the boiling fat. He gave them a few shakes in their wire basket, tossed them across the stainless steel counter and sprinkled them with salt from a giant aluminum saltshaker. Wanda licked her lips.

Thulin walked up to her as if in a daze and said, "Hey."

They talked for a while. Thulin showed her his eye. He popped it out and pretended to shoot it like a marble at her chest. Then he grinned his goat-like grin and popped the eye back into its empty socket again.

"Cute," Wanda said. Her hair was long and thick and black and lustrous. She had it tied into a ponytail with a red elastic band.

Thulin brought her over to where Ginny and I were standing. "Me and Wanda here's gonna get us a couple orders of fish-and-chips, then maybe head on back over to your place." He grinned his goat-like grin and casually groomed his wispy goatee.

Wanda smiled a shy, polite, half-smile and glanced over at us. Then looked down at her black Converse sneakers sticking out from under a pair of bell-bottom jeans. She had a pink plastic wallet in her right hand. The wallet was held together by the same red elastic bands she used to tie back her hair. We talked. Wanda was in the tenth grade at San Carlos High School. She'd come up on the Greyhound. Her parents didn't know it yet, but she wasn't planning on going back.

"I might need me a key, unless you're going to hang around," Thulin said.

"Did Jon tell you his poem, yet?" Ginny asked Wanda.

"No. He just showed me his eye." She brushed aside a strand of hair that had come loose from the elastic.

"So, what'd you think?" I asked her.

"I thought it was…unusual," she said. "What's his poem?"

"There'll be plenty of time for all that later." Thulin's forehead got all contorted like he was trying to give Ginny a secret signal to shut the fuck up.

"Come on. I want it hear it," Ginny said.

"I'm gonna break the chains of conformity…into a million shitty pieces."

"Yeah? And?" Wanda asked. She was still waiting to hear the rest of the poem. Ginny and I knew he was through.

"That's it," Thulin said. "That's my poem."

"It doesn't rhyme," Wanda said.

Ginny handed him her keys.

* 𝒢 𝒢 *

They were still at it when Ginny and I got back to the apartment. He and Wanda were louder than he and any of the other chicks had ever been. We could hear them from the hallway. I worried for a minute that they might be breaking things, but it was mostly just a lot of thumping and bumping and clumping.

When he finally brought Wanda back out into the living room, Thulin had the biggest shit-eating grin I'd ever seen. He had his arm around her shoulders. I'd never seen him with his arm around one of his chicks before. She was gorgeous. They were all pretty cute, but Wanda was hauntingly beautiful. Her hair was blacker than black. It glistened all purple and green, like a starling's wing in the sun, and her skin was creamy and flawless. Her lips were full and soft but always on the verge of a slight sneer. She had even white teeth when she smiled, but she didn't smile much. She was serious.

What was also extraordinary about Wanda was that she only fucked Thulin just that one time. He couldn't figure it out. Days went by. She wouldn't go away. Thulin didn't know what to do. He kept kicking her out. She kept not going anywhere. That was fine with Ginny and me. They were cute together. She wouldn't fuck him and she wouldn't go away. Thulin didn't get it; it was beyond the realm of his experience.

"So." Thulin raised an eyebrow. "When do you think you might be heading back to San Carlos, little girl?" He called them all "little girl."

"I can't go back there." Wanda laughed. "Are you crazy?"

"So, what are you planning on doing?"

"I'm not planning on doing anything, Jon." She blinked her eyes slowly and moved her lower lip. Her mouth was relaxed and slightly bored.

"Yeah, well, if you're going to be here, we're going to be here, like, together, you know?" He nodded in the general direction of the extra bedroom and smiled the goat-like smile that had always done the trick with every other chick.

"I don't think so," Wanda said.

"What do you mean, you don't think so? Who the fuck do you think you are? The fucking Queen of fucking Sheba?"

"Yes," said Wanda. "I am the fucking Queen of fucking Sheba." She made right angles of her arms and looked like a picture of a Pharaoh's wife on a pyramid.

"Hey, listen, man," Thulin said. "You're cute and all that, but you're gonna have to split. Period. I'm serious." He waved his thumb toward the door.

Wanda shrugged her shoulders and stared at him.

"Fuck it, then. *I'll* leave." Thulin opened the door.

"Could you bring us back something to eat?" Wanda asked.

When he came back with Chinese food and Wanda's usual can of Dad's Old Fashioned Root Beer, Thulin tried to get her to fuck him again. She wouldn't. He couldn't believe it. He kicked her out in as many ways as he knew how. Wanda examined the ends of her hair. She wanted them to get an apartment of their own. Thulin found a place around the corner on Page Street. He and Wanda moved into it together, but she still wouldn't fuck him. She wanted them to get married. He kicked her out of their new apartment again and again. She never left.

* 𝒢𝒢 *

During the wedding ceremony, Thulin kept shaking his head and rolling his eye and muttering obscenities into his wispy beard. He flipped the ring like a coin and kept trying to get the makeshift preacher to call it in the air. The preacher had some ocular trouble of his own. Gold wire glasses magnified his right eye. It seemed to float aimlessly over toward his hatchet nose like a dark, bloated tropical fish trapped in a tide pool.

Thulin and Wanda had met the preacher in Golden Gate Park. His name was Kirk. He looked like a picture of the Prophet Ezekiel in one of those ornate Victorian Bibles. They took him home with them, and while he was cooking his brown rice and broccoli, Kirk agreed, under the auspices of the powers conferred upon him by some guru in Nepal, to marry them, for better or for worse.

Wanda had the exact place she wanted to get married already picked out—up past the horseshoe pits, across from the fuchsia gardens, among ferns so gigantic they looked like palm trees buried up to their necks in black soil. Thulin didn't give a shit about any of that. He just wanted to get it the hell over with. During the ceremony, Kirk chanted some sort of chant he'd learned over in Tibet. Everyone knew what he was saying whether anyone understood it or not—well, everyone but Thulin. He'd gotten kind of monomaniacal. He didn't know anything but that he wanted to fuck Wanda.

When Thulin grabbed the ring out of the air for the last time and handed it over, Kirk looked through the circle formed by the ring and into the cloudless sky. Then he looked at Thulin through the ring. Thulin flipped him off. Then Kirk looked at Wanda through the ring. She smiled. There were tears in her eyes. Kirk's wandering eye settled on each of them. He put the ring onto Wanda's ring finger. It fit. That seemed significant. Kirk closed his eyes and bowed his head. Birds stopped twittering in the bushes. Then he opened his eyes and asked Wanda if she would take Jon to be her husband, to have and to hold. Wanda said, "Yes."

Thulin got a big shit-eating grin on his face.

Then Kirk asked Jon the same question. "Motherfucking, Jesus H. motherfucking fuck," Thulin answered.

Wanda bashed the bridal bouquet across his chest.

"Okay, okay, yeah," Thulin said.

Kirk dutifully repeated the question, like he'd be breaking his vows to the guru in Nepal if he didn't conduct the ceremony correctly. "Yes. Yes. Yes. For cocksucking Christ's sake, what the fuck more do you want me to say? I do. I do. Jesus fucking fuck."

Kirk deemed that to be sufficient. The ceremony was over. We all went back to Shrader Street—well, except for Wanda and Thulin—and when they finally showed up, he had another big shit-eating grin on his face, the biggest yet, the biggest ever.

* 𝒢 𝒢 *

A couple of months later Wanda was pregnant. Thulin couldn't believe it. He couldn't *fucking* believe it. He wanted to know if *I* could fucking believe it. We were having coffee in the doughnut shop on the corner of Haight and Shrader. He paid. He wanted to talk. I had wanted to go for a walk.

"What am I gonna do with a kid?" he asked.

"Kids are cool," I told him.

"Yeah? What kind of a place is this to have a kid in?"

"The same kind of place it's always been, Jon."

"Yeah? With this fucking war and shit going on? I don't know, man. And what about other chicks? What am I supposed to do about that? Be a fucking monk?" Then he got pensive for a minute and started speaking more softly. "We've been talking about naming him Jon. Except if it's a chick. Then I don't know what we'd do. Any name we pick, I fucked some chick with the same name. That's gonna piss her off, you know? We talk about all kinds of stuff, her and me. I really totally love the fucking piss out of her, but—fuck it. I can't deal with this shit."

"Wouldn't it be like starting all over…having a clean slate?"

"What are you talking about, man? You offed you and Ginny's kid, didn't you? So, what's this clean slate horseshit? I been trying to get Wanda to off the fucker. She won't do it. She's like all Catholic and shit. How'd you get Ginny to—have an abortion?" He must have seen that I wasn't amused.

"I didn't. It was her idea—her and her father's lawyer. They talked it over. It wasn't practical, she wasn't in any condition, and it was true, she wasn't, but…"

"You wanted a kid?"

"Yeah. I like kids."

"Hey, man, I groove with kids, too. But he'd also be, like, *around* all the fucking time, you know? Like fucking forever. Like fucking always. Pooping in his pants and shit—or *her* pants. Motherfuck. What would I do with a chick for a kid?"

"Like it," I said. "Love it. Take care of it. Feed it. Clothe it. Educate it. Take it places. Grow it up."

"Yeah, well, I don't know, man. We'll see."

Not long after our conversation at the doughnut shop, four or five months before the baby was born, Thulin dumped Wanda and moved back to San Mateo.

That was the last I ever saw of him. The next thing I heard was that he went to New Mexico and got his picture on the cover of *Rolling Stone.*. A couple years later I heard from Dick Joseph that he was killed in a drug deal that didn't work out.

Wanda was pissed off that Thulin dumped her. She didn't try to get him back or anything—that wouldn't have been her style. She took it out on him by naming his kid Popeye. She'd been going to name him Jon but decided at the last second to name him Popeye instead. Dick Joseph kept track of her, too. He kept track of everyone. According to Dick, Wanda got on welfare, went back to school and ended up working as a dental hygienist in a small, rural, community just outside Tallahassee, Florida—just the sort of town where a kid named Popeye would fit right in.

CHAPTER TWENTY-TWO

Haight Street

Wanda and Thulin getting married and having a baby, just like that, easy as pie, got me to thinking that was what I wanted to do, that was what I wanted Ginny and me to do. I wanted us to get married and live happily ever after. How hard could it be? If Thulin and Wanda could do it, why couldn't we? I wanted a kid. I wanted a house. I wanted a family, like my mother and father had a family. Ginny didn't want to do that. She wanted to be a muse. I went up to Oregon. She sent me this letter:

I am longing for unrest. My long subjugated, patronized, conde-
scended to, sneered at romanticism is now crying, "Let me live!" It's also
sneering back at me for cowardice, jeering at me for finding mundanity,
peaceful acceptance as the cure for internal turmoil. I want to be dishon-
est! I want to be deceived...skillfully. I want you to become romantic
and write books and love and hate passionately. Let's fall in love and eat
fire and have martinis out for dinner. Enough of all this realism and psy-
chological health—I call for the demonic elements—tragedy, yearning,
unrest, ecstasies, suffering. Wisdom's a bore, contentment a drag. Boy,
I'm glad God stays so neat all the time—and doesn't ever get boring.

He's so exciting, and it's safe to love Him too! I'm so glad you're gone. I can be so much closer to you. You can't armor me off. OH GOSH—I just REALIZED SOMETHING. YOW! About you! About me! (I don't want to talk about it now.) I know what. We can have a week for passion, yearning, romance, ect.—and one for serenity, calm acceptance and wisdom. They've just got to co-exist some way—and be pure too!!

I went back down to San Francisco in time for the Christmas of 1966—and we made it through another season of drunk, schizo insanity. She didn't get locked up in a psycho ward, but she got locked up in plenty of other places. A bartender wouldn't let her out of a bar on Haight Street after it closed. She called me. I went down there. They were listening to Chubby Checker on the jukebox. She was doing the twist. I banged on the door. Cops came. The bartender let her out. We went home.

The same sort of thing happened at the Straight Theater, not long after it opened again. This time it was some rock group. I got a whispery phone call. They had her trapped. They wouldn't let her go. I got up and got dressed and walked down there in the drizzly fog and wind and made a fuss. Some of the guys in another band found her, and Ginny and I went home. Guys were always kidnapping her when she was drunk. They wanted to keep her for themselves, I guess. The same thing happened at an art gallery, at a gas station on Van Ness and at a 7-11 in Noe Valley. She wasn't just crying wolf, no; she got herself into scrapes, no doubt about it. Some of them I managed to get her out of; some of them I didn't manage to get her out of.

Her Christmas troubles took their toll. I had been torn up into little pieces like Osiris and was being fed to the fishes in the Nile—she was eating my flesh like communion wafers; she was drinking my blood. After the worst of it was over, I went up to Oregon to recuperate again. When I went back down to San Francisco, she'd messed with a bunch of guys while I'd been gone. I was getting used to it.

Toward the end of March of 1967, I rented a room in a huge hippie crash pad in the Lower Haight, on the northwest corner of Haight and Pierce, to be exact, and messed with a fair number of chicks myself. It was sort of slick being a hippie for a while. There must have been fifty or sixty people coming in and out on any given day. I don't think anyone besides me was paying any rent and I wasn't paying much. *Morning Dew* and *Little Schoolgirl* played nonstop on about five different record players night and day—and chicks? *Whoa.* I felt like Thulin. There were big, young, blustery blondes up from Santa Barbara with sand in their underpants from sleeping on beaches and frail, fawnlike, doe-eyed chicks out from Boston and droll chicks from Mississippi with lilts in their voices and twangy chicks from Missouri—every kind of chick you can think of—Saskatchewan, you name it.

That was where I was living when I took a bus down to meet my mother at the airport. She had a layover in San Francisco on her way back from visiting my grandmother, who was dying, on and off, back in Michigan. The Grateful Dead were at one of the gates. I introduced them. My mother nodded her head and smiled her motherly smile and asked, "How many of you boys *are* there in your band?"

Jerry Garcia spread open his hand, the hand with one finger missing and said, "Five, five, an even five."

"Your mothers must be proud of you," my mother said.

On the bus back up to the city, I sat next to a girl who was running away from home. She said she'd just turned sixteen, but that might have been a lie. We spent a couple of days together in my room at the hippie crash pad. She was Italian. We came up with a new identity for her in case her parents had the cops after her. The name we settled on was Zita Silvano. We made up that she'd come out here from Bradford, Pennsylvania. She might have kept the name, for all I know. When her kids open up bank accounts they may use Silvano as their mother's maiden name.

I wasn't cut out to be the kind of hippie that was showing up in the Haight by then. It was fun to fuck a bunch of different chicks, sure, but the whole hippie thing was over by 1966. A few minds got blown on acid. That was it. The culture was ripe. It had nothing to do with the war or civil rights or free speech. All that riding around in flower power VW busses was the commercialization of the experience. The music, long hair, beads, dope, bare feet, brown rice, free love, *Mr. Natural*, psychedelic art, Timothy Leary turning and tuning and dropping, Tom Wolfe's *Electric Kool-Aid* hogwash, Cassady tooling Kesey's merry pranksters around in their funky bus—all that was nothing but advertising by people who'd already taken acid to get other people to take acid, and by then the advertising was getting mistaken for the only thing that *really* went on. A few minds got blown on acid. That was it.

After a few weeks in the Lower Haight, I moved back into the apartment on Shrader Street and Ginny and I lived happily ever after again for another summer.

* 𝓖 𝓖 *

Elliot came back into the picture sometime in May of 1967. He'd recovered from most of the short-term effects of his father having blown his head half off. He was going to school at the Art Institute and teaching a class in airbrush technique. He had a girlfriend, too—a cute little Korean chick with nice tits, extra slanty eyes, one of those Asian overbites and vestiges of some difficulty with the English language.

Ginny and I ran into them on Haight Street a couple times—the first time we were in the middle of the block, between Ashbury and Clayton. Ginny and Elliot were sheepish with each other. I kind of liked the cute little Korean chick myself. She was noticeably not wearing a bra and didn't seem to mind me looking down the front of her loose fitting paisley shirt. She seemed to sort of like it, in fact.

The cute little Korean chick kept trying to squeeze Elliot's Zippo out from the tight pocket of his jeans. He kept moving away, like he was embarrassed by her familiarity and obvious affection. That was it. That was all that happened. We went our separate ways. The next time we ran into them at the Drogstore Café.

When I first came up to the house on Clayton Street to rescue Ginny from Jim Moss, there was a drug store on the corner of Haight and Masonic. By the spring of 1967 it had become a restaurant, which for some arcane legal reason or other could not be called the Drugstore Café, so the owners named it the Drogstore Café.

Ginny and I were sitting on a couple stools by one of the big picture windows, eating big dripping hamburgers and hot skinny French fries out of yellow plastic baskets—with squirts of ketchup from a red plastic container on the side. Well, *my* ketchup was on the side. I always squirted a mound of ketchup onto the side and dipped my French fries into it.

Ginny squirted *her* ketchup like so many marks of Zorro all over her French fries. I put extra salt and pepper on mine. She didn't. She liked onions on her hamburgers. I didn't. We had separate likes and dislikes. We went around and around. I don't know how we lasted as long as we did.

Elliot and the cute little Korean chick shuffled up behind us. What the hell was her name? Kim? Chee? Ting? Tang? Bing? Bang? I can't remember. She was sure cute, though— ripped up Levi's, a boy's white button-down dress shirt tied into a knot above her tiny waist, flat brown skinny stomach and a little slit of a belly button I wanted to lean over and stick my tongue into—and she *still* wasn't wearing a bra. This time there were big gaps between the buttons of her shirt. She had on a man's tie sort of half tied and half untied. It might have been one of the Roos-Atkins ties from Elliot's closet. She said she was a performance artist—like Yoko, she said.

The only concession Elliot had made to the fashion trends of the times was that he had a small jade rooster on a leather thong around his neck. Other than that he might have been shuffling down a hallway at Hillsdale High in his maroon and black striped shirt and dusty Wellington Boots.

Ginny and the Korean chick cocked their heads and said, "Hi."

She and Elliot pulled up a couple stools and sat between us, looking out the window. Nobody said anything for a while. Elliot took a couple of my fries. The Korean chick eyed Ginny's fries but didn't try to take any. Ginny and Elliot never quite made eye contact. They almost did, several times, but kept looking away.

Finally, Ginny looked at Elliot and said, "Gosh. It's been *aaa*ges!"

Elliot was always so *sheepish* around her, so shy. He twitched his lips into and out of a bunch of little half smiles, looked down and said, "Not that long."

The Korean chick frowned.

"So what about all this hippie horseshit?" I asked.

"It's a groove, man. I dig it," the Korean chick said.

"I think it's not going to last more than another couple months," Elliot said. "I think people are going to put a stop to it. I think there are going to be troop transport trucks in the streets firing tear gas canisters into crowds of so-called hippies. Walter Cronkite will give it ten minutes on the news."

"Who's it hurting?" the Korean chick asked.

"Our brave young soldiers fighting a war in Vietnam." He narrowed his eyes. "Our way of life, the Constitution of the United States, the fabric of society."

"Do you really think that?" Ginny asked.

"No. But not many people pay attention to what I think."

"I do." Ginny looked right into his eyes. "I think you probably know way more about it than any of us." She laughed then, and said, "Oh, dear," and covered her mouth with a handful of her hair.

"I think everything's going to just keep changing and changing and changing, despite what anyone thinks," I said.

"Like how?" the Korean chick asked.

"Like who the fuck knows, you know?" I shrugged.

"Okay," Ginny said. "Let's each say what we would see if we looked out this exact same window in, oh, I don't know, let's say thirty years from now."

"You'd see the same things you're seeing today," Elliot said.

"I think there won't *be* a street corner in thirty years," the Korean chick said in stupid-sounding earnestness. "I think there'll be a war. I don't know who it's going to be between, but it's going to be the last war. Humanity will be obliterated."

"I think the exact opposite," I said—possibly to give us something to talk about if the Korean chick and I ever ran into each other alone on the street. "I think people will be flying around in little one man helicopters—like on the Jetsons. I think there'll be plenty of everything for everyone—no police or racial strife or pestilence or war. I think it'll be like looking out at the cover of a *Watchtower Magazine.* Lions will be lying down with lambs, swords will be beaten into plowshares."

"I think Elliot's more realistic," Ginny said.

"Than me? Are you nuts?" I said.

"Yes," she said.

Everyone laughed. That was it. Elliot and the little Korean chick had somewhere to go. They went.

CHAPTER TWENTY-THREE

Golden Gate Park

*T*hen it was the summer of 1967, the Summer of Love. Scott McKenzie sang his dork song about how everybody ought to go to San Francisco and wear some fucking flowers in their hair. It was far out. It was groovy. It was over.

Then it was early October, the Fall of Love. Ha! All the hippies gave Haight Street a funeral. Ginny got her ass thrown in jail. The guards squirted mace in her face. The skin peeled away from around her eyes. She looked like a raccoon.

It all started out innocently enough. The three of us—Kirk, the preacher from Thulin's wedding, Ginny and I—were on our way home after a rock concert at Speedway Meadows. Ginny and Kirk were drinking champagne. It was on the verge of the Christmas season again. I was a little fed up. Officer Garrens was the cop who arrested her. He was a notorious asshole—*The Oracle* and *The Berkeley Barb* wrote articles about what a notorious asshole Officer Garrens was. I'm getting ahead of myself, however—as is my wont. I'll start from the beginning.

gg

It was early October, a warm, sunny Sunday afternoon. San Francisco's like that. The weather's crappy all summer, but it gets nice again in the fall. Ginny and I had gone our separate ways that morning. We frequently went our separate ways by then. Our promiscuity had taken its toll. It had always been okay for her to fuck other people. There were always mitigating circumstances—she was drunk, she was blacked out, she didn't know what she was doing—but it wasn't okay for me. It hurt her feelings. Things got sticky. We broke bonds we hadn't broken before.

I was out wandering among the waifs fresh in from Kansas City and Des Moines. They were mostly making their way in the general direction of a free rock concert in Golden Gate Park. The Grateful Dead were going to be there, along with Quicksilver Messenger Service—the Quick and the Dead. It was going to be far out. It was going to be groovy. It was going to be out of sight. Big Brother and The Airplane were going to be there—that meant Janis Joplin; that meant Grace Slick.

I went past the little knoll we used to call Hippie Hill. Black guys in sunglasses smoked Kools. They beat conga drums. Their cigarettes stuck to their lips. A Golden Retriever had on a red bandanna. A little hippie chick in granny glasses threw a stick for the Golden Retriever to chase through the purple haze of dope and patchouli oil that was rising up like the Jimi Hendrix song playing on the little hippie chick's little hippie radio.

In the flat meadow in front of the knoll, college kids in Bermuda shorts threw Frisbees with one hand and drank beer with the other. A German Shepard leaped at a bright disk whistling above him. Neighborhood mothers sat on benches in front of the adobe rest rooms and talked and smoked and knitted long, colorful afghans, always with one eye on the children—boys and girls in clean shirts and tiny dresses wandering in the sandy dirt next to the merry-go-round or playing on the playground.

A little girl in red pigtails was backed up against the steel steps of the big slide by a frisky black Cocker Spaniel who was trying to lick her Mary Jane's. His ears dragged in the dirt. She reached toward him, cautiously, courageously, almost touching his wet nose. The dog let out a couple of elongated yips and tore off sideways, low to the ground. The little girl was disappointed...and triumphant, too. Nobody saw—well, except for me. I saw. I wanted a kid, a little girl of my own. I wanted to hang out with her, to keep an eye on her, to see the things she saw.

Beyond the park, streaks of bright colored cars flashed through the thick branches of cedar trees and scraggly pines bordering Lincoln Way. I followed the blacktop path around Hippie Hill and over toward the tennis courts. My running shoes were yellow and black, the color of bumblebees. I walked along the path without making a sound. Next to the clubhouse, one of the tennis players was tying his shoe against the slats of a green bench. A chain link fence kept the dogs out and the tennis balls in.

I stayed on the path over another hill or two, toward the conservatory, until I came to a little lake in the middle of nowhere. The lake had palm trees and huge ferns and rhododendron bushes crowded around it. The water was so thick with algae it looked like you could walk on it. There were orange clay cliffs around the lake. The cliffs were held together by the root systems of trees. I wanted to see what the lake would look like from the rim of the canyon and made my way up a narrow path, pulling myself along by grabbing onto saplings and exposed roots until I got to a ledge formed by the base of a eucalyptus tree—and just sat there for a while.

The lake was so chock full of green algae it looked solid, like a giant lily pad. It looked like I could jump off the cliff and land harmlessly on the surface of the lake like it was a big green trampoline. I'd bounce up and fall onto it again and again, and the lily pad would keep me dry and suspended above the surface of the warm water while the waves I'd made rocked me gently, like I was in a cradle.

There wasn't a breath of air.

It felt good not to have taken any drugs. I hadn't even smoked a joint with Dick Joseph when he'd come over that morning. I wanted a clear head. I had thinking to do. I was trying to figure out a way to get rid of Ginny. I wanted to dump her. I wanted her to dump me. I was tired. Fed up. She was too much trouble. Too much? I didn't know. How much was too much? She was a lot of trouble, yeah, but was she more trouble than she was worth? That was the question. That's always the question. She was worth a lot. She needed me. I found her when she was lost. I rescued her. I rubbed her back and told her everything was going to be all right. If I dumped her, she'd kill herself. I didn't know what to do. She would die without me. I would die without her. But I was tired. Worn out. Fed up. We weren't *going* anywhere. We were dicking around. She was too much trouble.

I wanted to jump off the cliff and land harmlessly on the lily pad lake. I wanted it to rock me to sleep like I was a baby in a cradle. But I also knew that it really *wasn't* a lily pad. It was a lake—a cold, wet, stagnant pond, crawling with thick algae and slick, rotted palm fronds and dead rhododendron blossoms and frogs and snakes and bugs—and if I did jump off the cliff I'd end up stuck in muck up to my neck and covered with slithering slime until someone came along and pulled me out, which might not be for a long, long time.

Nothing stirred.

The soles of my shoes had made waffle shapes in the fine orange dust leading to the base of the tree I was sitting on. A fly landed in the treacherous hair of my arm. It crawled and hopped and finally made a harrowing escape over onto the knee of the Levi's I was wearing. I wore the same frayed Levi's almost every day. They were faded. They looked like the sky. I had on one of the old tie-dye T-shirts I used to wear most days too—the one that looked like a faded sunset.

More insects began to appear. They came from nowhere and everywhere—spiders and mosquitoes and bees and ants and green dragonflies, glinting in the sun. The longer I sat there, the better I blended with the roots of the tree, the more things got back to normal. I saw a gopher. It wrinkled its nose. Squirrels ratcheted at each other in the underbrush. Songbirds sang, oblivious now of the commotion I'd caused. They flitted from branch to branch, squabbling among themselves.

It was like I wasn't there. It reminded me of what Elliot had been talking about in the living room on California Street—what the world would be like without him in it. The same as it would be without me in it, I imagined. He'd been in Vietnam. I was in San Francisco. The sky was blue. The grass was green.

How *can* you remember not being somewhere?

GG

Down at the other end of the lake, I noticed a guy in a shelter made out of tree branches. It was so well camouflaged that I hadn't seen it at first. He had a beard and long, graying hair tied back out of his sunburned face by a chamois headband. He was smoking a joint by himself in the sun. He didn't seem to have seen me—or he didn't give a shit if he had. I liked that. The guy had found himself a place to live, a home to call his own. He was having himself a peaceful Sunday afternoon.

Then there was the sound of disembodied voices coming from the direction I'd come from. The voices kept getting louder. The canyon amplified sound. The voices were jarring. Birds stopped singing.

"It was your fucking idea," one of the voices said. "I didn't want to buy the bitch no god damn shoes in the first place."

"You got the son of a bitches, I didn't. Since when do you do what I say? It was worth it, though. Just for the look on her face. That was almost as good as the look on *your* face." The other voice burst into disturbing, unnatural, laughter.

"Oh, yeah, it's fucking funny all right. We got us a god damn pair of girl's shoes and no pussy. That's fucking funny all right."

The bodies of the voices came over the crest of the hill leading down toward the lake and the canyon. They were two guys around nineteen or so, both in white T-shirts with the sleeves rolled up and both with new crew cuts, the kind they might recently have gotten in the army.

The one who didn't think it was funny was tall and skinny and had a fresh tattoo on the side of one of his biceps. A jagged scar was visible under the close-cropped black hair on his scalp. His companion was skinny, too, but shorter and blond, with a bright ring of acne around the back of his neck and pimples pinpointing his face. The tall one threw the shoebox at him.

"Here, you keep the fuckers," he said.

"You weren't gonna get no pussy, no matter what you bought the bitch."

"My ass," said the tall one.

"Not her ass, though, that's for sure. No way, Jose—here, I don't want these fuckers." The short one threw the shoebox back at the tall one.

The two guys had walked to the far side of the lake by then. They came unexpectedly to where the hippie was sitting under the branches of his shelter. The three of them froze momentarily.

"Hey, Moses, how'ya doin'," the tall kid said, at last, rocking back on the heels of his shiny black army boots.

The hippie didn't respond.

"Moses in the bulrushes," the blond kid said.

"I said, how'ya doin', man," the tall one said.

The hippie looked up at them. His legs were folded under his torso, and his hands were in his lap, fingers joined together. "I'm doing fine, thanks," he said.

"Well, that's good. That's good. That's good to hear," said the tall guy, clasping his own hands. "Say, listen, partner. We're kind of new here and was wondering if you might know where we could get us some pussy? Some hippie chick, flower child who might want to fuck herself a couple United States Marines?"

"No, man, I don't know."

"We got these shoes she might like." The short guy laughed.

"Sorry."

"Sorry don't cut it, Jasper."

"Look. You boys really ought to just toddle on off about your business." The old hippie shooed them away like there was a swarm of gnats in his face.

"You look, *asshole*. We asked you a civil god damn question. Maybe you got yourself a little hippie chick stashed in them bulrushes. How about you trot her ass out here and we fuck her for you, one at a time. How would that be?"

"Yeah, one at a time, that'd be nice," said the short Marine.

The hippie stood up. He was muscular, sturdy, relaxed. "Okay, let's do this thing," he said. "You both going to jump me like chicken fuckers?"

"Hey, hold up a fucking minute, man." The tall Marine held up his hands. "What's this we heard about how all you long hair hippie pricks is such big peace lovers? You want to fight us now, is that it? Well, shit." He glanced at his partner, feigning disappointment. "We come out here wanting to do like they say on the radio, you know? Make love, not war. Fuck us a flower child for free, and look what we get—some asshole looking for a fight. Is that what you want, dipshit?"

"Tell you what, Baldy." The hippie reached into the grass and weeds by his feet and picked up a small machete. "How about you make love with this? How would that be?" He pointed the machete lazily at the tall Marine's chest, like he was maybe drawing his attention to an algebraic equation on a blackboard.

"Hey, man, there's no need..." the tall one said. The Marines backed up and turned around, tripping over their own feet and each other's feet, just as the hippie let out a yell like an Indian coming down the side of a hill on a pony.

He swooshed the machete over his head and lunged toward the Marines. They ran. As they were running, the tall Marine tossed the shoebox over his shoulder. It caught the hippie square in the chest. The box came apart. The shoes went in different directions and the tissue paper they'd been wrapped in floated gently onto a small flowering bush. The shoebox slowed the hippie down for a second, but he kept after them until the whole pageant vanished over the ridge and out of sight.

I heard their army boots for a while, clodhopping against the asphalt, getting further and further away, heard the diminishing war whoops of the old hippie still chasing them. I was hoping they might come back, so I could give them a round of applause. I had it all pictured. It would have been like a curtain call.

The Marines would roll down the sleeves of their T-shirts. The tall one would wipe the grease paint tattoo off his bicep, and the short one would remove the rouge that had made the acne look so realistic, and the hippie would bend so low to take a bow that his long gray wig would fall off, and he'd catch it in mid air and laugh, as though that too were part of the act. I would have given them a standing ovation. I would have whistled and stomped my feet in the dirt. But they didn't come back.

GG

I got up from where I'd been sitting, went over to the other side of the lake and looked inside the hippie's house. There were a couple of cans of Sterno and an aluminum frying pan on the floor. I picked up the shoes. The shoes were more along the line of bedroom slippers, actually. They had low heels and were covered with brocade cloth, which was covered with hundreds of tiny, different colored beads, mostly white and pink, but a few were amber, and one or two were purple, like amethysts. I looked inside. They were size 5 ½ B.

They were too big for Ginny, but I picked them up anyway. I got the tissue paper out of the flowering bush and put it into the box and put the slippers on top of it and covered them with the folded tissue paper like I used to do when I sold shoes. I was a born shoe salesman. I could do it again. I could get a job down at Macy's or Magnin's. It hadn't been bad. Chicks came in. I sat on my comfortable stool and helped them into new shoes with a silver shoehorn and told them they looked gorgeous.

What had been wrong with that? I'd been good at it. Selling shoes was in my blood. I'd made decent money. I could do it again. I could get a place to live—maybe back down around San Mateo. I could look up Bonnie. She was cute— she looked like Brigitte Bardot, for God's sake—and she'd been in love with me. Why I'd ever gone out on a date with Virginia Good, I did not know. That had been what fucked things up with Bonnie, right there. That first date with Ginny. Motherfuck. What more could I have asked for? Sure, Bonnie was stupid. Sure, she didn't know what the fuck I was talking about half the time, but so what? She wasn't a raving lunatic drunk. She didn't get her ass kidnapped nine times a day. She didn't go on bus trips with Kesey and Cassady and who knows who any time you had your back turned for more than five seconds. Tortured young Assistant Psychology Professors weren't forever knock, knock, knocking on her cute little door down in Fritz Perls's hot tubs at Esalen. She didn't hang out with rock-and-roll assholes. She didn't smash typewriters and break windows and gouge slices of skin out of my god damn back. She wouldn't have wanted to fuck my best friend. She didn't spend Christmases in insane asylums. She wouldn't have killed our kid.

Bonnie would have loved our kid. She would have cuddled and cradled and nurtured our kid—him or her, both of them, a boy and a girl, all our kids. She would have cooked and cleaned and made the bed and changed diapers. She would have gone to the grocery store with our kids strapped in the basket of the shopping cart—and she would have fucked my brains out at the drop of a hat, both because she loved to fuck and because she wanted to make more kids. And it wasn't too late! Bonnie wore a size 5 ½ B! I remembered that.

I could have taken that beat-up old shoebox down to San Mateo. I could have gone up to wherever Bonnie may have been living by then and simply have said, "Hi." She would have dropped everything she was doing, no matter what it was, and we would have lived happily ever after, Bonnie and me and our nine happy kids and their ninety-nine happy kids. But I didn't.

CHAPTER TWENTY-FOUR

Speedway Meadows

Back in the main part of the park, crowds of people were still heading toward the ocean, toward the muffled sound of music coming from the bands. When I got to a conspicuous place along the path, I put the shoebox down where someone would be sure to find it. Another path converged into the one I'd been on, and all of a sudden there was a cute little black chick in a pair of red cutoffs walking ahead of me.

Her hair was dyed amber-blond and cut in a short Afro. The cutoffs were as skimpy as they could be and still have had a crotch. There were calluses on the backs of her heels. The skin of her calves glistened in the sun clear up to where her ass disappeared under the frayed cutoffs. If I dumped Ginny, there were plenty of other chicks around. There were plenty of other guys, too. We wouldn't die without each other. None of them was her, however; none of them was me. The only way you ever know what's going to happen if you do something or don't do something is to do it or don't do it and see what happens or what doesn't happen.

I turned onto a trail that led through the bushes. The black chick kept heading toward the ocean. I walked and walked. The trail came out by the buffalo paddock. Except for one of the calves, the buffalo were far away under their trees, munching on a broken bale of hay in the dirt around their shelter. The calf was scratching itself against the rough bark of a scrub oak by the fence. Its coat was half growing in for the winter and still half falling out from the summer. It looked hot and itchy and miserable and prickly. It stuck out its tongue and moaned. Its tongue was thick and purple and cracked—the way Ginny's got when she drank too much red wine. Maybe I'd see her through one more Christmas. Who else could? Nobody. Fuck.

The music kept getting louder—guitars, feedback, amplifiers—a woman was singing. It sounded like Janis Joplin. Through the foliage I could see thousands of people fanned out in front of the makeshift bandstand. I cut through some bushes and ended up behind the stage. It *was* Janis Joplin. Guys from other rock groups were lying in the grass, waiting, resting, talking to women, picking at the strings of guitars that weren't plugged in. There was a tangle of cable and wires that hooked the sound equipment together under the stage.

It all looked like a giant mess to me, everything hanging in great loops and knots under the planks of the platform. I had no idea how people ever got it put together in a way that made sense, and I especially didn't see how they ever got it taken apart again—but they did, they must have, there were always concerts again next week. I felt lighter, freer, relieved, encouraged. Things would figure themselves out.

Speakers throbbed. My eardrums throbbed along with them like we were all plugged into the same sound system through which Janis was wailing a little piece of her heart out.

The music shook into me from the ground up and made my dick tingle, like my legs were a big tuning fork.

I knew some of the musicians from Thulin or Ginny or Brenda. I didn't hang out with them—mainly because I didn't much care for the scruffy motherfuckers—but some of them had been over at the apartment on Shrader Street to buy drugs or to sell drugs or just to get loaded. They nodded at me and nodded among themselves and sometimes just nodded. Nobody knew anyone's name.

A couple hundred yards out beyond the platform, Speedway Meadows was wall-to-wall people moving like a big, colorful, symbiotic extension of the band, like a time-lapse garden of wildflowers opening up in the morning sun. Farther out, the crowd thinned into smaller groups sitting on blankets.

I started making my way back home. I still had some thinking to do. I picked my way through the crowd, touching people inadvertently. People smiled at me. I didn't smile back. They danced around me, breathed on me. I was jostled, toasted with wine, stepped on, ignored, excused, forgiven. The people in the crowd were from all over the place—some kid's madras shirt with the sleeves torn off had come from the J. C. Penney's in Yankton, North Dakota; the chick with horn-rimmed glasses and thick braids got her tire-tread Mexican sandals off a street vendor in Brooklyn.

I came to an area where the crowd had formed a circle around a woman who was dancing obliviously, all by herself. She was wearing a thin, faded, blue and white pioneer dress. I could see her breasts through the loose armholes. Her hair was long and straight and streaked lighter and darker shades of blond. The sun on her throat made her look vulnerable.

Sweat glistened on her forehead. Blades of grass poked up between her long, narrow toes. She didn't shave her legs.

Janis Joplin stopped singing. Silent, twangy reverberations from the sound system hung in the air for about a tenth of a second, then people screamed and yelled and clapped their hands, and the dancing chick fell into a heap of arms and legs and blond hair and faded blue fabric on the bright green grass.

Way at the back of the crowd, Ginny was sitting on a blanket with Kirk. They were drinking wine and talking about Nepal. He and Ginny had the hots for each other but hadn't done anything about it yet—usually she got drunk first. I sat on the edge of their blanket. The concert was over. People were dispersing. Fog was coming in from off the ocean. The wind had begun to blow. Leaves were falling.

"Let's get a bottle of champagne," Ginny said, like it was an unusually brilliant idea—a new idea, something she'd never thought of before.

"Sounds cool," Kirk said.

So we did that. Ginny and Kirk and I cut over to a liquor store behind Kezar Stadium and got a bottle of champagne and a couple of plastic champagne glasses. Ginny and Kirk were yucking it up, charming the pants off each other. I'd seen it too many times, but it was all so new to Kirk. He was enthralled. He'd forgotten everything he'd learned over in Tibet and Nepal and India, and all he wanted out of life from then on was to fuck Ginny. I'd seen that too many times, too.

𝓖𝓖

By the time we got to Stanyan Street, the champagne bottle was empty. We turned the corner onto Haight and were just about to the bowling alley. Ginny still had a little champagne left in her glass. It was dark by then. Fog diffused the light coming from street lamps. Two cops were walking toward us. One of them was swinging a nightstick. They were smiling, chatting, talking cop talk. Ginny laughed.

"What's funny?" one of the cops asked.

"Oh, I don't know. Just cops, I guess." Ginny shrugged and got that impish, Pied Piper of Cops look in her eye.

"Yeah?" the cop swinging the stick said. "We were just thinking the same thing about you long hair hippie freaks."

"How fortuitous that we're able to entertain one another," Ginny said.

"Ain't it though? You got some ID?"

"What for?"

"Just show me some ID."

"How's this?" Ginny gently flipped him off.

"That's not good enough. Diver's license, please."

"I don't have a driver's license. I'm not driving."

"How'd you like me to run you down to the station?"

"How'd you like my father's lawyer to sue your ass for harassment?"

It was an offhand remark. She sidestepped the cop standing directly in front of her and kept walking. Kirk and I walked around the other cop. When the three of us were safely past the cops, Ginny turned around and tossed the last few drops of champagne toward them. None of it actually got on either of them, but that was that, she had assaulted a police officer. She was under arrest.

Kirk ducked into the bowling alley. I reasoned with the cops. I told them she didn't mean anything, that she had a thing about cops. She was working on it. She was seeing a psychiatrist. "She's legally nuts," I told them.

"I don't think there is such a thing," said the cop with the nightstick.

"Hey, if you don't believe me, call her shrink," I said.

The cops looked at each other. Then, to my astonishment, they agreed to talk to her psychiatrist, like "legally nuts" might have been something they'd vaguely heard about in cop school.

Ginny and I got into the back of the police car. Officer Garrens was sitting in the passenger seat. He stretched his arm across the back of the front seat, turned sideways, readjusted his girth, looked straight at Ginny, and asked her in a calm, informative, lighthearted, jovial tone of voice, "You know what happens to little hippie chicks when they go to jail, don't you?"

"They get raped by fat ugly fucks like you?"

"Hey, you're quite the little spitfire, aren't you?"

"Suck my dick," Ginny said.

"First you get strip-searched. We take off your clothes and check your *orifices* for contraband. Then we have to hose you down to get rid of the lice and the bed bugs, and you get put into a holding tank with junkies and drunk street whores puking their guts out. There are snakes on the floor, bugs, cockroaches big as my thumb. All kinds of pesky little critters creep and crawl and slither around on the naked shivering bodies of smart-mouth hippie chicks who get their butts tossed in the can."

To give him the benefit of the doubt, Officer Garrens may just have been trying to steer Ginny away from a life of crime, but I doubt it.

The cop who was driving stopped in front of our apartment building and left the red and blue lights spinning silently on the police cruiser while the four of us went inside. I dialed Dr. Crockett's number and got the answering service. I knew I'd get the service, but it was an emergency. They'd track him down.

"I have to go potty," Ginny said.

"Hold it," Officer Garrens said.

Ginny crinkled up her nose and frowned and said, "You big meanie." She was a little unsteady on her feet. Then she said, in a more forceful tone, "I'm going to go potty *now*," and took a couple steps down the hall.

Officer Garrens grabbed her arm. "Hang on there, missy."

"Don't touch me." Ginny pulled her arm away.

Dr. Crockett came on the line. "Okay, I've got her shrink on the phone." I covered the mouthpiece. "He wants to talk to whoever's in charge."

"Tell this jerk cop to get his hands *off* me," Ginny called across the room.

"Nobody's got their hands anywhere," the other cop said and took the phone.

"Tell him I'm going to the bathroom," Ginny said and turned on her heel and started to march down the hallway again.

Officer Garrens grabbed a handful of her hair and yanked her back.

"Ow," Ginny said. Then she wheeled around and slugged Officer Garrens square in the jaw and brought her knee up into his crotch, and when he bent over from the pain, Ginny butted her forehead into the bridge of his nose. He made a sound like a moose and started sinking toward the floor.

I heard gurgling somewhere deep in Officer Garrens's throat. Ginny kicked him in the leg, just below the knee. Then she tried to kick him in the throat and in the head and to kick his red, huffing and puffing face, but the other cop was pulling her away by then. The three of them ended up in a pile on the floor.

The other cop managed to get his handcuffs clicked around Ginny's wrists, but her feet were still free. She kicked without aiming. She kicked and screamed while they were dragging her out the door of the apartment, and she kicked and screamed all the way through the long hallway, and she kicked and screamed as she was being yanked through the front door of the apartment building.

Out on the stoop, she caught her foot between the iron bars of one of the railings and lost a shoe when the cop twisted her leg loose. Officer Garrens had a towel over his nose by then and wasn't helping much. I saw Ginny's head hit against the doorframe of the police car when the cop finally managed to get her pushed through the door, but she didn't seem to take much notice. She kicked at the screen between her and the front seat. Every time she kicked the screen with the foot with the missing shoe, Ginny let out a yell. It hurt. You could tell. But that didn't stop her from kicking the screen again and again.

𝓖 𝓖

The next day I met Ginny's father's lawyer by the elevator at the Hall of Justice. He was a businesslike Boalt Hall kind of guy, fifty-five or so, getting ready to retire. When we got off the elevator at the jail, he went to the counter and filled out paperwork and after awhile, Ginny came out.

Blood had soaked through gauze taped over her upper left arm. Her hair was matted. Her face was splotchy under the fluorescent lights. She had an Ace Bandage around her right ankle. She couldn't see very well. The skin had peeled away from around her eyes. She looked like a raccoon.

"You look like a raccoon," I said.

"Thank you, dahling," she said in that brave, shaky, embarrassed, ironic tone of voice she used when she was getting out of one of the scrapes she'd gotten herself into. "I feel like Oedipus."

"You don't look like Oedipus," I said and smiled.

"I thought I was blind. I *was* blind! Then I could see— amazing."

"What happened?"

"I'd like to hear that myself," the lawyer said. "We might have a problem. The cop you kicked is in the hospital."

"I kicked a cop? Good," Ginny said.

"His nose is broken. There may be other serious injuries. I need to know whatever mitigating circumstances there may have…" Then the lawyer looked at her carefully for the first time and said, "My God, Ginny. What happened to your face?"

"The guards at the jail did it. They kept calling me over to the bars, then kept squirting mace in my face, right into my eyes. 'Come here, little girl, we've got something *nice* for you.' Squirt, squirt. They thought it was hilarious."

"How long did they do that?" the lawyer asked.

"For *aaa*ges and *aaa*ges." Ginny's eyes grew wider and wider.

"We need to get you to a doctor," the lawyer said.

* 𝒢 𝒢 *

Her father's lawyer got Ginny off on the assault charge. Then he sued the City and County of San Francisco for police brutality—or rather, to be precisely accurate, he counter-sued the City's suit against her for kicking the cop. The lawsuit went on for years. I had to have my deposition taken.

The main thing the City Attorney wanted to know was how many times I'd taken LSD. I couldn't give him an exact figure. Then he asked me what color my jacket was. I told him it was green. He said it looked more like brown to him. I looked down at one of the sleeves of my jacket and could distinguish fibers of both brown and green, along with some orange fibers and black fibers and even a few red fibers. I told him maybe he ought to take a sample of the fabric and send it to the FBI to see if they could tell him what the hell color it was. It looked green to me.

Eventually, the city settled the lawsuit. They didn't like their chances with a jury. Officer Garrens was a big son of a bitch. Ginny was barely five feet tall and had never weighed more than a hundred and four pounds in her life. The settlement money didn't quite cover attorney fees.

CHAPTER TWENTY-FIVE

Kentfield

$\mathscr{G}$inny's run-in with the cops and the ongoing lawsuit took some of the steam out of the Christmas of 1967. By her standards, it wasn't all that bad, just a scrape or two, a single abduction by a young black cab driver and a lame suicide attempt inspired by a Maxfield Parrish painting and a sudden feeling of kinship with Ophelia—she waded out into the little duck pond across from the Portals of the Past in Golden Gate Park, covered herself up with handfuls of vegetation and lay down onto her back in the shallow water, but didn't manage to drown.

She got a degree in psychology from San Francisco State in the spring. She was still short a few credits, but her father's lawyer got the school to give her the thing anyway. Her father sent her a note saying that he was proud of her.

Toward the end of the summer of 1968, we gave up the apartment on Shrader Street. Tom Piper was working as an engineer and had moved up to Marin County. Haight Street had turned into nothing but junkies and speed freaks. Everyone was moving up to Marin County by then. Tom had a house by a river in San Anselmo. Ginny wanted to live in a house by a river. Tom was glad to have her. Their relation-ship was still Platonic. He thought this was his big chance.

I stayed at Elliot's place in the city for a while, then Elliot and I rented a house together in Marin County ourselves, just the two of us. The house was in Kentfield. The backyard went clear up to the top of Mt. Tamalpias. There was a cement fishpond in the front yard.

The only reason Elliot and I could afford to live there was that the house was a wreck. *The Independent Journal* advertised it as a "Handyman Special." It needed things like a new founda-tion, rewiring and the plumbing replaced, but the first thing Elliot and I fixed up was the fishpond. It was full of dirt. It hadn't been used in twenty years. Ginny found the fishpond for us. We didn't know it was even a fishpond. We thought it was dirt. Once Elliot and I moved to Marin, Ginny spent most of her time over at our house. Poor Tom Piper, he was pissed.

After Ginny found the fishpond, the three of us went to work. We dug the dirt out of it and patched the cracks in the cement and painted it blue and filled it with water and put in a bunch of goldfish—brown goldfish, orange goldfish, black goldfish, Creamsicle goldfish, spotted goldfish, you name it.

Elliot got some old rusted wrought-iron chairs from his mother. We cleaned them and sanded them, and Elliot got a long extension cord for his compressor and airbrushed them a pretty shade of grayish-white, and we settled back in our wrought iron chairs around our freshly refurbished fishpond. We may not have had any wiring or sewer pipes, and some of the faucets might have dripped a little, but we sure had a hell of a place to sit around and wonder how we were going to *get* wiring and faucets that didn't drip.

⁂ GG ⁂

It was quiet out there. We didn't talk much. There wasn't a lot to say. Elliot was still in love with Ginny. She still knew it. We all still knew it. We all still pretended not to notice. Robins hopped around under the bushes. A Monarch butterfly fluttered from one rotting calla lily to another.

One of the fish was biting at the top of the water. They were just ordinary goldfish. One of them died now and then. The rest of them ate it. We found stringy orange carcasses lapping up against the powder blue shore. The fish biting the air was one of those bulbous, raisin colored things with flowing, useless fins.

The surface of the water reflected branches of the huge pine tree in the front yard. There were puffy clouds crawling across the sky. Ginny tossed a stone at the fish biting the surface of the water. The pond rippled. The clouds got jumbled up. The branches of the pine tree shimmered like a mirage. The goldfish all dove to the bottom of the pond, stabilizing themselves with their tails, taking lazy gulps of water.

"Why'd you do that?" Elliot asked.

"I hate that bug-eyed fucker. He keeps chasing Ondine."

"Who's Ondine?"

"The pretty orange and white one."

She'd named them all. Genghis Kahn. Ondine. Willow. Heloise. Abelard. Sri Ramakrishna. Semolina Pilchard. Mowgli. Raskolnikov. I forget the rest. There were about fourteen all together. Some were friends. Others were bitter enemies. A few didn't take sides.

Elliot and I got to be friends again. He tried to teach me how to paint. I was hopeless. He tried to show me how to use an airbrush. I was more hopeless. He tried to get me to dance like a flamenco dancer while he played his guitar. I laughed. Ginny danced like a flamenco dancer for him. He tried to teach me all kinds of things. I was as much a novice as he was a genius at everything he tried to teach me.

We had long philosophical conversations. He was still a pacifist. He asked me once if I had any idea how many living things nobody could even see—dust mites in the carpet, frail, sharp-nosed creatures clinging to grains of pollen the relative size of hot air balloons, infinitesimal little rhinoceros-looking things that spent their lives carting flakes of dead skin off the sheets at night. According to Elliot it was impossible to calculate the number of sentient organisms that got sucked into oblivion every time some insensitive brute took it upon himself to breathe.

"Half of all life on Earth's invisible," Elliot said.

"You're full of shit," I told him.

"Why?"

"Why you're full of shit? I have no idea."

"In what way, then, am I full of shit?"

"You want examples? Okay. In the first place, if you take it to its logical conclusion, everything's invisible. I mean, all anything's made out of is cells and molecules and atoms and electrons and stuff nobody can see, right? So that blows your whole theory right there. How can half of anything be invisible if everything is?

"And what makes you think anything's even alive to begin with? You think you're alive? Or me? You think I'm alive? Or some dust mite? How can that be? Because you think we are? If everything's nothing but inanimate atoms, what makes life? Tell me that. Do you know? No. Are atoms alive?

Name me one atom that's even partly alive. Nickel? Cad-
mium? Boron? That's what makes life such a big fucking
mystery—nobody can figure it out—and anyone who thinks
he can is full of shit. That's the definition. Thinking you
know anything means you're full of shit."

"Yeah?"

"Yeah."

"And where, exactly, did you learn all this?"

"From taking acid."

Elliot hadn't ever taken LSD. I had. Ha!

* 𝑔 𝑔 *

Ginny thrived over at our house. She was in her element.
Perpetual adoration. Elliot doted on her. She dug it. Elliot
sprayed urethane foam all over the walls and ceiling of one of
the upstairs bedrooms for her. It was Ginny's Room. She
kept her latest shrine there. He airbrushed the foam to make
the room look like she was in a tree. She said she felt like a
bird when she walked in the door. Like she could fly if she
wanted to. It didn't last, but the three of us liked being there
together.

I was working at a job as a vault teller in the city, on Montgomery Street, at the main branch of the Bank of America. By
the beginning of fall, Ginny and Elliot were alone with each
other all day. I didn't get home until after dark. She lounged
around half naked and told him nonsense stories while he
painted pictures of her.

One thing *didn't* lead to another. The pictures weren't rep-
resentational. The last thing they looked like was Ginny, but
they made you feel how he felt about her. He loved her. He

was in love with her. Why they never just fucked and got it the hell over with, I have no idea—out of consideration for me, I suppose, but that just made it worse. It was achingly romantic. He was Lancelot; she was Guinevere.

When I got off work, the bus let me out by the 7-Eleven on Sir Francis Drake. After you got past the smell of exhaust and the blink of neon from the highway, the street sloped down into what used to be a narrow, grassy meadow, back before civilization took over. Sometimes at night it seemed to get that way again. I imagined what it must have been like to be one of the coastal Indians who used to live there, taking refuge in the hollow of a dead redwood, peering up at the same incomprehensible shawl of stars. There was a street light every so often now, sure, and the road was paved and there was that stop sign at Madrone, but if you really put your mind to it you could still feel how it might have been to have been an Indian living in our little valley before civilization took over.

I remember walking home one night. It must have been November. It was cold. It was getting close to Christmas again. I wasn't thinking about being an Indian. I was watching my feet step on shadows of themselves. When I got directly under each of the streetlights, my shadow would disappear and a new shadow would grow out in front of me again. I heard a faint scream—probably from some TV. Then I heard a pretty good-sized pane of glass break and heard another scream, a louder scream. It sounded like Ginny. It was. Fuck.

I ran the rest of the way down to the house, crashed through the side door, ran up the back stairs, through the kitchen and into the living room. Elliot was sitting on top of

Ginny. He had her arms pinned to the floor with his knees and was trying to cover her mouth. His hand was bloody from where she'd bitten him. He looked up at me. He was scared. He wasn't acting. His cheek twitched. His mouth trembled. There were tears in his eyes. I didn't laugh. The living room window was shattered.

"Could you do this?" Elliot asked.

"Sure."

We traded places. I sat on Ginny while he tended to his hand. I didn't ask what had happened. It didn't matter. She was drunk. I was used to it. Elliot wasn't. That was the one thing I was always better at than Elliot—taking care of Ginny when she went nuts. I was a genius at taking care of Ginny when she went nuts.

* 𝓖 𝓖 *

Elliot and I had to move. It was the beginning of my fifth and final Christmas with Virginia Good. We all went our separate ways. Ginny stayed at Tom's place in San Anselmo. Elliot went to his mother's new house. I moved back to San Francisco, into a studio apartment on Central, across the Panhandle from where my newly married sister, Nicki, and her husband, Murph, were living on Fell Street. He'd settled down some since he used to hang out with Thulin and Ralph Wood.

Ginny still came over to my apartment a lot. It was well into December. It was probably my fault. I should have known better. We went over to Nicki and Murph's apartment one night. They had their Christmas tree up. There were lights everywhere and presents under the tree and Christmas cards on the mantle. Bing Crosby was singing Christmas songs. Their newborn baby boy, Myles Cadet Murphy, was asleep in his bassinet in their bedroom. Ginny got drunk and tried to fuck Murph on the living room floor in front of my sister and me.

I shouldn't have taken her over there. I knew how she got. Of course it was my fault. What the hell was I thinking? Nicki was sitting on the couch with a glass of wine in her hand, watching very closely as Ginny climbed into her husband's lap. Nicki never liked Ginny much to begin with. Most women didn't think much of Ginny. Some women liked her—Brenda and Mary had—but most women didn't.

Murph was cute about it. He frowned and shook his head and screwed up the corner of his mouth and raised his eyebrows and laughed uncomfortably while she put her arms around his neck and squirmed in his lap. Nicki looked at me. I was sitting across the room in an armchair. She looked back down at Ginny and her husband on the floor between us and looked at me again.

I shrugged.

She shrugged.

Nicki and I both felt sorry for Murph. He didn't know what to do. I got up, took Ginny by the arm, pulled her off Murph's lap. "Come on, we're going," I said.

"No. I need to know what he wants," Ginny said. "He needs to know."

"I don't need to know shit," Murph said. "I know everything I want to know."

"No. You don't. You need to know what you want."

"And you know what that is?" Nicki asked. Then she laughed. Then she frowned. Then she screwed up the side of her mouth and shook her head.

"I do. He knows, too. Murph knows. Don't you, Murph? Don't you?"

"Ginny. Shut the fuck up," I said.

I was pissed. Finally pissed. Permanently pissed. Fed up. Tired. Bored. I can't explain it. I'm not even going to try. It wasn't emotional in the least. It was factual. Enough was enough. Watching Ginny with Murph was the last straw. She was nothing but a drunk. You see drunks on the street. They come up to you in bars. They're boring. They're stupid. Nothing they do or say has any meaning. It doesn't matter whether they live or die—and suddenly somehow that was it.

I don't know what else she said. I don't know what else I said. Ginny eventually took off with a couple of Mexican garbage men at around five in the morning. The last I saw of her, she was on the running board of a Sunset Scavenger Service truck. I didn't care. I didn't want anything to do with any of it anymore, period, and went up to my parents' house in Oregon again.

Tom Piper got to handle the rest of Christmas that year. He thought he was up to it. He wasn't. Here's the second to last letter I still have. It doesn't have a date, but this one had to have been from sometime around Christmas of 1968:

Gerry: I am in a hospital—and have been for three days. But not me—a ream of identities all using this body. I have some kind of brain damage. The experiences have been HUGE—from deepest despair to laughter—never really happy though. I'm too sick. I must see you. And Elliot. You both I saw during "various" stages of minds and you are both quite different than ordinary humans. I am being fed through the arm by a bottle and through the fanny with something they put in. Before I had my last 2 pills I was a MESS MESS MESS and wanted to die. The pain was unendurable in my head and tum. I couldn't move and gagged which broke my head apart. OH I must tell you how it happened. Tom did it.. He hit me perfectly and I fell and broke something in my spine. I stayed home and was strange but quiet...no drinking...so drinking doesn't have anything to do with this one—finally I just fell in a swoon and went potty all over myself. He took me to Kaiser emergency where the doctors found blood in my spinal column and put me in ambulances for the city where I am now. They will do an EEG when I am well enough. (Damn—that's when they stick millions of pins in your skull and make you sit there forever.) Are you surprised at all this? I have no idea when I'll be plopped into a bramble of pain and other worlds again. Last night they had to make me naked and put ICE towels all over me to bring the fever down. It was AWFUL. ICKY. Now I feel OK except for a headache which is continual but less. There is something physically wrong in my head. I am SO weird from one minute to the next. WHERE ARE YOU? COME! I seriously may really KILL myself. That's all. Tom will mail this...bye...it's late.

Along with the letter, Tom Piper enclosed this note:

She's in the Kaiser Hospital on Geary Street. I didn't hit her. I threw her away from me. The doctor found blood in her spinal fluid from a probable burst blood vessel around the brain. They are keeping her in the hospital because the tests that they would have to make in order to know exactly what is wrong are quite painful and they can achieve the same result by merely keeping her under close observation. She has a temperature of 102. They are doing things to lower it. She has had a powerful headache continually since the fall. She is mentally confused frequently. The doctor said tonight that they would probably do another spinal tap Friday to see if she needs to remain in the hospital until some-time next week.

CHAPTER TWENTY-SIX

Cole Street

By the spring of 1969, I had recuperated up in Oregon long enough to have another go at San Francisco. I got a job at the phone company on New Montgomery Street. That was where I met Melanie. She'd had a kid when she was fifteen, a daughter, Wendy. Wendy had just turned four. Melanie and Wendy were living out in the Mission with a redheaded brick-layer named Dick. Wendy's real father was long gone. So were a bunch of other guys by then.

Melanie and I were alone in one of the elevators a week or so after I'd started working there. I'd noticed her before. She was cute...and shy—uncomfortable, maybe. I couldn't tell. She kept to herself. She didn't seem to have any friends. She had on a shiny green blouse, a short red skirt and a pair of red and green earrings and kept her head down.

"You look like a Christmas present," I said.

She glanced up briefly, looked into my eyes, and looked down again, all so quickly I wasn't sure I'd really seen her smile, but I had. I can still see it anytime I want—her slow, smoldery smile, her big shy eyes.

ɠ ɠ

The next day we walked up to Chinatown together. She had on a gray cotton dress. Some old Chinese guys were playing checkers under a cement pavilion in Portsmouth Square. Some other old Chinese guys were doing Tai Chi on the lawn. Kids jumped on and off the merry-go-round. We got a couple of hot dogs and found ourselves a cement bench to sit on.

Melanie treated everything she touched as though it got its feelings hurt as easily as she did. She let the hot dog bun melt in her mouth awhile before she nudged her teeth through it and bit into its tender, fragile skin. Then she chewed slowly, moving the bite of hot dog and bun gently up and down inside the warm pink walls of her pretty chipmunk cheeks. I was wearing a pair of thin cotton khaki slacks, without any underwear. My dick stirred. She might have noticed.

Nothing ever got very verbal with Melanie. Why talk about things you can just *do*? Ginny, on the other hand, holy shit, she thought there was no point doing stuff you could just *talk* about. They were as different from one another as two people could get. Ginny was hard. Melanie was soft. Ginny had a tiny mouth; Melanie's mouth was wide and slow and luscious. She wore thick, creamy, red lipstick. Ginny thought makeup was silly and stupid and bourgeois. Her eyes were small and piercing and luminous and blue. Melanie's eyes were huge and warm and green and gray and swallowed you up in comfort and generosity and hospitality. She thought one thing at a time and got nervous when she had to talk, and when she did talk, Melanie got straight to the point. Ginny always double-edge sworded everything; for every good there was a bad—she never just flat out, unequivocally did or said or even *thought* the tiniest little two-bit thing. Melanie was immediate, direct, uncomplicated.

"Is that a birthmark?" I brushed a small discoloration on the inside of Melanie's thigh. She was wearing sheer white tights. Her dress had a prim, white lace collar.

She looked right into my eyes. Her innocence scared me. Then she reached over and deliberately folded her fingers gently over my not quite yet completely throbbing dick.

On our way back to work, I put my arm around her shoulders. She reached back, slipped her hand across the back of her neck, gently lifted her hair out from under my arm and let it rest more comfortably *over* my arm—and wow was her hair ever pretty, glinting all red and gold and chestnut in the sun.

* 𝒢 𝒢 *

Melanie and I met up at a Laundromat out in the Mission after work the next night. It was Friday. Dick the bricklayer was away for an obligatory weekend in the Army Reserves. I gave Wendy sticks of Juicy-Fruit gum and lit books of matches for her to blow out while her mother took the clothes out of the dryer. We went upstairs. Melanie folded laundry. Wendy spit in my face. Her spit tasted like Juicy-Fruit gum.

"Ooo, that feels good," I said.

Wendy spit in my face again. She wasn't being playful. She was spitting in my face because she didn't want me there. I didn't blame her. I shouldn't have been there. Here they were, this nice little family, a mommy and a daddy and a little girl. What was *I* doing there? I wanted to fuck Melanie, yeah, but that was about it.

And what, for that matter, did Melanie want me over there for? She wanted to fuck me, too, I presumed, but there had to be more to it than that. She probably wanted me to fall utterly in love with her forever. I didn't want to do that. I was still in love with Ginny, for one thing. Yeah, I was fed up with her. She was a drunk. She was nuts, she drove *me* nuts—but that didn't diminish the fact that I was in love with her. What's being fed up with someone ever had to do with being in love?

Wendy spit in my face again, and suddenly all the second thoughts I was having vanished. Hey, spit in my face all you want, kid—I'm going to stay here and fuck your mother whether anyone likes it or not. Ha! Eventually, Wendy got tired of spitting at me—or maybe she just ran out of spit—and fell asleep on the bed. Melanie scooped her up and laid her down onto a little mattress in the walk-in closet and covered her with blankets.

Melanie and I touched each other's faces. I put my hand under her pretty hair, and rubbed the back of her neck, and she put her arms around me and we kissed each other and held each other and took off our clothes and made love with each other for a long time next to piles of folded clothes still slightly warm from the dryer.

In the early, early morning, crouched next to a window across the room, Melanie was looking out at the orange sun coming up over the rooftops. She was smoking a cigarette. She smoked lots of cigarettes. True cigarettes. True Blues. She smoked cigarettes and chewed the skin around her fingernails and rested her chin on her knees and wound her hair around one of her fingers, looking for split ends.

Wendy was sound asleep. She was snoring. Her tangled blond hair covered her pillow. Her left arm was cuddled around an inflatable Easter bunny with buckteeth, a big smile and a wink in one of his bright blue eyes. There were empty gum wrappers everywhere.

I was picking up one of the gum wrappers when Dick came home. He just walked right in the front door like he lived there. His weekend in the Army Reserves had ended early. I didn't say anything to him. He didn't say anything to me. He knew it wasn't my fault that I was there. I put my clothes on and left.

I didn't find out until later what happened after I was gone. First he threw some of Melanie's clothes out the window. Then he slapped her. Then he pulled her hair and slapped her again. Then he closed the door to the walk-in closet where Wendy was sleeping and fucked Melanie on the floor until her knees bled and turned her over and fucked her until she had rug burns on her shoulder blades.

Jealousy's an aphrodisiac. Melanie didn't resist. She didn't say a word. She let him fuck her until her knees bled and let him turn her over and fuck her until she had rug burns on her shoulder blades, and when he was through they knew it was over, and he was sad, and she wasn't, and that was that.

* 𝒢 𝒢 *

The next day Melanie called me from a pay phone, and I picked her and Wendy up in a rented car. They were standing in front of the Shell station on the corner of 20th and Valencia. Wendy was dragging her inflatable Easter Bunny by one of its inflatable ears. Melanie had a suitcase and a black eye and a cut lip.

I was living in a house with a bunch of other people over by Eighth Avenue and Clement. Melanie and Wendy stayed there with me for a few days, then the three of us got an apartment on Cole Street, not far from Ginny's place on Clayton. It had been five years—almost exactly to the day—since I put one of my mother's fancy teacups into a bag, took a bus up to Haight-Ashbury and rescued Ginny Good from Jim Moss.

After a while I was in love with Melanie—not utterly, but I definitely liked her a lot. She was an oasis. A sanitarium. Somewhere I could go to keep getting over Ginny. I had to get over Ginny. It was all very logical. She was nuts. She was a drunk. So what if I was in love with her, I had to get over being in love with her. Melanie would come in handy. She could absorb me, distract me, love me, like me, fuck me, laugh at my jokes. That was what I had in mind.

What Melanie had in mind was a lot more clear-cut. Things were either yes or no with her, on or off, true or not true. She was either in love or she wasn't. There were no two ways about it. And she was in love with me. Suddenly. Just like that. Boom. She couldn't help herself. It just happened. Nobody analyzed it. I had a job. I was good with the kid. It was obvious I liked her. I listened to her. I talked to her. I was interested in how she got to be who she was and loved that she was in love with me. That was the only thing that ever mattered to Melanie. Being in love—what it felt like, how it made her feel. All she wanted was to show me how much in love with me she was; all she wanted was to fuck and fuck and fuck.

She was good, too—really good. She'd had years of unabashed practice, years of experimentation with all sorts of different guys with all sorts of different ideas about what it took to be a good fuck, and Melanie had picked up something from each of them—wow, was she ever a good fuck.

Melanie had just turned fourteen when she used to wait outside the W. T. Grant Store in Citrus Heights for Wendy's father to come along on his motorcycle and take her to the fields by the river to fuck. She fucked him among the thistles and the whirring of flying grasshoppers while they listened to the rippling of the river. There were other men after Wendy's father—short-term guys, long-term guys, smart guys, dumb guys, nice guys, assholes—anyone who really wanted her could have her.

Melanie *wasn't* like a four-year-old kid. She didn't need anybody to be the Daddy. She didn't need to be drunk. She was a pretty little nineteen-year-old with big, serious eyes who, if she knew anything, sure knew how to fuck—and she was in love with me! On top of all that, she loved to take acid. There was nothing in the world Melanie liked better than to take LSD and fuck. That was all we did. You want to go to the movies? No, let's take acid and fuck. She didn't even say it. She didn't have to say it. LSD was an aphrodisiac. Love was an aphrodisiac. We wore ourselves out.

And it was working. I was getting over Ginny. Sure, I missed her. I missed how we used to be together. How she used to hide. How I used to find her. How I knew what to do when she went nuts, how she needed me, how she taught me everything I knew, everything I know, how fun we were with each other, how funny. But I also had Wendy, and Wendy wasn't *like* a four-year-old kid, she *was* a four-year-old kid. Ha!

We dug each other, Wendy and me. We galloped down the sides of sand dunes like horses and found sea shells on the beach and watched the sun set and watched the sky turn all purple and pink from one side of the horizon to the other.

Wendy would point up at the sky and say, "Ooo, pretty." Then she'd point down at a piece of polished glass shimmering in the sunset and say, "Ooo, pretty." Then she'd pick up a small rotting octopus and say, "Ooo, pretty." There was almost nothing Wendy didn't think was worth mentioning. She made up for all the talking Melanie *didn't* do. Wendy jabbered all the time. Sometimes she fell asleep in the middle of a sentence and finished the same sentence the first thing the next morning. I had all kinds of things going for me. The memory of Ginny was fading fast.

Wendy and her mother had no idea I was just using them. Wendy thought I was her dad. Melanie thought I was her boyfriend, her husband, the love of her life. She thought we were together. We were. I was. But, still. I was older than her. I was twenty-seven by then; Ginny was twenty-eight; Elliot was twenty-six. We knew more than Melanie did. We'd been through more. Melanie was a kid. She'd had a tough life, sure, but she couldn't begin to understand the things that had been going on with Ginny and me for the last five years.

* 𝒢 𝒢 *

Around the middle of June, I heard from Elliot again. He called me one night. He and Ginny were living together in L.A. I'd known by then that they were living together, but I'd been immersed in Melanie and hadn't paid it much mind. Elliot's phone call made the fact that they were actually *living* with each other more concrete—sleeping in the same bed, doing the things people do. He fucked her.. She fucked him.

Shit. They had two turtles. The turtles had names. They were happy. His voice sounded apologetic—not guilty, exactly, he knew I was living with Melanie by then, too—but he sounded apologetic nonetheless. I was jealous. Fuck. I was utterly in love with Ginny all over again.

I didn't mention the details of Elliot's phone call to Melanie. She knew Ginny and I had lived together on and off for years and that Elliot and I had been friends since high school. She thought it was perfectly natural that the two of them had gotten together after Ginny and I split up. I was scared to tell her anything different. She was fragile. She wanted me to be as much in love with her as she was with me. Was that so much to ask? She wanted to believe that, like her, I only had room in my heart to be in love with one person at a time. But that wasn't true. I had more room in my heart than that. Melanie wouldn't have understood. She was like one of those little African antelopes that, when it catches the scent of a lion, leaps straight up and starts running before its feet even hit the ground. That I was still in love with Ginny would have been the scent of a lion. It would have been like a lion roaring in Melanie's face. So I told her that Elliot called. I told her that he and Ginny were living together in L.A. That was it. That was all I told her.

CHAPTER TWENTY-SEVEN

Sutro Heights

*T*hen one day everything fell apart forever. Wendy was staying with her grandmother in Sacramento. Melanie and I had each other all to ourselves. We hopped on two or three busses and ended up out at the end of Geary Street. There was a park there—Sutro Heights Park. Two cement lions crouched on squat cement pillars with a daunting, heavy black chain strung between them at the entrance to the park. The chain normally wouldn't have been that big a deal, but Melanie and I were so stoned on acid it took us forever to climb over it.

Once we finally got past the chain and the lions, we pulled each other by turns up the stony path until we came to the crest of a hill and stumbled into the remnants of concrete gun emplacements left over from World War II. They were covered over with ice plant and lichens. The heavy artillery in the bunkers had been aimed out at Japanese war ships that might have come steaming under the Golden Gate. It was going to blow them to smithereens. I knew my history. I didn't try to explain any of it to Melanie. She had an innate aversion to facts of any kind.

It was foggy but unusually warm that day. The ocean was gray. Seabirds cried to each other. I saw the whole bloody conflagration as it might have taken place—Japanese destroyers knifing toward the city, big guns blazing through slits in the concrete, shells landing like geysers, ships exploding, Jap sailors crying like seabirds.

Melanie was busying herself with the building of waterfalls. She pushed tiny drops of water, like mercury from a broken thermometer, into a larger drop of water at the center of a fleshy lichen. Then she swept that drop of water along with one of her fingernails into a bigger drop of water until it grew too massive to remain contained by its inherent surface tension and flooded over the walls of the lichen like a waterfall.

The cascading water sent a shock of surprise through her. She was more sensitive than a spider web. The least little whisper of air sent electrical currents of surprise and delight through her, from the top of her head to the tips of her toes. She started making a big drop of water out of little drops of water on the glistening surface of a fern frond. Melanie liked the feelings of things, the way they tasted and smelled and how they made *her* feel. She touched the fern the way she would have wanted to be touched if she were a fern. She touched the fern as though she were touching herself. It was sexual. The fern was getting aroused. So was I. Everything she did was sexual, sensual; it gave her pleasure to give pleasure.

The park had a gazebo. We went into the gazebo and sat down. Its rafters had been painted over and over with thick white paint. Drizzle from the fog clung like jewels to the strands of a spider web in one of the corners of the structure.

The surfaces of the benches crawled with the graffiti of generations. I climbed up and hung upside-down by my knees from one of the rafters. I could feel the blood bulging the veins in my forehead, throbbing through my temples.

Melanie had just put on fresh lipstick. Her girlishness took my breath away. I went boneless as an octopus with my hair and my head and my neck and my arms dangling down, and closed my eyes. Melanie put one of my fingers into her mouth. I felt the nipple of one of her breasts move under her silky shirt and touched it with the tip of my tongue.

"God, I love you," I heard her say.

I opened my eyes and slipped one hand through a space between the buttons of her lilac blouse. Where my mouth had been there was a wet spot, like a purple heart.

"I think," I said. "My head. Is. Going. To. Explode."

Melanie didn't say anything.

I climbed down and sat next to her and tried to talk again. "Acid," I began. And stopped. And started again. "This." I stopped. "This is a stupid drug to try to talk about...or on...or in...or under. Hey, did you know. That. When I was in the seventh grade. I memorized. The only thing I ever memorized?" Melanie didn't answer, but I assumed she wanted to know what it was. "It was a list of prepositions," I said. "They were in a thick, flimsy, red, paperback book. I still know them. Want to hear?" She still didn't answer, but I knew she'd want to know, so I told her. "In, on, into, over, under, to, at, by, for, from, of, off..."

"Huh?" Melanie said.

"Never mind." I laughed.

Then Melanie stretched out on the wide bench and laid her head in my lap. The ends of her hair brushed the floor.

She closed her eyes. Nerves made a muscle twitch lazily in one of her cheeks. Her mouth was open. Her tongue rested comfortably against the backs of her bottom teeth. I smoothed out one of her eyebrows and rubbed the muscles where her jaws joined, right where the muscles of *my* jaw ached. That was when Melanie asked the fateful question. She was just trying to make conversation, I guess, but it was the fateful question, nonetheless.

"Are you jealous of them? Ginny and Elliot?"

I didn't answer right away. That was it, right there. That was all she needed to hear. My heart broke. I felt my heart break in my chest. I got tears in my eyes. Waves of sadness and regret washed over me. Yeah, I was jealous, sure, but the thing that really got me crying, the second wave of sadness that welled up was that in that tiny fraction of a second I wasn't in love with Ginny or Melanie or anyone. I wasn't in love, period—love, schmove, stick it up your ass. What the fuck does it mean, anyway? Love. What does *that* mean, Ginny had asked when we were on the floor of her apartment on 45th Avenue. I didn't know. I don't know. I've never known. I'll never know. You can't trust the shit is all I know. It comes and goes. It wasn't something I could explain to Melanie at the moment, so I just didn't answer and started to cry instead. I tried to stop crying, but that just made it worse.

The drug no doubt affected the way Melanie saw it, too. She never forgot it, that brief hesitation, the momentary pause, then all that crying and trying not to cry. She saw things simply, directly. She saw things for what they were, and what she saw was that I wasn't in love with her, that I'd never been in love with her, that nobody had ever been in love with her and that nobody would ever be in love with her no matter what she did. That broke my heart even more. I wanted to tell her that wasn't it. But I couldn't. She wouldn't have believed me. She wouldn't have heard. She wouldn't have listened. She saw what she saw. She'd seen what she'd seen.

You had to go all the way back to before Melanie was born to know how really mean and cruel and unfair it was for her to have seen that I wasn't in love with her. You had to know that Melanie's mother was already pregnant with her when she met the guy who eventually married her. Nobody bothered to tell Melanie that. The guy who married her mother treated Melanie like shit because she wasn't his kid. She thought she *was* his kid. That was the cruel part.

He slapped her and pulled her hair and beat her with a stick until she cried. She didn't cry easily, either. She was brave. She was stoical. She had too much pride to cry. But once he started swatting his stick across Melanie's bare legs, he didn't stop until she cried—and what it felt like to her was loathing, hatred, unadulterated dislike. She didn't know what she'd done to deserve to be beaten with a stick. The only thing she could figure was that she'd just been born bad, like no matter how hard she tried to be good she could never be anything but bad—and she tried to be good all the time. Everything she did was good. She washed the dishes until they sparkled and shined the faucet handles and cleaned the toilet bowl and got A's in school and didn't talk back and kept her room spotless—but no matter what she did or didn't do, the guy who married her mother shook her and slapped her and pulled her hair and beat her with a stick because she wasn't his kid.

Melanie's mother didn't interfere. She felt sort of guilty that her husband had to feed, clothe, educate and generally put up with some other guy's child, but she didn't feel all that great about her daughter being beaten with a stick, either. She's the one I blame as much as anyone—well, next to me, I guess. I blame myself for everything. At least there came a time when Melanie found out that the prick really *wasn't* her father and she could make some kind of belated sense out of it, but with me it was like I was mean and cruel and unfair on purpose.

"Yeah, I guess," I said, when I was finally able to answer the question she'd asked what seemed like a hundred years ago. "Sometimes."

"Oh," she said.

That was all she said. But her eyes went out of focus and she looked like she'd been hit on the top of her head with a ball peen hammer. I wasn't in love with her. I never had been. Nobody ever had been. Nobody ever would be. That was the only truth she knew. It hurt.

I tried to fix it. I tried to tell her about love, about what I had meant, but that just fucked things up even worse *again*.

"Elliot," I said. "Elliot used to quote the Bible all the time. There was a thing from the *Song of Songs* he used to say."

Then I stopped and got fucking tears in my eyes again, another fucking lump in my throat, another fucking ache in my heart.

"'Stay me with flagons,' he used to say." A picture came into my mind—Ginny drunk, her otherworldly blue eyes blacked out, pulling at the ends of her hair, shuddering, shivering, shaking her head, trying to be sane, trying to see things as they really were, laughing, saying, "Oh, dear," Elliot and me trying to comfort her.

"'Stay me with flagons; comfort me with apples, for I am sick of love.' That was all I was trying to say," I said.

Melanie had no idea how to respond to that. It didn't seem to make any sense to her. It didn't make any sense to me by then, either. We somehow made our way back home again, but that was the day everything fell apart forever, all the same.

GG

Well, that was the beginning, anyway. If it had just been that, that I hadn't been utterly in love with Melanie for a minute or two, on acid, in a gazebo in Sutro Heights Park sometime in the summer of 1969, things might have figured themselves differently. But it wasn't just that.

A few weeks later, rather than simply avoiding the subject of Ginny and Elliot altogether like anybody with any brains would have done, I exacerbated the Bejesus out of it by coming up with the brilliant idea that the four us ought to all just live together. Ha! How fucking stupid of an idea was that?

I know exactly how it happened, when and how and maybe even why. I was in the shower, watching the water stream down my body, down my stomach and down my legs and off my feet and down the drain—like my life, I remember thinking. That was when I had the clearest picture I've ever had of anything, a picture of Ginny and Elliot and me and Melanie all living in a big house together. It was a fantasy, sure, but I didn't see anything *wrong* with it. I didn't see why we couldn't just *do* it. I thought we could all just fuck each other and cook and clean and have each other's babies and things. I told Melanie about it when I got out of the shower.

All she had to do was say no. But she didn't say no. She didn't say anything.

CHAPTER TWENTY-EIGHT

The Garden of Eden

*O*kay, this part gets a little tricky. Toward the end of 1969, Melanie and Wendy and I moved to Sacramento for a year or so, but the idea of the four of us all living together was still percolating, and when we moved back to the Bay Area again at the beginning of 1971, I still didn't see anything wrong with it. I thought, at the very least, that it wouldn't do any harm to just maybe *try* it sometime and let the chips fall where they may. Man, was I ever wrong about *that*.

After we came back from Sacramento, we lived in an apartment by the San Mateo Municipal Golf Course. I sort of eased Melanie another step in the general direction of living with Ginny and Elliot by encouraging her to fuck other people. I wanted her to get over the idea of being jealous—to see that she could be with other people without it diminishing the affection we had for one another. I wanted her to find out for herself that I would be even more in love with her than ever.

So she started fucking other people. I'm pretty sure that what Melanie had in mind was that once she actually went out and fucked someone, I really wouldn't like it and we could forget about the whole absurd notion of the four of us all living together. It was the early seventies. These were all such early seventies things to do—getting a bunch of people to all live together like *Bob and Carol and Ted and Alice*. We may even have had a lava lamp there for a while.

I remember this one guy in particular. He was a bartender at the Off Broadway. I never met him. I just remember him. Melanie was a dancer by then. She'd started working at topless bars in Sacramento, and when we moved back to the Bay Area, she worked at the clubs on Broadway. She was the headliner in a love act at The Garden of Eden. Her picture was in *Playboy*. Melanie and the bartender at the Off Broadway had the hots for each other the minute she started working there.

"It's just really...physical," she said.

"Hey, so fuck him and get it over with."

"When?"

"Whenever you want."

"Tonight?"

"Okay."

"He'll bring me home, then. Don't wait up."

I did wait up, however. I waited up all night. I waited up until around five the next morning. I can still hear her footsteps on the sidewalk. The sun was about to come up. Birds were singing so excruciatingly loudly I didn't see how they could keep from tearing their poor little pink gullets out. I expected the sidewalk to be strewn with dried up sparrows' throats. I expected them to crackle under my shoes the next time I went outside. The front door opened. I could barely hear it because of the birds. Our bedroom door opened. The birds stopped singing.

"So?"

"I thought you'd be asleep."

"I'm not."

"What do you want to know?"

"Did you fuck him?"

"Yes."

"What's up and down your arms?"

"Hickies."

"From him?"

"No. I did it to myself."

"While he was fucking you?"

"Yes."

"Did you suck his dick?"

"Yes."

"Did he eat your pussy?"

"Yes."

"Did you come?"

"No."

"Why not?"

"I just didn't. Do you want me to take a shower?"

"No."

"I probably should."

"No. You shouldn't. Really. Just come here."

Jealousy may have been an aphrodisiac, but it was also kind of a bitch. I didn't want Melanie fucking everybody in town. Well, I did and I didn't. It was all part of the preparations that needed to be in place.

The next guy, she fucked five days a week. That was her job. She got weekends off. I forget his name. He lived in Foster City and owned a couple of the clubs on Broadway. He paid Melanie to clean his house and fuck him. Some days she didn't bother cleaning his house. After awhile I didn't see how she could possibly have any reservations about at least *trying* the idea of the four of us all living together.

In the meantime, Ginny and Elliot had moved up from L.A. and were living in a Taoist commune in the Santa Cruz Mountains. The commune was run by some old Chinese guy by the name of Gia-Fu Feng, who, along with his young Caucasian girlfriend, had written a book about the teachings of Lao-Tzu. The people in the commune ran around naked all day. They greeted the sun in the morning, said good-bye to the sun at night and ate organic vegetables and lentils and brown rice.

Melanie and Wendy and I went down there one weekend. Wendy dug it, but it wasn't Melanie's cup of tea. She liked wearing clothes, for one thing. Clothes were pretty. She liked how they felt. She liked how they made her feel. No one wore any make up, either. She felt out of place. If that was what I had in mind about us all living together, I could forget it. It wasn't what I had in mind. What I had in mind was you pick the people you want to live with and live with them—like a family.

I got a job at the San Mateo Public Library. We moved to a nice house on a quiet street in Burlingame. I had money coming in. Melanie quit working and stayed home with Wendy. I had my mind set on us all living together more than ever. I'd done enough. She'd fucked plenty of other people and, to my way of thinking, the time had come to just try it and see.

Elliot stayed with us for a couple weeks during the Christmas of 1971. Ginny had wrecked the dining room at the commune. They'd had to leave. She was in a private mental hospital in Santa Cruz. Melanie and Elliot got to know each other on their own terms. They didn't do anything unto-ward—nobody was trying to push anything on anyone—they just got to know each other. They liked each other. They talked. They were shy with one another.

He drew pictures of her and told her she reminded him of Cordelia—she *was* Cordelia, actually. If you really want to know what Melanie was like, go read *King Lear.*. Elliot and Wendy finger-painted in front of the fireplace. Nobody watched TV. See. It was like a family. Just like I knew it would be. Melanie admitted it hadn't been bad, but she was still glad Elliot left when he did.

Six months later Ginny and Elliot showed up together; arm in arm, hand in hand. That was when the shit hit the fan.

* 𝒢 𝒢 *

Melanie and Wendy and I were living in our cozy little house. We had a fig tree in the back yard. I was working at the library. I wore suits and ties and belonged to the employee credit union. Melanie and I were more in love than ever.

Some weekends we still took acid and lounged around out in the hammock in the backyard and watched hummingbirds and bumblebees leave jewel-encrusted vapor trails among the fig leaves and thought we were Adam and Eve. She was happy. I was happy. Wendy was happy. Susie was happy.

Susie was a shiny black squirmy little part Labrador Retriever and part Dachshund who'd followed Wendy home from school one day and kept getting knocked up by the next door neighbors' Kerry Blue Terrier. The neighbors com-plained that Susie enticed him over there because of his cham-pion blood lines, although why Susie would have done that we had no idea, since all she ever got out of it was a minimum of seven of the ugliest yapping little blue-skinned puppies you ever saw. Wendy used to have to spend two or three days over in front of Safeway getting rid of the little bastards out of a cardboard box marked "FREE PUPPIES."

But the next-door neighbors swore it was a conspiracy to contaminate the racial purity of the Kerry Blue Terrier breed. Their dog wouldn't have anything to do with the champion bitches they tried breeding him with. His heart belonged to Susie. The next-door neighbors also had a bomb shelter and thought World War II had been lost—which may have accounted for some of their views on racial purity.

In the summer of 1972, Susie had just had her latest batch of ugly puppies. There were nine of them this time. Every morning, bright and early, Melanie waded out into this huge warm whimpering pile of black and blue flesh, carrying a speckled roasting pan full of hot Puppy Chow, and Susie's puppies went berserk. They engulfed her ankles and licked her feet and bit at her toes and looked up at her in utter adoration with their newly opened eyes—while Susie sat on her blanket like it was a throne, squirming and wagging her entire body with such pride and gratitude and dismay that Melanie had to make a conscientious effort to keep from laughing out loud for fear Susie might get her feelings hurt.

Melanie and Susie were the two happiest creatures in all creation. Melanie was almost complacent. This was the way she wanted to live—knee deep in newborn puppies, trying not to laugh out loud. All she wanted was to shine the faucet handles, clean the toilet bowl, bake enchiladas and have me love her forever. And we were doing that. There wasn't anything wrong with it. I was happy. Wendy was happy. Susie was happy. Her nine ugly puppies were happy. Everyone was happy.

There wasn't anything wrong with anything. We had the next-door neighbors to gossip about and the people at work to gossip about and movies to go to and the Sunday paper to read and a brand new Safeway a block away. But, despite the fig leaves and the hummingbirds and the bumblebees and Susie's puppies and the rest of all that unbridled bliss, I still had it in mind that you only live once and that there are things in life you have to try if you get the chance—if for no other reason than just to know for sure that they really won't work—and Ginny and Elliot and Melanie and me all living together like one big happy family was still one of those things.

CHAPTER TWENTY-NINE

Burlingame

*D*ick Joseph had stopped by that morning while I was at work. Elliot and I had known Dick Joseph since he was a freckle-faced kid in high school. By the summer of 1972, Dick Joseph had a bushy red beard.

Everyone liked Dick Joseph—Ralph, Thulin, John White, me, Elliot, Ginny, Melanie, Wendy, Susie—we all liked Dick Joseph; nobody didn't like Dick Joseph. He was like a gadfly; he hung out with everyone. One of the things Melanie liked about Dick Joseph was that he didn't read anything but Russian novels. He *refused* to read anything but Russian novels. He eschewed all books but Russian novels. That cracked her up. Dick Joseph wouldn't even *hear* about any books but Russian novels.

"I'm reading Faulkner," Melanie would say. "*Light in August.*"

"Fuck Faulkner. Faulkner eats shit." Dick put his hands over his ears, closed his eyes and repeated the names of Russian novelists like a mantra. "Leonid Andreyev, Fydor Dostoyevsky, Mikhail Sholokhov, Ivan Sergeevich Turgenev,

Vladimir Nabokov, Mikhail Sholokhov, Aleksandr Solzhen-
itsyn…"

He made her laugh.

Melanie loved books. She read and read, but there were
always so many more books yet to read. Dick Joseph got her
to think about maybe just reading French novels or English
novels or American novels, but she didn't. She read everything—Indian novels, South American novels, you name it.

Another thing Melanie liked about Dick Joseph was that
he sold drugs—predominately cocaine, but he dabbled in marijuana, crystal meth and downers when he could get them at a
fair price. Melanie loved barbiturates—barbiturates and
books. She and Dick Joseph sat around the kitchen table that
morning and talked about Russian novels while he manicured
a couple of pounds of marijuana. When he was through, Dick
Joseph gave Melanie a little jar of Nembutal and left the stems
and seeds from the marijuana in a trash bag under the sink.

* 𝒢 𝒢 *

Ginny and Elliot showed up at around six in the evening.
She was carrying a small, round, light blue overnight case. He
had on a faded camouflage shirt and was carrying a couple
half-gallon bottles of Gallo Pink Chablis. I had just gotten
home from work. I was in the kitchen. Melanie was cooking
enchiladas and telling me what she and Dick Joseph had
talked about when he'd stopped by that morning.

I still had my tie on. I was tired. Wendy was coloring in a
coloring book on the cool tiles in front of the fireplace. The
sun was shining through the kitchen windows. We hadn't
been expecting Ginny and Elliot. They just showed up.

We drank wine and ate enchiladas. The sun went down. Wendy went to bed. The four of us went into the living room and drank more wine. Melanie took a few of the Nembutal Dick Joseph had given her. I opened a bag of tortilla chips, brought them out to the living room in the big popcorn-popping pan we used to use, and put them on the floor in front of Melanie's chair. It was her special chair. No one else sat in it. Ginny and Elliot and I all sat around on the floor in front of the popcorn pan.

Melanie wasn't very sociable. Ginny kept trying to get her to talk, to open up, to say what was on her mind—to yell or kick and scream and throw things if that was what she felt like doing—but Melanie didn't feel like doing any of those things. She didn't feel like talking. Ginny made a halfhearted attempt to get the ball rolling.

"You can't just sit there," she said. "I mean, you can if you want, I guess, but if you don't want us here, you should just say so. Talk about passive-aggressive. Gadfrees! What if I threw stuff at you?"

Melanie cocked her head slowly and looked directly into Ginny's eyes.

Ginny picked up a handful of tortilla chips and tossed them in a slow arc toward Melanie. A few stuck in her hair. Melanie looked at me. Ginny looked at me. I didn't say anything. Elliot and I looked at each other. Nobody said anything.

"This is absurd. What if I threw the whole pan?" Ginny laughed, picked up the popcorn pan and tossed what was left of the tortilla chips across the room at her. Melanie looked like a little maple tree with dried up tortilla chips hanging from her like autumn leaves, and still she didn't say anything.

Then Ginny stood up, picked up the empty popcorn pan, walked over and started bonging the pan onto Melanie's head—Bong! Bong! Bong! I watched. I thought Melanie was going to say something, but she didn't. She just sat there. It hurt, sure, you could see that, but she was brave, she was stoical, she had too much pride to show that it hurt. Elliot got up and took the popcorn pan away from Virginia.

He held up one finger. "No hitting."

"Oh, dear." Ginny covered her mouth and peeked impishly out from under her bangs. "I'm sorry."

Around midnight, Elliot went over to Melanie and sat on the arm of her chair. He put his arm around her, pushed her hair away from her face and tried to kiss her, but she'd taken so many of the Nembutal by then that she was pretty close to catatonic—she didn't resist; she just wasn't enthusiastic. He didn't push it. He got up and went out the back door—to sleep in the hammock, I presumed. It was a warm night.

Not long after Elliot left, Melanie passed out in her chair. I took the last couple of Nembutal she still had clenched in her fist, put them into my pants' pocket, carried her into our bedroom and put her into bed with her clothes on.

That left Ginny and me alone in the living room. She was drunk. Blacked out. Her eyes had clicked off. The light in them was gone. She was oblivious. I had a hard time even recognizing her for a while. Putting things out of your mind changes them. She was different from how I remembered her. I had her all tucked away in pat memories of how we used to be together, and now here she was, right in front of me, out like a light, and I wasn't quite sure who she even *was* anymore.

There were scars that hadn't been there before, scars on her face, on her hands. She was older. There were lines around her mouth and at the corners of her eyes. The whole time we were together came cascading back—how we met, how she'd been so unattainable, so young, so sought after, how she'd taught me everything I knew, everything I know, how she laughed, the way her mouth used to go—and for a second I just wanted to forget about Melanie and Wendy and Elliot and my job and my house and Susie and her puppies and everything I had or wanted to have and run away together, just the two of us, Ginny and me, just run and run.

"I'm going to put on my jammies," she said.

She took her suitcase into the bathroom. When she came back she was wearing a light blue flannel nightgown with a picture of Raggedy Ann on the front of it. She sat on the floor with her knees apart and her feet under the backs of her thighs. She was wearing her usual white cotton panties. Her hair hid her face. She peeked out from under her bangs. We talked and touched each other's hands. She shook her hair away from her face. She was deranged. She had no conscience or guilt or guile. We talked in whispers and laughed because we were shy—we'd known each other so well for so long it was funny that we could still be shy.

It wasn't until practically dawn that we finally got up off the floor and went over to the couch. I still had my tie on from work. It was loose and my shirt was unbuttoned, but that was the first time I'd noticed that I still had my tie on. I left it on. I just took off my pants. I pushed her nightgown up above her tiny tits and pulled her white cotton panties off one leg and left them on the other leg and fucked her.

By then it was mainly something we had to do—for my sake and her sake and Elliot's sake and Melanie's sake—so we could say, okay, we did it, and let whatever was going to happen just hurry up and happen. We wanted to see how it was going to play itself out—so we fucked on the couch and got it the hell over with.

✦ ❦ ❦ ✦

When we were through, Ginny and I went into Melanie's bedroom. Ginny was still unsteadily sipping at a glass of wine. The sun was barely up. Elliot was in the back yard. I saw one of the arms of his camouflage shirt hanging over the side of the hammock. Steam came up from the grass. Robins were hopping around. Melanie was sound asleep. The pillow had made wrinkles in her cheek. Some of her hair was in her mouth. There were still a few stray tortilla chips here and there. I sat on the edge of the bed and asked, "Are you awake?"

Melanie made some lip smacking noises and swallowed. I shook her shoulder. She opened one eye and smiled and said, "I'm not sure. Am I?"

"We need to talk."

"What time is it?"

"Early."

She closed her eye again and pulled on my arm like she was trying to get me back into bed with her, like she didn't know I hadn't been sleeping next to her all night, like it was just another innocent morning.

"I have to tell you something," I said.

"Tell me later."

"Ginny and I had sex on the couch last night."

Melanie opened both eyes and blinked.

Ginny made her way over to the other side of the bed. She was still in her Raggedy Ann nightgown. She reached her tiny, tentative hand out to touch Melanie's hair, to comfort her—and Melanie, sweet, meek Melanie, mild as a mouse, sat bolt upright, reared back and slugged Ginny square in the mouth with her fist.

Whack!

It was a solid shot—straight to the jaw. Ginny reeled backwards and somewhat sideways. Her elbow smashed through the window against the far wall, the one that faced the house next door, the one with the bomb shelter in the basement.

"Hey!" Ginny frowned and looked down at the cut on her elbow. "Ow!" She looked plaintively over at me, held up her arm and said, "That hurt."

Then Melanie threw things. Ginny ducked. Melanie's aim was accurate, but Ginny had amazingly quick reflexes for someone as drunk as she was. A hardbound copy of *Magic Mountain*, a pair of pinking shears and a frilly table lamp all went flying straight at Ginny's head.

Elliot was standing in the doorway by then. Melanie came tearing out of bed, still in the clothes she'd had on the night before, and made a beeline toward Ginny with a wild look in her eyes, like she was going to scratch Ginny's eyes out, like she was going to wring her scrawny neck or grab her by the hair and bash her face into a wall again and again until Ginny was dead.

Ginny squeezed past Elliot, went into the bathroom and closed the door. Elliot and I stood in front of the door and didn't let Melanie get past us. Then Wendy was standing behind Elliot, rubbing her eyes. When she saw Wendy, Melanie calmed down some. I got Wendy ready for school—had her brush her teeth and get dressed while I made her a peanut butter and jelly sandwich.

After Wendy was gone, the cops showed up. The next-door neighbors must have called them. We were all out in the living room again, by then. Melanie was in the same chair she'd been in the night before. She refused to look at the couch. Ginny and Elliot were sitting on the floor. I was standing next to Melanie's chair. Ginny had changed out of her nightgown. Melanie was trying to light the filter end of one of her True Blues when I saw at least six uniformed police officers on the porch, peering in through the windows.

I opened the door. I didn't exactly invite them in, but I did open the door. Cops came rushing in, tripping over themselves, fanning out into all the other rooms in the house, looking everywhere. When they found the stems and seeds Dick Joseph had left in the trash bag under the kitchen sink, the cops were stoked. The one who found the dope held up the trash bag like it was Medusa's freshly chopped off head and said, "Well, well, well, lookie what we got here."

Melanie and I were under arrest. Since they didn't live there, Ginny and Elliot were free to leave. Melanie and I were taken to jail in separate squad cars.

They never would have found the Nembutal in my pocket if I had managed to stick them down the crack in the back seat of the cop car like I was trying to do, but I had these handcuffs on, see. I felt like Houdini—all twisted up like a contortionist, trying to push the squirmy little yellow bastards out of my pocket so I could slip them down the crack in the car seat, with my hands handcuffed behind my back.

One of the cops looked over his shoulder at me.

"What do you got there?" He frowned.

"Just a little Nembutal," I said.

CHAPTER THIRTY

Manitou Springs

*A*fter our drug bust, Ginny's father's lawyer got me off on some sort of Fourth Amendment technicality, but Melanie pleaded no contest to a misdemeanor and had to meet with a probation officer in Redwood City. She had to take a bus. It was a hassle. We got kicked out of the house in Burlingame and lived different places during the next year—San Bruno, Belmont, San Carlos. Susie got lost in the shuffle.

Melanie didn't trust me anymore. She didn't believe I was in love with her. Being in love with someone you don't believe loves you is unbearable. She got a headache every day. She tried all kinds of things to make it go away. Red wine worked—usually a little over half of a half-gallon jug of Gallo Chianti did the trick—or maybe the headache was still there but just didn't hurt anymore. Either way, the next morning it was back worse than ever. Melanie started sipping wine earlier and earlier in the day. She'd soaked the label off of an old Skippy Peanut Butter jar and used that as a wine glass.

After six months, the backs of her teeth had turned maroon, but the wine had stopped working altogether. Her head hurt nonstop, day and night. The only thing she could think of that would keep her head from hurting was to kill herself—and it was all my fault, of course. If I could have somehow loved her enough, if she could have believed me, she would have been fine. The headaches would have gone away. She would have been happy. But I didn't love her enough. I couldn't—and after the stunt I'd pulled with Ginny and Elliot, she wouldn't have believed me if I had. She didn't believe a word I said by then.

It went on and on. I brought her cold washcloths and took her to emergency rooms when she swallowed too many over the counter sleeping pills and dutifully visited her in the psycho ward at Mills Hospital.

Melanie and I had to not be together anymore, that was all there was to it. Living with me was killing her. We had to split up. That was the only logical, practical, reasonable, work-able solution—unless I wanted her dead. And I didn't want her dead, I wanted her alive, I wanted her to get better, I wanted to help her, to fix her. I loved her. I wanted to love her. I couldn't. She was too sad. It was a vicious circle.

I finally got her and Wendy moved into a big old two-story house near downtown Sacramento. They had the whole first floor all to themselves. Some junkies lived upstairs. I was convinced that the only thing that was going to keep Mel-anie from killing herself would be for her to fall in love with someone else, and the only way she was ever going to fall in love with someone else was going to be for her to be on her own. Being in love with me was killing her. It wasn't doing me much good, either—or Wendy, for that matter—it wasn't doing anyone any good.

* 𝒢𝒢 *

300

A month or so after I got Melanie and Wendy situated in Sacramento, I went to see Ginny in Colorado. It was the summer of 1973. She was living in Manitou Springs, right below Pike's Peak—not far from the Cave of the Winds. After the imbroglio in Burlingame, she and Elliot had gone their separate ways. Elliot stayed with his mother and Ginny ended up in a commune in the Rocky Mountains. The same bunch of people from the commune in the Santa Cruz Mountains had moved the whole kit and caboodle to Colorado. I took my vacation from the library in August, stopped off at Melanie's for a few days, then drove to Colorado.

By the time I got there Ginny had been kicked out of the commune and was living in a little gingerbread cottage by the edge of a forest. She lived alone but had taken up with a group of people who espoused some conglomeration of New Age gobbledygook. The first few days were fine. We were shy with each other, unsure of ourselves, not exactly uncomfortable, but tense, wary, noncommittal. We still had a lot in common, though, and slept in the same small, soft, springy bed together.

We got a ride up to the top of Pike's Peak, then got lost trying to find our way back down again. It got cold. It snowed. Then it got dark. We thought we might freeze to death. We built a fire and made up stories about how, centuries later, people would discover our skeletons. When the sun came up, we weren't lost after all. The town was just waking up behind the next little ridge of rocks. All we had to do was walk a couple hundred yards farther, and we could have slept in a nice warm bed.

The day after that, some of Ginny's New Age buddies started showing up. They had some kind of loose affiliation with Elizabeth Clare Prophet. I never really got to the bottom of it all. They talked about St. Germaine, the Archangel Michael and some bunch of glowing guys they called "Ascended Masters." They all wore pastel clothes and had faraway looks in their eyes, and every two-bit thing that ever happened to any of them had some big cosmic purpose for the good of all mankind.

They adored Ginny. She fit right in. Every two-bit thing she ever did her whole life always had some big cosmic purpose. I understood practically nothing of any of it. We had grown apart. She had leaped a few rungs ahead of me up the spiritual ladder. We all go at our own pace. Or maybe all her New Age claptrap was just too much of a pain in the ass, even for me. I still liked her. I couldn't help but like her. I'll always like her—but her New Age buddies and me didn't hit it off at all. I left before the week was up.

* 𝒢 𝒢 *

All I wanted by then was to get to back to Melanie's while I still had a few days vacation left. I wanted my feet back on solid ground. I missed her. I missed Wendy. I was craving a little common sense. Less than a week with Ginny had convinced me once and for all that Melanie was the girl for me. I was finally ready for us to settle down and live happily ever after like a normal god damn family.

That was all I thought about the whole time it took to get back from Colorado. Elliot and his religious upbringing crossed my mind briefly as I blew by the Mormon Tabernacle, but I didn't want to think about him anymore, either. I didn't want to think, period. I had everything all figured out. All I wanted was to marry Melanie and have her and Wendy and me all live happily ever after. I sped past the Great Salt Lake and the Bonneville Salt Flats like they were a mirage.

In Winnemucca I stopped at a pawnshop and bought Melanie an engagement ring. It was just a cubic zirconium, but the guy at the pawnshop found me a dusty black velvet box to keep it in so I could spring it on her in style. I would have told her it was a cubic zirconium, too. Melanie would have appreciated that it was a cubic zirconium. She wouldn't have wanted me wasting our hard-earned money on a real diamond any more than I would have wanted to waste our hard-earned money on a real diamond. And because it was just a cubic zirconium, I could afford to go all out. It was the biggest cubic zirconium in downtown Winnemucca. It was huge. It was gigantic. It was a cubic zirconium as big as the Ritz.

For a while there, coming down out of the Sierra Nevadas, Zelda Fitzgerald was all I could think about. And I didn't want to think about Zelda Fitzgerald. Fuck Zelda Fitzgerald. I wanted Zelda Fitzgerald out of my mind completely. I didn't want to think about Gurdjieff or Virginia Woolf or Marcel DuChamp or Bach or Saint Germaine or those glowing guys or anyone anymore. All I wanted was to marry Melanie and live happily ever after. I would have been a bricklayer. I would have been or done anything Melanie wanted me to be or do. I would have gotten down on one knee. I would have begged. If it hadn't been so late I would have brought her flowers. I would have paid top dollar—no second hand freesia or wilting baby's breath—I would have brought her long stemmed roses, as many as I could carry. But it was too late. By the time I got into downtown Sacramento, all the florist shops were closed.

Driving around among the alphabetical streets, trying to find her house, I pictured how happy she was going to be that we were finally just going to get married and live happily ever after. Melanie might even cry a little. They'd be tears of joy. I could see them in her loving eyes. Then, wow, would she ever fuck the fuck out of me the rest of the night and the next night and the night after that—maybe even once or twice during the day. Ha! I was so in love with Melanie I was going to die.

CHAPTER THIRTY-ONE

Sacramento

*T*he way I had it pictured wasn't how it turned out. While I'd been with Ginny in Colorado, Melanie had fallen in love with someone else. I know I'd convinced myself that she needed to fall in love with someone else, but I had changed my mind by then.

Oops. Sorry.

The guy she'd fallen love with sold heroin for a living. He made a lot of money at it, but it didn't turn him into a jerk. I liked the guy. The top of his head was bald. He looked like Shakespeare. I didn't blame Melanie. He was good for her. Shooting up heroin cured her headaches—along with all the other aches and pains she'd had for longer than she could remember.

Heroin's an analgesic, a painkiller. You inject it into the blood that goes straight to the pain centers of the brain. And the euphoria Melanie got from being free from the aches and pains she'd had all her life—physical, psychological, emotional, spiritual, you name it—gave her mind and her body and her soul a peace and quiet and a joy she'd never known. She *loved* heroin. It took her breath away. It was heavenly.

And to the guy who gave her the heroin, she was grateful beyond words. I was sorry I hadn't thought of it myself. But I hadn't. He had.

GG

Melanie was alone when I finally found her house. I saw her through the front window. She was sitting under a dim lamp with a yellow lampshade, reading Proust. Proust was her friend. Thomas Mann was her friend. Nabokov was her friend. Anthony Trollope was her friend. She had all kinds of friends—Angel Miguel Asturias, that *Hundred Years of Solitude* guy, Isaac Bashevis Singer, V. S. Naipaul, V. S. Pritchett, James Purdy, Alberto Moravia, Christopher Isherwood and that Mishima guy, the list went on and on—she had a whole world of friends.

She always had a book to read and always read it carefully and patiently, cover to cover, before she picked up another. Her hair had some red in it, like she'd been out in the sun. I knocked on the door and heard her clear her throat. She always had to clear her throat before she said anything. She was perpetually shy.

"It's open," I heard her say.

I went inside. Melanie had on the white silk nightgown I'd bought her just before the debacle in Burlingame. She hadn't been expecting me. She'd been expecting someone else. She didn't stand up. She just sat there with her finger marking her place in her book and looked surprised that it was me—surprised and frantic and disappointed and possibly even a little triumphant. She cleared her throat again.

"What are *you* doing here?" She frowned slightly.

"I just got back," I said.

"You can't be here. Someone's coming over."

"Who?"

"A friend."

"I need to talk to you."

"Not now, you don't."

The guy got there. He didn't knock. He just walked in like he lived there. She introduced us. We shook hands. I forget his name. I've blanked it out. He had a limp, sort of fishy handshake. He was frail, delicate, almost effeminate— with long, cool, thin fingers and dark pretty skin and big bovine brown eyes and a smooth shiny bald head with wisps of baby-fine black hair around his ears.

He was reserved, cautious, smart, playing it just right. I liked the guy. I couldn't help it. He was cool. Melanie marked her place in the book with a fringed bookmark, got out of her chair and stood quietly beside the guy. He touched her hair. She looked worried. I didn't exactly like it that she was wearing the nightgown I'd given her—not because I'd given it to her, but because it was a little too risqué to be parading around in in front of some guy we hardly knew. I guess I hadn't quite completely gotten the picture yet.

They seemed to presume that I would go away, but I didn't go away. I stayed. I stayed the whole night. Whatever was going on between them, I wanted to see with my own eyes. I didn't want there to be any doubts in my mind. I didn't want there to be a possibility that I may have misunderstood what was going on between the two of them. I stayed. I saw. There weren't any doubts; there were no misunderstandings.

It seemed to be okay with the Shakespeare guy that I stayed. He and Melanie looked at each other and shrugged as if to say it didn't matter to them one way or the other who else wanted to hang around, they were going to get loaded anyway. He went out to his car to get the dope.

Wendy was asleep in the only bedroom. Melanie used the living room for *her* bedroom. There was a big, freshly made bed with lots of pillows against the far wall.

"You may not enjoy this," Melanie said when we were alone.

"Look. I'm in love with you," I said. "I've been a huge asshole, I know, but I'm totally in love with you. That's what I need to tell you."

"That's not what I need to hear."

"I got you this." I took out the black velvet box with the engagement ring in it. "I want to marry you. I want us to get married."

Melanie looked like she was going cry. She didn't say anything—she just looked like she was going to cry. It didn't look like she was going to cry from happiness, however; they weren't going to be tears of joy.

The guy came back. I slipped the box into my pocket. The three of us went out to the kitchen. Their junkie paraphernalia was stashed behind the silverware tray in one of the drawers. There were homemade syringes and bent spoons and matchbooks and cotton balls and a new length of powdered latex.

Melanie went first. The Shakespeare guy tied off her upper arm deftly, like he'd done it a hundred times. The veins in the crook of her elbow got engorged.

"God, you've got good veins," the Shakespeare guy said. He bent down and kissed the inside of her left arm. The ceiling light reflected off his bald head.

Melanie had a few healed puncture marks in the biggest of the veins. The heroin was brown. His connection was the Mexican Mafia.

I had never seen Melanie more interested in anything than she was in that long, bright, skinny little homemade hypodermic needle getting closer and closer to the vein in her arm. It was like the guy was teasing her. It was like foreplay. He moved the tip of the needle across the surface of her skin and her eyelids fluttered. Then he stuck it in. She winced a little, and a trickle of blood seeped into the syringe.

The anticipation was making her sweat. She so badly wanted that mixture of her blood and his heroin to gush from the shaft of the syringe into her blood—and when it finally did, her whole body sighed such a huge sigh of relief it made her almost fall off her chair. She slumped down. Her nightgown slid up the sides of her legs and the crotch of her panties came into plain view. They were black silk, with bright red clusters of cherries. The guy pulled the needle out. He reached over and wiped off the drop of blood on the inside of her arm with a fresh sterile cotton ball.

Then it was my turn. The guy didn't get cute with me. With me, he was efficient. He tied off my bicep. I clenched my fist. He drew the mixture of heroin and boiled water up from the spoon through a new ball of cotton, pricked the skin of one of my veins, let the needle relax, flicked the nipple on the end of the syringe until I could see my own blood turning maroon and velvety brown inside the syringe. Then he shot the whole works back into my vein—and pretty soon I noticed I was numb. It was like a dream. I could pinch myself and it didn't hurt and I didn't wake up.

All of a sudden, I felt sick to my stomach. I'd heard heroin made people nauseous the first couple of times, but there were other things going on, as well. As soon as the stuff had gone all the way through me, I was racked with guilt and remorse and regret and such all-consuming love for Melanie I thought I was going to throw up. I *was* going to throw up.

I didn't want her doing heroin. Junkies are bad. They rob people and fuck people and don't give a shit about anything but staying strung out. I wanted us back in Burlingame, out in the yard, with Susie's ugly puppies nipping at her ankles. I wanted us to get married and live happily ever after. I had the god damn engagement ring in my pocket, for Christ's sake. What the hell more did she want? Of course it was my fault. I knew that. I didn't blame the Shakespeare guy. I didn't blame Melanie. I blamed myself. I was the one who had fucked Ginny on our couch. I was the one who had made Melanie feel so bad she had a headache every day, the one who made her so sad she wanted to die. I was the one who dumped her in Sacramento and took off to see Ginny again—and now here I was, tired, dirty, unshaven, reeking of tabouli and New Age claptrap, thinking I could make it all up to her with some two-bit phony engagement ring...and the worst part was that even with all *that* going on, I didn't feel a thing. I couldn't feel, period—not anything. I was senseless. Anesthetized. Numb. Nothing hurt. Nothing felt good or bad, either one.

I barely made it into the bathroom before I started throwing up everything I'd eaten the whole time I'd been in Colorado—all that hummus and tofu and broccoli. I threw up things I didn't remember eating. I threw up things I never ate—live lizards and dead palm fronds and soggy parakeets and stuff that looked like it came out of a Dr. Seuss book.

Oobleck!

Bartholomew and the Oobleck.

Ha!

I was throwing up gobs of increasingly green oobleck all over Melanie's brand new bathroom—which then got me to thinking about every other Dr. Seuss book I ever read. I couldn't help it. Ever since my mother read *And To Think That I Saw It On Mulberry Street* out loud to me when I was five, my imagination has always just taken off on me. I'm like the kid in the book. Marco. I see a tired old nag pulling a rickety old one-horse cart down a quiet street in Brooklyn and have it turned into elephants and giraffes pulling a big brass band in no time. I wanted it to stop, but it didn't. My imagination went on and on, loaded on heroin or not loaded on heroin. Where did it come from? I didn't know.

It got to be sort of funny, though. I looked into the toilet bowl and wondered, wow, where the heck had *that* come from? Maybe it was my appendix. Tonsils? Adenoids? What did adenoids look like? What the hell were adenoids, anyway? What did they do? I could hardly wait to tell Melanie and the Shakespeare guy all about what fun I'd been having puking my guts out in her new bathroom. I had a whole comedy routine all worked out. It was hilarious. It was going to make them laugh until their stomachs ached.

When I got back into the living room, the Shakespeare guy and Melanie were in her bed together and didn't look like they were in the mood for comedy. It would have been a tough audience, no matter how funny I might have been.

GG

It's hot in Sacramento in the summer. Even at night. You don't need blankets. You don't need clothes. Even a sheet's too much. The two of them were lying in her big bed with no clothes on. It was like *Nashville Skyline*, like *Lay Lady Lay*. The window was open. There were a few candles burning on the windowsill. There wasn't any breeze. The flames didn't flicker. They flared up when the wax overflowed and left a new piece of the wick exposed, but the flames didn't waver.

The guy was propped up in a pile of pillows pushed against the wall. His arm was under Melanie's head. Her face was nuzzled into the side of his neck. Her hand was lying limply on his chest. His clothes were hung neatly over the arm of the couch. Melanie's white nightgown and the black panties with bunches of cherries on them were on the floor.

I took off my clothes and got into bed with them. I don't know what the hell I was thinking. Maybe I was thinking, hey, Melanie had tried things *my* way, the least I could do was to try things *her* way. Her way was that she wanted to be with this guy. Okay. That was all right. I'd just go ahead and be with the son of a bitch, too. I couldn't imagine that she didn't want to be with me, period. I couldn't imagine that she *only* wanted to be with this guy. I was deluded. Her way was that she didn't want me there. I refused to believe it. She was absolutely in love with me and always had been and always would be. She couldn't help herself. Why the hell else would she have been killing herself all that time? Because she couldn't help being absolutely in love with me forever no matter what, that's why. I couldn't conceive of it being otherwise. That's what deluded is—if you know you are, you're not. I was deluded. I stayed. I stayed the whole night.

The candles smelled like vanilla. They flared up and died down and flared up again. The guy was passive. He didn't move. He didn't smile; the muscles in his face smiled all on their own. His eyes stayed sort of half opened and half closed, like it didn't matter whether he was asleep or awake. Everything he did was involuntary. Even his dick kept getting bigger and bigger all by itself as Melanie's hand made its way slowly down the lean involuntary muscles of his stomach.

Pretty soon her fingers were creeping tentatively around in wisps of his pubic hair. She propped herself up on one elbow and slid her whole pretty naked little body down the side of his bare chest. She opened her eyes briefly and looked over at me as if to reiterate that I *really* might not enjoy what was yet to come—that if I had decided by then that I wanted to leave after all, I should probably get up and leave.

Melanie had a certain knack, a way, somehow, of making a guy feel like his dick was as important to her as it was to him. The Shakespeare guy was making it all the easier for her, too, by staying so cool, so aloof—lounging there with such aplomb. Her long pretty hair brushed his nipples. The intellectual concept crossed my mind that I ought to have been kind of turned on myself, but I wasn't. My own dick was shriveled up to about the size of an acorn buried somewhere near my left kidney.

I covered myself up with a corner of one of the sheets and decided it must have been the heroin. But the Shakespeare guy had done at least as much heroin as I had, and he certainly wasn't having any trouble with *his* dick. It must have been Melanie. She was having the same effect on him she used to have on me. Now he was the cocky one, the beneficiary of her unbridled affection. That's the trouble with guys. Chicks bestow all this unbridled affection on them and they get all cocky and full of themselves, then use that cockiness to beat up on the chick that gave it to them in the first place. I'd been supplanted, replaced, aced out; it was him she was with, and she was with him in as profound a way as she'd ever been with me.

The preliminaries were over. Melanie had built up to it long enough. She was sucking his cock right in front of my eyes. I could see the vacuum making dimples in her pretty chipmunk cheeks. She seemed to be enjoying herself as much with him as she ever had with me. She gave it a rest now and then, toyed with him—licked him up and down playfully, bit the side of his cock with her teeth, nibbled at him.

After he was good and ready, Melanie straddled the guy like she was getting on a horse. She slipped his cock up inside her like a saddle horn. He was moving some by then, but his movements were still effortless. It went on like that forever. They fucked each other interminably. She rolled him over on top of her and held onto the sides of one of the pillows. He turned her over and fucked her like a frog. He turned her onto her side and fucked her sideways. She put one of her legs on his shoulder and he fucked her with her leg on his shoulder. She liked it. So did he.

I didn't like it, but I was too stoned on heroin to know what I liked or didn't like, too stoned to know what I was see-ing or wasn't seeing. She wasn't fucking me. I knew that. She was fucking some other guy. She was fucking the fuck out of some other guy the way she used to fuck the fuck out of me. I knew that much. After the initial, mind-numbing, immobilizing bliss, the heroin seemed to act as a sort of time-release aphrodisiac for the two of them. They were like morning glories, winding around and around each other for hours on end. I was pretty much just out in the audience. I had a front row seat, yeah, but that was about it.

Melanie reached over and patted my head during intermissions—while the guy was taking a leak or eating a peanut butter sandwich—but then he'd come back and fuck her some more. They put the *Kama Sutra* to shame. It was an impressive performance, a regular *tour de force*. If I had been a critic, I would have given it all the stars I had to give. I'd seen enough but had nowhere else to go and couldn't have gone anywhere anyway, due to being too loaded on heroin to move.

When the sun started to come up, they were still at it. The heroin had worn off a bit. I kept falling into a kind of trance. I still hadn't slept since I'd left Colorado. I guess you could call it sleep, but I kept waking up. One time I woke up, I was over on the couch. I didn't know how I had gotten there. Another time I woke up, the guy was gone. I had no idea how that had happened either.

Melanie and I were alone. She was still in bed. She had her nightgown back on and was winding the ends of her hair around her fingers, looking for split ends. It used to drive me nuts the way she wound her hair around her fingers, looking for split ends, but it didn't drive me nuts anymore. I loved seeing her wind the ends of her hair around her fingers. I could have watched her wind the ends of her hair around her fingers forever and have been happy for the rest of my life.

Sunshine streaming through the dust in the air made it feel like we were under a microscope. Everything was too clear, too magnified. The candles had melted into puddles. The bed was punctuated with apostrophes of pubic hair. There was a big semen stain in the shape of a question mark. Melanie looked stunned.

Wendy came into the living room, then. She was rubbing her eyes. She stood in front of me. I shook her by her shoulders and said, "Hey, kid."

She yawned and said, "Could you take us to the zoo today?"

"Some other day. I really can't today."

"Mom would like it, too. Huh, mom?"

Melanie didn't say anything.

"I've got to go," I said and looked over at Melanie.

If she had said I didn't have to leave, I wouldn't have left, but she didn't say I didn't have to leave. She didn't say anything. I had to leave. I left.

CHAPTER THIRTY-TWO

Hillsborough

From that hot night in Sacramento in 1973 until around the end of 1977, I pretty much have to extrapolate. I must have quit my job at the library and must have moved up to my parents' house in Oregon again. Wendy sent me a piece of red construction paper with tiny, blue cutout hearts pasted onto it for Valentine's Day one year, but I only know that because I still have it in my little pile of letters and things. Melanie didn't send me anything. Not a word. Nothing. She was like that. The only thing that's stuck in my mind of those four years is a long empty dull blank ache.

At some point during that time, based solely on an old airline ticket in my pile of letters and things and the most rudimentary of recollections, I flew out to Colorado to rescue Ginny. She and Elizabeth Clare Prophet had a confrontation of some sort—possibly having to do with a man. Some of Elizabeth Clare Prophet's people were after her. Ginny was hiding out. She needed to be rescued. We drove her car back to California. There was a blizzard in Wyoming. It was around Christmas. Ginny was probably nuts. I didn't care. My heart belonged to Melanie. She was all I ever thought about. I thought about her all the time. When we got to San Francisco, Ginny dropped me off at the airport. I went back up to Oregon. She cried in the car in the parking lot. I didn't.

I also have a letter Elliot wrote me around then. The postmark on the envelope is November 24, 1974. In the letter he said he was sorry for any hurts he had inflicted on me.

Eight months later, I got the last letter I ever got from Ginny Good. It was postmarked August 25, 1975. She was living in the Berkeley flatlands with a guy named Ross—one of her New Age buddies from Colorado. The first page of the letter is just a picture of a guy with knobs on his knees, playing what appears to be a zither, with a small Christmas tree growing from his forehead. Under the picture it says. *"I can't write so doodles must do."* On the next page there's a Picassoesque clown patting the cheek of a twelve-legged, round-faced female French Poodle with a perplexed smile and antennae growing from her forehead who's saying: *"Hello. My name is Twoodle Bumskulltear. I am walking on smog. Not air."* Then the letter begins in earnest:

I so need a non-male friend. I wish you did not identify with a gender. I would like to come up there, but I don't trust you. I don't trust anyone. Too late. Money all gone. Me screwed up. Yep—dead. I was robbed and raped last week. Really. People broke in and did it. Took everything. I hadn't made love or had sex once except for the aforementioned rudeness on the part of the aforementioned intruders. I suppose I could have tried to enjoy such a rare occurrence. Everything all gone. Even my new library card. I lay around sick and don't have spirit to get a job or join a group or do anything...I WANT to Lots...but seem stuck to invisible can'tfly paper. No car—(doesn't work) no way to fix it cuz no money. I just want a girl roommate, but am so stuck I can't even

muster that. My hatred for the sex game is eating my guts out—it's kill-
ing me slowly but I can't deny what I see and I wish I were blind.
Women are going to have tyrannical power and deserve it! Oh doobrot. I
am so determined not to drink so the emotional whammies cause "psy-
chotic behavior." Yesterday was a scream. I joined B'rer Rabbit, jumped
into the raspberry bushes, and stuck sticks into the offensive eye, the mid-
dle one, toward the right. Wanted to die so poured Rit dye in the bathtub
and laid in it and changed color. Really. It was a symbolic act. More
went on. It was much like our scenes. You and me. Me in the closet at
the motel—remember? Or burning the curtains? Not drinking makes
me nutty. Anyway, yesterday was extreme and rare and I'm glad of it. I
feel more me that way, really—this dumb other pretend stuff and keeping
cool is Really Crazy. Oh, well. I love what you sent. Gads, I wish we
could be FRIENDS and do sex too. Oh, well. No hope that centuries
of conditioning in me could be overleapt in a single lifetime's bound.
Well, bound is right, but not the kangaroo kind. Gotta go, here comes
hubby. Yuk. I love Ross but not the predetermined roles that pollute
and use love—rolls and rolls of roles. Krapps Last Tape never comes.
Oh, no! Not the Last Tape! What to do? Play 'em all over. Krapp!

Somewhere around the end of 1976, I stayed with Elliot in
Palo Alto for a couple of weeks. His mother had become
something of a real estate mogul. She'd used the house she'd
gotten out of the divorce from Elliot's dead dad to buy more
property, then she kept buying more and more properties,
using one to leverage the next, until, by the end of 1976, she
was worth maybe ten million bucks. One of the properties
she owned was an apartment complex in Palo Alto. Elliot was
the resident manager. His mother had remarried. She was living in Hillsborough. Her new husband was another real estate

guy. Between the two of them they bought or sold half of San Mateo County every couple years or so.

While I was staying with Elliot in Palo Alto, I managed to get myself out of the paralyzing obsessive depression I'd been wallowing in for longer than I thought anything could go on and was finally able to function well enough to get a job as a telex operator at the Bank of America up in San Francisco again.

Elliot was still painting. It was his skull period. He used to sit on the living room floor with the barrel of his dad's .38 caliber revolver pointed at his forehead and stare at the bullets in the chambers until the gun hallucinated itself into a skull of one sort or another. Then he'd hurry up and go paint a picture of what he'd seen. The skulls were all different. Some were pretty; others were menacing and scary.

* *G G* *

Another year or so later, Melanie and I got back together. That was a surprise. I'd about given up on her by then—not quite, but almost. The daily doses of heroin had started rotting her teeth and were causing her hair to fall out in gobs, so she had gradually weaned herself off heroin and onto methadone and had gradually weaned herself off the Shakespeare guy and onto a guy who was on methadone, too. The new guy had swastika tattoos from prison gang affiliations.

Melanie called my parents' house. My mother gave her my phone number in San Francisco. Two hours later I was in Sacramento. I packed her and Wendy and their meager belongings into a U-Haul truck, and we all moved back to San

Francisco while the swastika tattoo guy was at a biker convention in Bakersfield.

We lived in a little Victorian house behind a big Victorian house out in the Mission for a couple of years. Eventually Melanie got off methadone and got into eating huge healthy cauldrons of broccoli, zucchini, parsley and green beans. Her hair grew thick and lustrous and pretty again. Her teeth stopped falling apart. I parlayed my experience as a telex operator and my innate ability to lie on a resume into a job selling computers. Then I got another job, selling a different kind of computer, and another, and another, each more remunerative than the last. I wore suits and ties, took clients to lunch and filled out an inflated expense report at the end of every week.

I never forgot that Melanie had been in love with other guys, but I also never forgot that it had been my fault in the first place—and the two equally bleak recollections canceled one another out. I had practically nothing to do with Ginny or Elliot anymore. Melanie never mentioned them. I didn't bring it up that she'd been fucking her heroin boy day and night for the last four years, either—not to mention the swastika tattoo guy. We had a sort of mutual emotional nonproliferation pact. I didn't think it was exactly fair—I mean, one measly indiscretion on our couch in Burlingame didn't quite seem the equivalent of fucking the Mexican Mafia and the Aryan Brotherhood nonstop for four years, but hey, who said anything about fair? That was the deal. We had to live with it. We lived with it.

Melanie went to work for an insurance company. We had plenty of money. We moved into an apartment on the outskirts of the Tenderloin and settled into a quiet, comfortable, mutually considerate routine that would have taken ten years to settle into with anyone else. On Saturdays Melanie I went to Brother Juniper's Breadbox for breakfast and, afterwards, stocked up on groceries down on Geary Street. Sometimes Wendy came with us, but usually she wasn't around. On Sundays I watched football on TV. Joe Montana was just starting to come into his own with the Forty-Niners. It was an exciting time to be living in San Francisco.

We had a little trouble with Wendy. It's kind of complicated to try to get into. Wendy missed a lot of school, didn't respond well to discipline and did way too many drugs for a twelve year-old. We had a lot of trouble with Wendy, actually. She ended up in Camarillo for stealing cars. Stealing cars was nothing compared to what she could have ended up in jail for. She was a handful. Oh, well. Our moderately comfortable life together went on and on, day after day, for years. We had our ups and downs. They resolved themselves with equanimity. Melanie was relatively happy. I was relatively happy. We were content.

𝒢𝒢

Then one day, out of the blue, Elliot called me up. It must have been in1980 or so. I didn't know who he was. I had put him and Ginny so completely out of my mind that I didn't recognize his voice for a minute. Then he sounded like his same old fidgety self again. He told me, in that halting, roundabout way of his, that we had made a pact ten years earlier, that we had promised each other that no matter what we were doing, we would get together on such and such a day—which happened to be the next day. I didn't remember making that particular deal, but he and Ginny and I used to make all sorts of long-term deals with each other all the time, so it didn't seem unreasonable. We talked some. He was living at his mother's house in Hillsborough. Elliot gave me the address. I wrote it down.

I had an appointment at Alumax in San Mateo later on the next day, anyway. I'd been trying to get in to see those guys for months—so that might have been on my mind. Getting Wendy out of jail might have been on my mind. Slowing down my back swing might have been on my mind. Trying to get free tickets to *A Chorus Line* might have been on my mind. It had to have been around in there somewhere that I'd been eating ice cream cones with Donna McKechnie in Sausalito when she got all huffy on me and told me I sounded like a crass tabloid reporter.

I had on a suit and tie. My Adam's apple itched. I had a hard time finding Elliot's mother's new house. Whoever came up with the street plan for Hillsborough must have been instructed that its primary function was to keep the riffraff out. Roads meandered aimlessly, around and around. There weren't any numbers on the houses. Finally, I recognized the green Jaguar his mother used to drive. It was in the driveway with a tasteful "For Sale" sign in the back window.

His mother answered the door. Apparently they still had the same deal they used to have back in San Mateo. Her mouth still turned down at the corners. There were a few lines in her face that hadn't been there before, and she wasn't wearing the same sheer white silk bathrobe she always used to wear, but her eyes were as sparkly green and flirtatious as ever. She smiled. She was happy to see me. I still liked making her sad mouth smile. She showed me into the living room.

At first everything seemed fine. Elliot looked older. I may have looked a little older myself. How old were we by then? Thirty-seven? Thirty-eight? Wow. We were old. It had been a long time. A lot had happened.

Elliot's mother's new house was full of jade and Persian rugs. There was an Olympic-sized swimming pool outside. She had pointed out the pool and had mentioned its size on our way into the living room. Maybe she thought I might want to buy the place; everything she owned seemed to be for sale. I was thinking she might know someone I could sell computers to, too.

Elliot was sitting on a royal blue Chinese wool rug on the living room floor. He wasn't wearing his brocade smoking jacket. He was wearing a Pendleton shirt and a pair of Levi's. The rug had a pastel flowering bush woven into it. I bet it had cost a pretty penny, but I also bet it was worth more than they paid for it—everything in the house looked like it probably appreciated to the tune of about twenty bucks an hour. Elliot wasn't listening to Yma Sumac or *Sketches of Spain*, either one. He wasn't listening to anything. He was just sitting there in a half-lotus position, with his head bowed and his hands resting palms up on the insides of his knees.

I sat in front of him without saying anything, the same way we used to sit there not saying anything when we were in high school. After I'd been there for maybe half an hour, Elliot excused himself, went into his room and closed the door. Five or six minutes later, he came back out into the living room again.

"What did you do? Take a leak?"

"Nah," he said. "Brezhnev's worried about getting oil into Vladisvostok."

"Brezhnev's in your bedroom?"

"He called me on our phone."

Actually I hadn't heard a phone *ring*, but it didn't seem like a good time to argue with him. I sat there uncomfortably while Elliot confided to me what he'd been up to since I'd last seen him. He spoke in fits and starts, always diffident, never one to toot his own horn. Somewhere along the line, Elliot had acquired a controlling interest in one of the big Japanese trading companies—Marubeni, I think it was. He wasn't bragging, he was just answering questions. Brezhnev needed a favor now and then. I smiled. I may have looked at my watch.

Elliot also owned a sizable share of Wendy's Hamburgers. He'd named the company after Wendy, as a matter of fact— our Wendy, my Wendy, Melanie's Wendy. He'd used a picture of her in the logo—a little sketch he'd made of her that time he stayed with us in Burlingame. She'd had her hair in pigtails the day Elliot drew the sketch. Wendy's was just getting off the ground, but Elliot had big plans. He wanted franchises in the Soviet Union. Brezhnev could open doors. It was strictly business. Tit for tat. You scratch my back I scratch yours.

"You're full of shit," I told him.

"Yeah? Come on, I'll show you."

He stood up and motioned me to follow him down the hallway and into his room. When we got there, sure enough, there was a little red plastic toy phone on the floor. What more proof did I need? Who but Brezhnev could it have been? It wasn't funny. Only Elliot had heard the phone ring. Brezhnev spoke English. They kept it a secret from the State Department to avoid putting translators out of work. Brezhnev was a union man; Elliot was a full-on, free-market capitalist, but they accommodated one another in the interests of global trade.

Elliot wanted people to pay attention to him. He'd always wanted people to pay attention to him. Not many people did anymore, including me. I barely paid any attention to him at all. I had this appointment, see.

Then he showed me some pictures he had painted. He took down one of his mother's big Abrams art books and pointed out a Botticelli, a Goya, a few Vermeers. He'd painted them all. Reason didn't faze him. He knew what he knew. He was classically crazier than a fucking loon. There were gaping holes in his personality. He was hanging on to remnants of who he used to be. He had made himself into famous painters—dead or alive, it didn't matter. He was a diplomat, a statesman, a world power, a Renaissance man sitting cross-legged on a Chinese rug in his mother's living room, shooting the shit with Brezhnev, sending off urgent cables to the Shah of Iran, getting the oil situation straightened out in Vladivostok.

Go nuts, he seemed to be saying. It's the only way. He was coming up with such pitiable, off the wall, megalomaniacal stuff it was hard even to pretend to laugh. I used to just laugh. Even when the things he did weren't all that funny, I used to be able to laugh. But this just wasn't funny. There wasn't anything funny about it. All the quaint little psychological quirks that used to make me like him had run amok. He was as transparent as a soap bubble about to burst. His whole life had been one long series of jolts that he'd been able to defend himself against, somehow or other, by hook or by crook, but now that one of them had broken through, all the rest had come tumbling in after it.

As we sat there, it became obvious to me that the jolt that had made the initial breakthrough had been Ginny. He was still in love with her. He would always be in love with her. I made the mistake of asking him if he had heard from her.

"So what's going on with Ginny? Do you know?"

His eyes lit up. He smiled one of his twitchy smiles and leafed through the big Abrams art book again, pointing her out to me. There she was in a Goya, and there she was again in one of the Botticellis—and that was Ginny standing by a window in one of the Vermeers. He stopped at the Vermeer and shook his head and bit the inside of his lip and said, "You probably won't appreciate it, but getting the light right through that window was a bitch. Ginny was an angel. She glowed."

"No, I appreciate it," I said. "It's beautiful."

"Thanks." Elliot was proud, but modest—still a little shy, still a little guilty, maybe. Ginny came into his room at night, he told me. She modeled for him the way she used to model for him at the house in Kentfield, the way she no doubt modeled for him when they were living together in L.A. The two of them talked while he painted pictures of her—just chatted, not about anything special. She was fine. She didn't mention me much, no, but I didn't have to worry, she was happy, she was doing okay.

I forget exactly how the pictures got into the book, but he had an explanation. He had explanations for everything. He was so sure of himself it was hard *not* to believe him. Maybe he *was* buddies with Brezhnev—and the women in the paintings did all sort of look a little like Ginny. I mean, who can say? Maybe she was the reincarnation of all the women in the paintings, and he was the reincarnation of Goya and Botticelli and Vermeer. He was so calm and peaceful and at ease that something like that could have been going on, couldn't it? It would have broken my heart if he were just completely crazy. I didn't want my heart broken. I didn't have time to have my heart broken. I had to get over to Alumax pretty soon.

* 𝒢𝒢 *

The next day Elliot shot himself in the head with his father's .38-caliber revolver. Sure, of course, obviously I should have known he might have been going to do something like that. I *did* know. But it could also have been symbolic, therapeutic—like Ginny dying herself in a bathtub full of Rit dye. I probably could have done something about it, too—which was very likely why he'd gotten me over there in the first place. We hadn't made any deal ten years ago; he was getting ready to blow his brains out, is all. He probably wanted me to talk him out of it.

People, when they're getting ready to kill themselves, sometimes make elaborate, ceremonial preparations. They make a big show of settling old accounts and patching up past misunderstandings, but what's really going on is that they want you to talk them *out* of killing themselves. They don't just come right out and say, "Okay, I'm going to be blowing my brains out now, so if you want to talk me out of it, now might be a good time to start talking." No. That's not the way it works. The way it works is that you've got to figure it out for yourself. You've got to decide whether you want to interfere or not. That's part of the deal. It's not really all that tricky. They want to be talked out of it. But I didn't get it. I

328

didn't figure it out. I guessed wrong. I'm not trying to justify anything. Or maybe I am. Who the fuck knows? Not me.

Sure, I was a little wrapped up in myself. I've always been a little wrapped up in myself. Who isn't a little wrapped up in himself or herself? We're all a bunch of fucking water spiders, skimming over the surface of everything, face to face with nothing but our own stupid reflections. All I had to do was look. All I had to do was listen. But I didn't. I had this appointment, see.

When I was leaving, his mother gave me the same sort of imploring look that she used to give me twenty years earlier when Elliot had stayed in his bed that whole year after he'd walked in on her boning the Lebanese real estate guy on the drain board. What should she do? Only this time it was also like she was blaming me, too, like if it hadn't been for me, Elliot never would have gotten mixed up with Ginny and none of this would have happened. I might have given her something of an imploring look myself.

How was I supposed to know what she should do? What could I tell her? Your son, Mrs. Felton, is off his fucking rocker. He's crazy as a loon. He's nuts. He's insane. You should lock his ass up somewhere before he blows his poor fucking brains out, like your poor fucking husband blew his poor fucking brains out, like his poor fucking father blew his poor fucking brains out. But what *could* she do? What could anyone do? Bake him cookies? Call the police? Call the fire department? Get Army Intelligence over there? What? Love the crazy motherfucker? How the hell was I supposed to know? He was *her* kid. She had to do with him whatever the fuck she was going to do with him.

That was about all I could tell her, and I didn't even tell her that. I didn't tell her anything. I needed to find my way out of the maze of winding streets in Hillsborough and get over to Alumax before two. It was a solid lead. I stood to make a lot of money.

CHAPTER THIRTY-THREE

Scenic Hills

I didn't find out Elliot killed himself until way later. Dick Joseph told me. He'd dropped by to see Elliot one day, as was his wont, and Elliot's mother told Dick Joseph that Elliot had shot himself in the head with his father's revolver a month ago the previous Thursday. I went through my appointment book and figured out it must have been the day after I'd last seen him. I called Ginny to tell her. The phone rang and rang. She never answered. I tried several times a day for a week or more. Then the number I had reached was no longer in service.

I asked a guy I was in the middle of selling around a million bucks worth of computers to at Levi Strauss whether *he'd* seen Ginny lately. They used to go to the same AA meetings over in Berkeley. He pinched the sides of his chin and wrinkled up his forehead and said, "I think she might be dead."

"Really?" My face got hot.

"I could be wrong," he said.

"Can you find out?"

"I'm going to a meeting tonight, sure. You're coming by tomorrow, right?"

"To pick up the *signed* contract from your nit-picky boss, I am, yeah."

The next day, it was true. Ginny Good was dead. The guy at Levi's pinpointed the exact time and day. One of his friends had been the one who found her. The way the Levi's guy heard it was that she had overdosed on Excedrin PM and the better part of a fifth of gin. He stressed the gin more than the Excedrin—AA guys get sanctimonious when it comes to alcohol and people in the program.

"Shows to go you," the guy said.

I wasn't entirely sure what he meant by that, but I didn't ask. He didn't know I knew Ginny very well. I did, though. I knew her as well as I've ever known anyone. I knew her well enough to know that killing herself would have been more along the lines of an accident. She'd tried to kill herself hundreds of times; she'd been trying to kill herself since she was six. I don't think she thought she was ever actually going to die. Elliot killing himself was more conscious, more deliberate; you pretty much have to pull the trigger of a .38 caliber revolver on purpose.

When I finally got the chronology sorted out, Ginny and Elliot both died on the same day—probably pretty close to the same time—as if it had been some kind of a cosmic suicide pact. Elliot would have liked that. He was always kind of a romantic. Whether Ginny would have liked it or not, I couldn't tell you. I didn't like it, I can tell you that. I don't like dead people. I've never liked dead people. Dead people piss me off. Dead people can go fuck themselves.

Well, except for my father, I guess. He's the only dead person I can think of who doesn't just totally piss me off. He didn't kill himself, though. He didn't want to die, not at all, not ever, not one tiny little bit. It took a lot to kill him, too. It took cancer—some weird, semi-rare kind of cancer called carcinoid syndrome.

It had been growing inside him for ten years. None of his doctors had the slightest clue. That his nose had turned increasingly purple was the only overt symptom anyone might have spotted, and we all just thought that was because he'd been something of a drunk for the last fifteen years or so. None of us paid much attention to his poor purple nose. He got more stomachaches than normal, too. His doctor didn't know what was causing either of the symptoms. His doctor was an idiot. Yeah, well, it was probably good that his doctor was an idiot. I don't think any of us would have wanted to know that he'd had cancer for ten years—three months was long enough. Up until then, all we knew was that his nose had turned purpler and purpler and that he was always running out of Rolaids.

Some specialist did exploratory surgery. It was no big deal. It was mainly just to shut my father up, to humor him, to prove to him once and for all that the pains in his stomach came from eating too many peanut butter sandwiches on Wonder Bread. While the guy was poking around in there, the wall of my father's large intestine fell apart, disintegrated. Gobs of pus and cancer came oozing out.

The surgeon cleaned it up as best he could, sewed my father back up again and said he had a month to live—six weeks, tops. My father fought it every step of the way. At the end of the six weeks, he was still going strong. Well, strong might be too strong a word, but he was still alive.

* ꙅ ꙅ *

I went up to Ashland to hang out with him while he died. It was only for a few weeks. I'm sure plenty of people have had the once in a lifetime chance to hang out with his or her father while he was dying, but I'm not sure anyone got to hang out with someone who didn't want to die as much as my dad didn't want to die. He *really* didn't want to die, not one bit, not at all, not ever. No matter how much it hurt. No matter how much weight he lost or how much shorter he grew or how many morphine induced Indians with tomahawks were surrounding the house and breaking the windows and chopping down the doors, he didn't want to die no matter what.

Sometimes it made sense to him to take less morphine and deal with the pains in his stomach on his own. One of the ways he did that was by imagining that he was fishing. It may have looked to the casual observer like he was propped up on pillows in a rented hospital bed, but in reality my father was out in a rowboat on Howard Prairie Lake, fishing his guts out. The pains in his stomach were fish. He'd feel one nibble the bait, give the line a little tug to set the hook, then gingerly bring it up the side of the boat and slip the hook out of its mouth and solemnly club it to death. That felt good for a second. Then he tossed the line back in to try to catch another. Sometimes one of the pains slipped off the hook halfway up the side of the boat and hurt all the more. The pains that got away were really pissed. They were like barracudas. They dove deep into the organs inside his abdomen and bit into his nerve endings with sharp, pissed off, barracuda teeth. But no matter the pain or the fear or the delusions that beset him every minute of every day, he did not want to die.

He tried everything he could think to try. He was making deals right and left. Some of his deals got sort of silly. One morning he wrote a check to God in the amount of five thousand dollars and put the check on the bright sunny windowsill in the kitchen where God would be sure to find it. Now, five thousand bucks may not sound like a lot of money, but it was more money than my father ever had in any bank account in his life, and he gave it all to God on the off chance he might not have to die. He tried anything he could think of, any off-the-wall hope in hell.

He called Art Linkletter's 800 number and ordered one of those Craftmatic beds. Art Linkletter had looked my dad straight in the eye and had told him personally, man to man, that if he really didn't want to die all he had to do was to go to the phone, pick up the receiver, dial the 800 number and order himself a Craftmatic Bed—and my father dutifully tottered over to the phone and ordered one.

I tried to talk him out of it, but trying to talk him out of things he had his heart set on led to the same inevitable conclusion—hey, if he wanted a Craftmatic Bed, what the fuck, he deserved a Craftmatic Bed.

"You don't need no god damn Craftmatic Bed," I said.

"You don't know what I need." He shook his head and looked at me—and he was right, of course, I didn't, but I didn't think Art Linkletter did either.

His deals got downright preposterous during the last couple of days. A news story on Dan Rather gave him a brilliant new idea—an absolutely sure fire way to keep from dying. He was more animated than he'd been all week.

First, he needed his chain saw.

He was tilted back in the La-Z-Boy. I'd just given him more morphine. I've never tried to describe my dad, but if I had to, I'd say he looked kind of like a cross between Humphrey Bogart and Don Knotts. He'd wasted away some—he still looked like himself, but he'd wasted away. His hair, which he always slicked back like Humphrey Bogart, was oily from the sickness and stuck in odd, curly shapes to his scalp. He hadn't been able to take showers.

The hospice ladies gave him sponge baths. He liked getting sponge baths from the hospice ladies. He flirted with them and made them laugh and seemed to think that the reason they were giving him sponge baths was because he flirted with them and made them laugh. Well, except when he got sad; then he knew perfectly well that no god damn hospice ladies were going to be giving him no god damn sponge baths if some fairly well informed physicians didn't think he was going to die, and probably pretty soon.

"Go out in the workshop and bring me my chain saw," he said.

"What do you want your chain saw for?"

"If you don't know, don't ask." That seemed to make as much sense as anything Yogi Berra ever said. Every nonsensical thing my father ever said always made all kinds of sense. I brought the chain saw into the living room.

"Now get a cube of butter," he said.

"Butter?"

He looked at me as if it were inconceivable to him that his own son could ask a question as stupid as that at a time as crucial as this. Then he relaxed, let it go, like it was a little late in the day to try to teach me anything new.

"I suppose you know I love you," he said, finally, as if he'd utterly given up on the idea that I'd ever amount to anything.

"Yeah," I said.

"Have I ever told you?"

"No."

"Did you ever want me to tell you?"

"No."

"Oh, boy," he said.

I couldn't tell whether he was just reacting to one of the pains in his stomach or whether he was just glad he hadn't ever had to say he loved me. He supposed I knew. I got the butter.

Then he wanted me to rub the butter onto the teeth of the chain saw. Somehow or other, the rubbing of a cube of butter onto the teeth of his chain saw was going to keep him from having to die. He didn't know how, exactly, but that did not in the least deter him from having me rub butter onto the teeth of his chain saw. The butter got soft. The chain saw gleamed with a patina of fresh soft butter. When the first cube was gone, I asked if he wanted me to go get another one.

"Do you think it's doing any good?" he asked.

"I don't know."

"I don't know either."

"I don't see how it can do any harm."

"Maybe we should try one more."

The next night he wanted me to break into Chuck Anderson's office. Chuck Anderson sold insurance. His offices were down at the end of our street, on Siskiyou Boulevard. There was this book, see. The book was in the lower left hand drawer of Chuck Anderson's desk. All I had to do was break into his office, jimmy open his desk, take out the book, erase my dad's name and put the book back into the drawer.

If your name was in the book, you were going to die, but if you could somehow manage to talk your blithering idiot of a son into breaking into Chuck Anderson's office and erasing your name, hey—who would be the wiser? I didn't break into Chuck Anderson's office. I thought about it, but I didn't do it.

My dad got everyone in on his deals. He had Nicki's husband Murph blow up several pairs of latex hospital gloves, tie them all together into a big bunch and hang them from the ceiling fan. Then he had Murph turn the fan on as slow as it would go. That was going to keep him from having to die. All kinds of things were going to keep him from having to die. None of them did.

We canceled the Craftmatic bed. The butter didn't do the chain saw any harm. God never cashed the check—last time I looked, it was still on the windowsill. I got to hang out with him the whole time, is all I know. That was cool. Well, some people might not have liked it. It got a little heart-wrenching here and there, but it was kind of funny here and there, too. Dying of cancer wasn't funny, no. There wasn't anything funny about it. It mainly meant that we had to stay alert—the way you have to stay alert with a little kid. He was like a little kid in so many ways. It was amazing to see how strong his potty training had been. He'd do anything to get to the bathroom. If there wasn't anyone to help him, he'd try to go on his own and end up flat on has face in the hallway. That wasn't funny at all.

But the kid from Domino's asking the undertakers how to get to the house behind the house next door while they were wheeling my dad's dead body down the front steps was sort of comical. The kid was just trying to do his job. So were the undertakers. They didn't want to stop what they were doing, but they didn't want to be rude, either. They were torn. Besides, they didn't know how to get to where the pizza was supposed to be delivered anyway. Marya had to step in and tell the Domino's kid what he needed to know. There's a path between our house and the house next door, see. It's hard to find in the dark.

Marya did everything the whole night. She's Nicki and Murph's daughter. My niece. She was the one who found him. We were all out in the living room singing *Say Goodbye*. If you've never heard it, it's a long song. A ballad. It goes on and on, verse after verse. Some guy by the name of Pappy was wooing the Widow Norton. Pappy and the Widow Norton were out on a date, out on a jamboree—and when Pappy brought her home at sun up, old man Norton raised his gun up:

> *"Say goodbye, say goodbye. Say goodbye, say goodbye.*
> *Say goodbye to the old apple tree.*
> *They cut the tree down for a casket,*
> *Put the apples in a basket,*
> *And buried poor Pappy 'neath the tree."*

"Mom," Marya said.

Her tone was unmistakable. We stopped singing and went into my father's room. His eyes were open. They still had some expression in them, too, but it wasn't an expression of anything any of us wanted to see for long. I pushed his eyelids shut. Nicki started wailing like a Palestinian banshee woman. She was practically doing those ululations they do—then she blurted out: "He loved me. From the day I was born. To the day he died."

I thought that was sort of a slick thing to say. I stole it off her for what I said about him at his funeral. We put a cribbage board in the coffin with him. That was probably pretty stupid. I mean, what you are when you're dead is a hunk of meat. They have to hurry up and get you to the funeral home and shoot you up with embalming fluid or you start to rot. What use a rotting hunk of meat may have had for a cribbage board was beyond my ability to comprehend, but we put a cribbage board in the coffin with him all the same. There wasn't much my father liked better than a rousing game of cribbage with one of his kids or some of the guys down at the Elks.

We put a mouth organ in the casket with him, too, in case he ran into anyone who might need cheering up. He had a knack for cheering up a person by playing the mouth organ. He'd have been lost without one, so we stuck his favorite Marine Band Harmonica in the lapel pocket of the double-breasted brown pinstripe suit he used to wear back when he was still selling insurance.

GG

When we finally got to the cemetery, Mandy and Marya sang *The Rose*. Mandy is Nicki and Murph's other daughter. She was around fourteen at the time. Marya was seventeen. Mandy's middle name is Rose. Amanda Rose Murphy. And there was a picture of a rose on the front cover of the program the undertaker passed out. Roses turned out to be kind of the floral theme of the whole funeral. I don't know whether anyone planned it that way. Printing programs was part of one of the more moderate packages the funeral home had to offer. *The Serenity Prayer* was on the back cover.

Marya laughed some during the first few verses. She wouldn't have picked *The Rose* as the song to sing—in fact she wasn't sure she could get all the way through it without barfing due to the sickening sweetness and sentimentality of the lyrics—but it was the only song she and Mandy both knew on such short notice, and once they got into it, the lyrics seemed to get more and more appropriate.

By the time they got to the last couple of verses, they were belting it out like they were Ethel Merman, both of them, two Ethel Mermans. Funerals are supposed to be sickeningly sweet and sentimental. Marya wasn't laughing because she was nervous. Nobody was nervous. She was laughing because she was crying. She was laughing because her mother was crying and her father was crying and her grandmother was crying and her uncle was crying. Marya was laughing because everyone was crying. She couldn't help it. Everyone crying was making her laugh. Mandy wasn't laughing or crying, either one; she was mainly concentrating on doing a good job of the singing of the song and didn't think much of her sister cracking up in the middle of her performance.

To counteract some of the sickening sweetness and sentimentality of the whole affair, there was a donkey in a field not far away, a donkey that hadn't been fed in awhile judging from the sounds he was making. He kept braying during the most somber moments. We all thought that was a nice touch. My dad would have liked a donkey braying during the eulogies at his funeral. He could bray like a donkey with the best of them. I adore my father. I will always adore my father.

Murph accompanied his daughters on the guitar while they sang *The Rose*. Then he sang *You Are My Sunshine* all by himself. Murph said it had been my father's favorite song.

Yeah, well, he was probably right. It probably was. My father had all kinds of favorite songs.

Then, God, I don't know what the hell happened after that. My mother, I guess. My mother got up from her folding chair in the front row. She walked across the grass in a pair of sturdy black shoes and stood with her back to everyone and put her hand on the coffin. It was a plain pine box, part of the same moderate funeral package she had picked out. She gave the box a comforting pat, then turned around and faced everyone.

There were maybe a hundred or so people there. People we hardly knew—grizzled old World War II fighter pilots from the Elks, guys my dad sold insurance with, guys he sold cars with, guys he sold storm windows with, guys he got drunk with and played poker with. And there were flowers everywhere, flowers of all kinds and of all descriptions. There were flowers on my mother's dress, tiny little sprigs of bachelor buttons and lilies-of-the-valley. What she said was simply that a song had been going through her head for the past few days. She didn't know where it had come from; it had just been going through her head the last few days.

"It's an old song," she said. "Maybe from the thirties. It's just been going through my head. I don't sing very well, either. As most of you know." Then she sang it. A cappella. Accompanied by no one:

"Out of a blue sky,
The dark clouds came rolling,
Breaking my heart in two.
Don't leave me alone,
For I love only you.

You're as sweet as a red rose in June, dear.
I love you, adore you, I do..."

That was as far as she got. We have it all on videotape. Myles did the videotaping. Myles is Nicki and Murph's only son—the oldest of their three kids. He was the newborn baby boy asleep in the bedroom the night Ginny tried to have her way with Murph then took off with garbage men, instead, lo those many long years ago. Myles never was much of a talker. I don't know whether it had anything to do with Ginny or not. He was a hell of a funeral videotaper, though.

When my mother sat back down and it was my turn to say a few words, I started out by saying some slightly off color things I knew would get a rise out of my dad's buddies from the Elks. There was a period of time when my father took to calling everyone "Frog-Ass." I don't know why. But, because of that, the guys at the Elks nicknamed him "Froggy." I told the story of how Dick Joss was fixing my car one day and I mentioned to him that he and my dad played poker at the Elks. Dick Joss asked me my dad's name. I told him. My dad's name didn't ring a bell. Then he said, "Oh, Froggy!"

They chuckled in fond remembrance.

Then I said that stuff I stole off of Nicki—only the way I said it was that my dad loved *me* from the day I was born until the day he died. Ha! That pissed her off. I knew it would. Well, what the fuck, two people can think the same thing, can't they? I mean, is there some kind of patent on pathos? I don't think so, but that was the first thing Nicki mentioned when it was her turn to say a few words.

"First, I'm pissed that my brother stole what I was going to say, but I'm going to say it anyway. My dad loved me from the day I was born until the day he died."

Then it was Tuney's turn to say a few words. She's the single lawyer soccer mom web designer who's sticking all this on the Internet for me. Tuney was holding her daughter, Maggie, in her arms—but Bucky, who was six or seven at the time, was on his hands and knees, lifting up the skirt around the bottom of the casket and looking down into the hole into which the plain pine box containing his grandfather's dead body was about to be lowered.

Tuney said we both got it wrong, that the fact of the matter was that her dad had loved her from the day *she* was born to the day he died. The line got a different kind of chuckle every time.

* 𝒢 𝒢 *

After everyone else was gone, Tuney and Myles and Bucky and I all hung around at the cemetery for a while. We stomped on the sod. Myles did more videotaping. We kept hearing the donkey.

Driving back to the house, we stopped and figured out where the braying was coming from, then drove over there. A family of local ranchers had just finished feeding the donkey and giving him water—a husband and a wife, and their five-year-old daughter. Tuney told them we'd just come from a funeral. "We kept hearing this donkey." She lifted her outstretched arms up toward the cloudless heavens.

"Oh, we're sorry," said the father of the local ranch family.

"No, no. We liked it. It would have made my dad happy as shit," Tuney said, without any hint of her usual reluctance to use bad language in front of kids.

"What's his name?" Bucky asked, pointing to the donkey.

"Geezer," the daughter said. Then she dug the toe of her shoe into the dirt and eyed Bucky furtively through her strawberry blond bangs.

Tuney and I cracked up. Myles smiled, too, although he was about as big on showing emotion as he was on talking.

"What's so funny about Geezer?" the little girl asked.

"Nothing. Really. Nothing at all," Myles said very seriously.

Tuney and I cracked up again, and by then we couldn't have said why we had cracked up the first time, either. Geezer wasn't that funny of a name. It was a good name. We couldn't have made up a better name if we'd tried.

The farm family waved to us, got in their truck and drove away. Tuney and Bucky and I fed Geezer some of the carrots they'd left. When we ran out of carrots, we fed him handfuls of long grass. Geezer still brayed now and then as he ate the carrots and the grass out of our hands. He curled up his lips and dripped snot out of his nostrils and showed us his huge teeth. Myles got it all on videotape.

CHAPTER THIRTY-FOUR

Colma

Anyway. By the time I heard Ginny and Elliot were dead, they'd already been buried. I didn't know where and I didn't ask. Melanie and I kept doing the things people do. I got different jobs selling different computers that all did pretty much the same thing—communications stuff. The computers I sold were precursors to the Internet. If I had stuck with it I would have been at least a billionaire by now, but I didn't stick with it.

Melanie kept working for the same insurance company. Wendy kept getting into more and more trouble. New trouble. Different trouble. We got her out of as much of it as we could. I started playing golf. I sucked at playing golf, but that was what I liked about it. It was a challenge. I like a challenge. Every time I had a spare hour or so, I'd go to a driving range and hit golf balls or practice putting on the putting green. When I had time to play nine holes, I played nine holes; when I had time to play eighteen, I played eighteen.

I used to take Melanie and Wendy out to the driving range with me when they least expected it. They'd think we were going Serramonte, and I'd swing by the driving range over in Colma and hit a bucket of balls. The driving range was up against the west side of San Bruno Mountain—not far from the Chinese Cemetery where I took that Norma Arce chick in my hot pink '53 Ford convertible nine million years ago.

There were black and white sheet metal signs marking off the distances at increasingly elevated points up the side of the mountain—yard markers, they're called. 100. 150. 200. 250. Like that. When you hit one of the signs there was a loud crack and another dent showed up in the sheet metal. I liked denting the signs. I was a shitty golfer, but I was good at making dents in the yard markers.

I also liked the whole idea of hitting golf balls into the side of San Bruno Mountain. It felt like I was trying to knock the god damn mountain down. It's hard to knock a mountain down by hitting golf balls into it. I barely budged the son of a bitch. I rarely got the balls past the 200-yard marker, but that didn't stop me from *trying* to knock the god damn mountain down. It was probably therapeutic, like playing golf every day for two and a half years when I first came up to Ashland had probably been a little therapeutic, like writing this book has no doubt been therapeutic.

gg

I remember this one day in particular. The three of us were at the driving range in Colma. Melanie stayed in the car and read one of her books. She never went anywhere without a book to read. Wendy went over behind the maintenance shed and tried to score a joint off of one of the scruffy grounds keepers. She had a knack for scoring dope off of scruffy guys. She was always on the lookout for scruffy guys off of whom to score a little dope when she had a minute or two to spare.

When I was through trying to knock down San Bruno Mountain by hitting golf balls into it, Melanie and Wendy and I stopped off at a fancy cemetery in Colma to feed the ducks. If you've never been to Colma, it's all cemeteries, wall-to-wall cemeteries. The one we went to was the biggest, the fanciest, the most exclusive. All sorts of famous San Francisco rich people were buried there—Crockers, Fleishackers, you name it—the place was so fancy it had its own private duck pond. Wendy and Melanie were over feeding the ducks. They were cute together. They're *still* cute together, only now it's all six of them—Melanie and Wendy and Melissa and Amber and Caitlyn and that other one, the other new one. Fuck. I forget her name. It'll come to me.

I ought to get them all up here one of these days, Melanie and Wendy and my four darling grandchildren. I could take them out to the golf course. They could feed the five families of Canadian Geese. I could introduce them to my golfing buddies. Johnny Pelosi would like that—Felix, Knapp, Bergeron, Wallace, Ford—they'd all like it. They all have families of their own.

Anyway, Melanie and Wendy were feeding the ducks. I was tired. My neck was sore. I sat down in the grass and leaned against the side of one of the headstones. There were cherubs on the headstone—curly-headed, angelic-looking kids with their cheeks puffed out. Below the cherubs, the headstone said:

"In Loving Memory"

Leaning against the grainy gray granite felt good. It was cool and soothing against the back of my aching neck. The harder I leaned against it the better it felt. I closed my eyes and could feel wisps of fog coming from off the ocean. The fog wasn't cold. It tasted like fish, some bony, bottom-dwelling scavenger fish, like the fish Elliot used to catch after his father shot himself. That was probably *how* Ginny and Elliot came into my mind—from the taste of fish in the fog.

The *way* they came into my mind was like a dream, but better; like a fantasy, like a vision. They were both in new bodies. They'd been reincarnated into fairy bodies, tiny little Tinkerbell bodies, with greenish-white lights inside them, like Ginny's body and my body had been down inside that burnt out old tree stump in La Honda. But this time it was Ginny and Elliot. Naked. Cavorting. They weren't in a redwood forest, though. They were in a jungle, a warm, steamy rain forest.

They were swinging on vines, landing on shaky branches, losing their balance, catching it again, singing Yma Sumac songs to each other across the lush valleys, thin and white as newborn children among the dark branches. And they were beckoning to me, beckoning to me with their arms, like we were kids and they wanted me to come out and play. They were happy. Elliot was flat-out laughing—there wasn't anything twitchy about it. He couldn't talk he was laughing so much.

Ginny could talk. She yelled at me, in fact. She called across the gulf between us with her hand around her mouth and her cheeks puffed out like one of the cherubs on the headstone, like she was Little Boy Blue, like she was blowing her horn:

"Come on, dodo, don't be scared. You can fly! See! Watch!"

She grabbed a long vine and swung like Tarzan from one tree to another, righted herself like a small gymnast on a balance beam, and called over to me again:

"Did you see? It's easy. You can do it. You can!"

I felt like I was standing on the edge of a precipice—like that scene in *King Lear* where Edgar leads Gloucester to the extreme verge of one the cliffs of Dover. I got vertigo. I could feel myself falling. They weren't that far away. If I jumped, it would be okay. It would be like that ant jumping off my arm in La Honda. My arms felt like they would turn into wings if I jumped. I could glide down and land next to them on one of the branches and—poof—I'd be in a little Tinkerbell body of my own.

* 𝓖 𝓖 *

I told Melanie about it when she and Wendy came back from feeding the ducks. When I got to the part about Ginny telling me I should jump off the edge of the cliff, Melanie said, "I wouldn't try it if I were you."

"It was just sort of a fantasy."

"I wouldn't trust anything either of them ever said."

"They're dead," I said.

"They may be dead, but that doesn't mean they're not still nuts."

Melanie had a way of putting things into perspective. They probably are still nuts. They're probably a lot happier, though—cavorting around in their new fairy bodies. They might even have met up with my dad—I'm sure that wherever they all are, it's the same place. Ginny and Elliot would have introduced him around. My dad would have liked that. He wouldn't have cared whether they were nuts or not.

He might have tried to teach Ginny and Elliot how to play cribbage. I mean, he had the damn cribbage board, didn't he? But, wait a minute. I can't remember whether any of us thought to put a deck of cards into the casket with him. Oh, man. I think we forgot. What the hell good is a cribbage board without a deck of cards? Yeah, well, I'm sure some other kid had brains enough to toss a deck of Bicycles into his or her dead father's coffin. I like the idea of them all playing cribbage together. Maybe dead people don't piss me off, after all—maybe they all sort of look out for one another, show each other the ropes. Hell, I might even *like* dead people. Hey, what's not to like? Ha!

CHAPTER THIRTY-FIVE

I-5

*O*kay, that's it. That's all I'm saying. I'm done. Now all I have to do is get my sister to stick the sucker up on a website for me while the interest in elephant polo is still at its zenith. Have I said everything I need to say, though? Man, I hope so. Do I still want someone to sue me? Not really, no—I mean, they can if they want, sure, anyone can sue anyone for anything, but you have to be hurt in some way in order to win. There have to be damages. So, did I say anything that hurt anyone? I don't see how it could have, besides it's all true—and truth is an absolute defense. Ha! If you believe that I got a bridge I could sell you.

I guess there's an off chance that Barbara Kalinowski might have construed my depiction of her as an invasion of privacy, but from what I remember of Barbara Kalinowski, she used to kind of like having her privacy invaded—the more someone invaded her privacy, the better she liked it.

As for Ginny, I heard recently that after she died her body was cremated and her ashes were scattered around on Mt. Tamalpias. It comforted me to think that some of her ashes might have been blown by the breeze or washed by the rain down to the house in Kentfield where she and Elliot and I all lived for awhile—the house with the fishpond. I figure the fishpond is probably filled up with dirt again by now—dirt, ashes, twigs, dead birds, whatever—time for someone new to dig it out, no doubt, paint it blue, fill it with water, throw in some fish. Start fresh. I don't know for a fact what happened to Elliot; I am sure he got buried, but I don't know where.

What about Melanie, though? Have I said everything I need to say about her? She's still around, getting by from one day to the next. She's still shy, not given to saying much more than needs to be said. We don't live with each other anymore, but I still like her a lot. We went our separate ways. She became a Buddhist. I see her sometimes when I visit Wendy and my four darling grandchildren, each of whom I still, to the best of my ability, spoil rotten and dote on to distraction— Melissa, Amber, Caitlyn and...god damn it. What the hell is that other one's name? I'm so fucking senile, I still can't remember. She's a cutie, though. The last two are twins, not quite four years old yet. I can see them in my mind's eye—all curly headed and cherubic—but I can't for the life of me think of the other one's name...

Rachel!

Ha!

* 𝄢 𝄢 *

Okay, that's really it. If I think of anything else to say, I'll maybe write a whole 'nother book some day, but I wouldn't hold my breath if I were you. I'm totally out of my settlement money. I'm totally out of everything. I seriously have to go get a job. I've already checked this morning's *Medford Mail Tri-*

bune, as a matter of fact. McDonald's is advertising for a shift supervisor. I circled it. I'm going there as soon as I get done with this. I'd be the boss of a bunch of high school kids. How cool would that be? Way cool, if you ask me.

I'm happy. If I had to explain why, I couldn't do it in a million years—all I know is that after telling Ginny Good I was going to write a book about her someday, after threatening to write a book about her for longer than I can remember, I finally just sat down and wrote the fucker. Now I can go get that job at McDonald's in peace. I'm excited about it. I'm looking forward to it. I hope I can start first thing tomorrow morning. In fact, if you're ever on I-5 going through Medford, Oregon, stop by and say hi. Tell me you read my book on the Internet and I'll see to it you get extra pickles on your Big Mac—anything you want, relish, onions, ketchup, say the word. I'll be the shift supervisor. It'll say so on my nametag. I'll have some authority. The high school kids will hop to it when I tell them to.

"Yo, Jimmy, extra pickles on the Big Mac for my buddy, here. He read my book. Ha! Is that slick, or what?"

Holy shit. I haven't even applied for the job yet; I don't even know who Jimmy is, and he's right here in the room with me. Past, present, future, it doesn't matter. All kinds of people are right here in the room with me. T. S. Eliot's over by my mother's Christmas cactus, reading *Cats.* He's reading aloud. We are having a PARTY! We are! The neighbors must think I'm off my rocker. Ginny's here. Elliot's here. Thulin's up in the back yard by the horseshoe pits, smoking dope with Ralph and Wanda and Popeye and Dick Joseph. Nicki and Murph are shaking their heads. My poor dead dad's running around like a gadfly, flipping everybody off.

There are all kinds of people running around, real people, fake people; you name it—Edmund, Edgar, Bartholemew Cubbins. I half expect that crazy old coot, the king himself—ay, every inch a king—to show up. Wait a minute! Wait a minute! Who's that knocking at my door? Who's that knocking at my door? I have to stop. I have to stop. I can't stop.

The feeling I have right now is the same feeling the crazy old king has toward the end of the play there where he's sitting by the side of the road, dazed and amazed and whacked out of his skull, with flowers and thistles and brambles in his hair like he's on his way to a free rock concert in Golden Gate Park and he says what he says. What was it, though? Fuck. He says something really extra slick, but I can't for the life of me remember what the heck it was. Son of a bitch! I forget. I fear I may not be in my perfect mind. I have to go look it up.

Okay, okay, check it out. Act Four. Scene Six. Here's what the old coot says, word for word:

"None does offend, none, I say none. I'll able 'em."

That's not a bad way to feel. It's the feeling you get when you've done things you thought you'd never do and have had your heart desiccated and ground down to around the consistency of talcum powder and suddenly it somehow gets itself, like, reconstituted or some damn thing. You *like* people again. You can't help it. You love people; you love people no matter what. And that makes you happy. It's like what Ginny said at the end of one of her letters:

"I love and am good."

That's it! That's what I feel like. I love and am good. I'm sure there's probably some fancy Greek word for a feeling like that. If I had any kind of decent education, I'd probably know what it was, too, but thanks to Mrs. Miller, I don't got no decent education. Yeah, well, I'm *glad* I don't got no decent education. I don't want no decent education. Once you start reducing everything down to a bunch of fancy Greek words you don't know what you even *feel* anymore. I'm grateful to Mrs. Miller. I love Mrs. Miller.

How long the feeling might last, I have no idea. Probably not long. Oh, well. Something else is bound to come along to replace it—some other feeling, some other thought, some other thing—who the fuck knows what. Not me.

GG

Okay, god damn it, that's really, really it. I quit. Well, except maybe for just this one last tiny little thing. It's something I wrote a long time ago. It might even have been part of that so-called journal I used to send to Ginny back when I was trying to get her to like me. I might have read it out loud in Gordon Lish's night school writing class at the College of San Mateo when I wasn't quite twenty-one yet and still had my whole life ahead of me. Those are the kinds of things you think about when you've got your whole life behind you—the things you used to think about when you had your whole life ahead of you. It's all I'm saying, I know that. It's the end:

I killed a bird once. With a bow and arrow. I killed it on purpose. It was a starling. Its wings looked like oil slicks. I snuck up on it from behind a tree. The starling didn't move. I couldn't miss. I didn't. The arrow stuck into the ground with the bird halfway up the shaft. Still alive. You could see down its throat. Its pointy tongue and jagged pink gullet were coming up with such blood curdling shrieks I didn't know what to do. I took it into the house. My mother was doing dishes. She turned around and saw the bird flapping on the shaft of the arrow and screamed. That made the bird screech all the louder. They were a duet— screeching and screaming, harmonizing with each other like dog whistles in my ears.

I took the flapping bird back outside and dug a hole in the ground and pushed the arrow into the bottom of the hole and covered the bird with dirt, buried it alive, and stood on its grave with both feet and pulled out the arrow with both hands. Dirt stuck to the shaft where the bird's blood had been—and if we went back there right now, just you and me, if we hopped on a plane, flew to Detroit, got ourselves a Hertz Rent-A-Car, drove to Royal Oak, found the same spot and dug it up, that bird would still be there, still alive, still squawking...

—Ashland, Oregon
February 2004

About the Author

Gerard Jones grew up in Michigan and moved with his family to California in 1960. He has been writing an odd amalgam of fiction and nonfiction on and off his entire adult life. This is his first book. He is also the creator of the website *Everyone Who's Anyone in Adult Trade Publishing.* He now lives in Ashland, Oregon.